UNITY AND FRAGMENTATION IN PSYCHOLOGY

Psychology has always defined itself as a science and yet it has lacked the theoretical and methodological unity regarded as characteristic of the natural sciences. Nicolò Gaj explores the topical question of unification in psychology, setting out a conceptual framework for considerations of unity and disunity, and exploring the evidence of its fragmentation. He takes a critical look at the history of the most prominent attempts at unification, and at the desirability and feasibility of the whole project. The book represents a unique and valuable attempt to address the issue of unification from a philosophical perspective, and via a combination of theoretical and empirical research.

Nicolò Gaj is a clinical psychologist at San Raffaele Hospital, Milan and member of the Research Unit for Philosophical Psychology at the Catholic University of Milan, Italy.

"Gaj has produced a book at the intersection of psychology and philosophy, and shows sophistication in both areas. He tackles the important question of unity in psychology by drawing on the insights of philosophy. This work should be of value to readers from both fields."

– George Stricker, PhD, American School of Professional Psychology at Argosy University, Washington DC, US

"Psychology has long suffered from an identity crisis. Is this often fragmented field one discipline or many? If it is indeed one field, what undergirds it? How does psychological research relate to psychological practice? This important and provocative book should help to launch a greatly overdue debate regarding the unification of psychology and the extent to which it is a desirable goal in its own right. Researchers, practitioners, teachers, and students interested in the future of psychological science will find this book to be a valuable and stimulating read."

– Scott O. Lilienfeld, PhD, Samuel Candler Dobbs Professor, Emory University, US

"As psychology as a science has developed at the intersection of a number of domains of human thought and practice, it is destined to experience tension between fragmentation (i.e., its tendency to deviate toward a proximal 'other' field, as, for example, biology for biological psychology, education for educational psychology, or business for industrial and organizational psychology) and unification (i.e., its need to self-define as a science distinct from neighboring sciences). This tension, various attempts at its resolution, and the consequences of specific resolutions have been explored by a number of thinkers at different stages of the existence of psychology as an independent science. This book by Nicolò Gaj makes a fine contribution to this exploration, underscoring the continuous nature of this tension, presenting its modern outlook, and outlining directions for its future investigation, as the science of psychology continues to define and redefine itself."

– Elena L. Grigorenko, Emily Fraser Beede Professor of Developmental Disabilities, Yale University, US

"Psychology has always had a variety of theoretical perspectives and there have been numerous attempts to unify the field. This book examines the most recent attempts and provides some insight into why they have failed. It is a book that everyone who is interested in this subject should read."

– Adrian C. Brock, Independent Scholar, Manchester, UK

"This comprehensive and thoughtful book is an important and creative contribution to the growing literature on the values and problems associated with monistic and pluralistic worldviews. Nicolò Gaj focuses largely on issues surrounding unification efforts in psychology in contrast with the vexing problems associated with the enormous diversification of contemporary psychological theory and practice. Gaj recognizes however that psychology is not alone in its struggles with the dizzying proliferation of emerging new scientific methodologies and the ever-expanding boundaries of all the sciences."

– Wayne Viney, Emeritus Professor and Emeritus University Distinguished Teaching Scholar, Colorado State University, US

UNITY AND FRAGMENTATION IN PSYCHOLOGY

The philosophical and methodological roots of the discipline

Nicolò Gaj

Routledge
Taylor & Francis Group

LONDON AND NEW YORK

First published 2016
by Routledge
2 Park Square, Milton Park, Abingdon, Oxon OX14 4RN

and by Routledge
711 Third Avenue, New York, NY 10017

Routledge is an imprint of the Taylor & Francis Group, an informa business

British Library Cataloguing in Publication Data
A catalogue record for this book is available from the British Library

Library of Congress Cataloging in Publication Data
A catalog record for this book has been requested

ISBN: 978-1-138-11890-4 (hbk)
ISBN: 978-1-138-11891-1 (pbk)
ISBN: 978-1-315-65257-3 (ebk)

Typeset in Bembo
by Taylor & Francis Books

Printed and bound in Great Briatain by Ashford Colour Press Ltd.,
Gosport, Hampshire.

This book is dedicated to those who perceive the need and acknowledge the value of a theory of practice in psychology.

Science walks on two legs, namely theory and experiment ... Sometimes it is one foot which is put forward first, sometimes the other, but continuous progress is only made by the use of both.

(Robert A. Millikan, Nobel Prize Lecture, 1924)

CONTENTS

ILLUSTRATIONS

Figures

Tables

PREFACE

The search for unity in science parallels the birth of Western philosophy, from Ancient Greece to the advent of Christian monotheism (Agazzi, 2000; Cat, 2014). From the origins, philosophers and other thinkers have dealt with the object of knowledge, the phenomena of reality, whose features and interrelations are investigated with different kinds of procedures. In very general terms, at the core of the issue are questions such as: in what sense is the world, and the knowledge of it, one? Is there a unity underlining all phenomena, based on an original substance or force? Can the unity of nature be affirmed on the basis of a set of (many) original substances or forces? Is this unity reflected in the nature of procedures used to obtain knowledge about the world? These and related questions initiated the debate between the two opposing theoretical positions of monism and pluralism.[1]

These two positions introduce the problem of the method (or methods) science should use to investigate the different phenomena of reality. Objects and methods are central concepts in the debate dealing with the unity of science: the former deals with metaphysical principles (what really exists), the latter with epistemological ones (how we know what exists).

It is plausible that the appeal of the notion of unity (of nature as well as of science) comes from the assumption that truth or usefulness is equivalent to simplicity, and unity is the quintessence of simplicity. In a traditional outlook, unity is considered as simple and plurality is not; simplicity is seen as a virtue in the scientific enterprise. From the viewpoint of scientific practice, simplicity results when there is only one conceptual system of science (Oppenheim and Putnam, 1956) that constitutes a frame for the study of all phenomena of reality. This is a methodological perspective in which simplicity is a sort of prescribing, regulating principle for the study of every kind of object: scientists should not postulate "new entities or new attributes unrelated to those needed for the study of inanimate phenomena" (Oppenheim and Putnam, 1956: 13).

A famous principle that warns us not to multiply theoretical entities is known as Ockham's razor. Why should we accept this principle? In the view of Oppenheim and Putnam, one reason to uphold the property of simplicity is because a simple theory is more useful than a complex one. In this case, simplicity is an indication of another theoretical virtue, namely practical utility. This is a case of epistemic simplicity: among theories with the same empirical content, scientists should prefer theories that are easier and have a simpler structure. Although the decision to use a theory doesn't mean that it is believed to be true (Kukla, 2001). Another possible answer to the previous question stems from a metaphysical view based on the presumed simplicity of the universe. In this case, the property of simplicity in a theory is advisable because it would bring us nearer to the essence of reality, that is indeed simple, i.e., reality would be composed of a relatively limited number of principles, forces, or substances which reciprocally interact. In this case, simplicity is an indication of another virtue of a theory, its possession of a truth value. This can be described as a metaphysical simplicity whereby simplicity is deemed to be a characteristic of entities and processes of the universe (Kukla, 2001). It is worth noting that simplicity itself is not an intrinsic virtue which can be valued for its own sake; rather, simplicity is a derivative virtue, a property that we are justified in seeking on the basis that it leads to an intrinsic virtue of a theory such as utility or truth. In other words, simplicity can be considered to be an index of something else.

This brief illustration of the link between the notion of unity and simplicity shows how concepts such as utility, truth, language, methodology, and metaphysics are linked to the central issue of the unity of science and how many conceptual layers make up the problem of the unity of science. The very expression "unity of science" hides different perspectives (Hacking, 1996). For example, the "unity" side of the problem deals with singleness or singularity, which means uniqueness, alterity, and diversity in comparison with something else. Unity is a feature that discriminates something valued. The concept can also be interpreted as integration, an ideal status where different parts are arranged and organized as a whole. Moreover, unity conveys the notion of harmony (Wilson, 1998) which is strictly linked to the issue of integration which in turn leads to the concept of functional interconnection where every single part has a specific and reciprocal role in the whole (Kauffman, 1995). Looking at the "science" side of the expression, we can find the singular as well as the plural form. From a methodological perspective, "unity of science" conveys that there is one, and only one, reliable way to investigate the world. The singular form (unity of science as opposed to sciences) suggests the notion of diversity and superiority of science, conceived as a compact whole, in comparison with other methods of knowledge. In contrast, "unity of sciences" conveys that there are many kinds of science, possibly with different objects and methods, but unified by virtue of some common ground. There are many ways to investigate the world, which nevertheless can be somehow unified, perhaps on methodological grounds.

Such a variety of points of view is similarly detectable in psychology. The fragmentation of psychology has long been identified by eminent authors (Bühler, 1927; Vygotsky, 1927) and still stimulates heated discussions among scholars. Even now, there is a significant literature dealing with the issues of unity, disunity, or frag-mentation in the field of psychology (for an overview, see Yanchar, 1997; Yanchar and Slife, 1997; Sternberg, Grigorenko, and Kalmar, 2001; Goertzen, 2008). What exactly is fragmentation? What is fragmentation about? Or, conversely, what does unity mean, or what should it mean? Should we be concerned about fragmentation, or just consider the fragmentation of psychology as a matter of fact? On what grounds is psychology definable as fragmented or united? Can unity/disunity of psychology as a scientific discipline influence its social status and organization? The present work has been conceived on the grounds of these and similar questions, in the belief that a better understanding of the status of psychology as a scientific discipline would benefit its strength and efficacy, both on theoretical and practical levels.

Some aspects of scientific unity or disunity – of science and psychology – will be discussed in the course of this work. In particular, Part 1 deals with general issues regarding science and unification. This can be considered as a sort of introduction that serves to provide a useful framework for the issues later debated. Part 2 regards psychology and its status as a fragmented discipline: different aspects of fragmentation are identified and their relationships are explored, in order to provide a framework where these aspects can be sorted out. Part 3 deals with some of the main theoretical attempts to solve the problem of fragmentation in psychology as it is interpreted by the authors whose models are presented. For each proposal, a descriptive part is followed by an analysis of the main issues raised by the conceptual aspects of the model presented. Part 4 specifically deals with the state of fragmentation of clinical psychology, which is an interesting field considering its double aspects, of theory and practice. This analysis is achieved through the investigation of its definition, mission and scope, as they are specified by the American and Italian psychological community. Part 5 presents an empirical study, whose aim is to explore the way a sample of Italian psychologists represents the discipline, considered as a science and as a profession. In the conclusion, the outcomes of the research will be compared with the reflections emerged in the course of the work, outlining the need for a new means of connecting theory and practice in psychology.

Note

1 The terms "monism" and "pluralism" here refer to very broad metaphysical positions about the nature of reality.

References

Agazzi, E. (2000). What does "the unity of science" mean? In E. Agazzi, and J. Faye (eds.), *The Problem of the Unity of Science* (pp. 3–14). Singapore: World Scientific Publishing.

Bühler, K. (1927). *Die Krise der Psychologie*. Jena: Fischer.

Cat, J. (2014) Unity of science. In *Stanford Encyclopedia of Philosophy*, http://plato.stanford.edu/entries/scientific-unity

Goertzen, J. R. (2008). On the possibility of unification. The reality and nature of the crisis in psychology. *Theory and Psychology*, 18(6): 829–852.

Hacking, I. (1996). The disunities of sciences. In P. Galison and D. J. Stump (eds.), *The Disunity of Science. Boundaries, Contexts and Power* (pp. 37–74). Stanford, CA: Stanford University Press.

Kauffman, S. (1995). *At Home in the Universe*. Oxford: Oxford University Press.

Kukla, A. (2001). *Methods of Theoretical Psychology*. Cambridge, MA: MIT Press.

Oppenheim, P. and Putnam, H. (1956). Unity of science as a working hypothesis. In C. Kenneth Waters (general ed.), H. Feigl and M. Scriven (eds.), *The Minnesota Studies of Philosophy of Science*, vol. I (pp. 3–36). Minneapolis, MN: University of Minnesota Press.

Sternberg, R. J., Grigorenko, E. L., and Kalmar, D. A. (2001). The role of theory in unified psychology. *Journal of Theoretical and Philosophical Psychology*, 21(2): 99–117.

Vygotsky, L. S. (1927/1997). The historical meaning of the crisis in psychology: A Methodological investigation. *Collected Works of Vygotsky*, vol. 3, New York: Plenum.

Wilson, E. O. (1998). *Consilience. The Unity of Knowledge*. New York: Knopf.

Yanchar, S. C. (1997). Fragmentation in focus: History, integration, and project of evaluation. *Journal of Theoretical and Philosophical Psychology*, 17(2): 150–170.

Yanchar, S. C. and Slife, B. D. (1997). Pursuing unity in a fragmented psychology: Problems and prospects. *Review of General Psychology*, 1(3): 235–255.

ACKNOWLEDGMENTS

This book has been long in its development, and somehow took root from questions which emerged when I was a psychology student nearing graduation in 2003. At that time, I had been studying a lot of psychology and related areas. However, the more I gathered knowledge about the subject matter to which I chose to dedicate my professional and scientific life, the more I became confused about the nature of psychology and the professional role of psychologists. I was quite nervous, because shortly thereafter I would become, myself, a psychologist!

What exactly is psychology? What does it mean to be a psychologist? What should I have done as a psychologist? What should my competences have been as a professional? How could I recognize a "psychologically competent behavior" in my professional practice or in the professional practice of colleagues? These and other worrying questions came abruptly to my mind. I was stricken as I had thought that taking degree courses in psychology would have provided answers, rather than more questions concerning psychology! Unfortunately, that was the hard reality. My confusion became even worse when my internship started and, later, when I began my doctoral program in clinical psychology at Vita-Salute University, Milan, in 2005. At that time, I had the valuable opportunity to meet and work with various professionals from whom I learned a great deal. However, the way they worked, the way they conceptualized and approached problems, the methodological and theoretical devices they used were very different. Sometimes, incommensurable. And they were all psychologists belonging to the same professional and scientific community.

My confusion became tolerable soon after graduation thanks to the interest I began to develop in philosophical psychology. The theoretical reflection on psychology as a scientific discipline provided categories and concepts by means of which I could put some order in my thinking. Many other questions were raised, but my growing professional experience and fruitful work in the theoretical field led to my decision, in 2009, to start a doctoral program in philosophy of psychology at Catholic University, in Milan. The program provided the occasion to organize, integrate, and examine in depth the considerations I have developed over the years on the issue of psychology and its fragmentation. This book is the outcome of my research work from 2009 until now.

I am profoundly indebted to each person who, directly or indirectly, contributed to my professional and scientific education. In particular, Antonella Morandi Corradini, Professor in Philosophy of the Human Sciences at the Catholic University of Milan, has offered much wisdom and guidance in the development of my scientific and philosophical awareness through working together over the years. This work would not have been the same without my friend and colleague Giuseppe Lo Dico, whose human and scientific support has been essential over the years. Antonella and Giuseppe significantly influenced the development of the methodological and philosophical positions I support, and the elaboration of this book. I am thankful to Renzo Carli and Fiammetta Giovagnoli from Sapienza University of Rome, without whose kind and competent support the empirical study would not be possible. I am grateful to my older and wiser colleagues at the Clinical Psychology and Psychotherapy Unit, San Raffaele Hospital, in particular to Raffaele Visintini, for his valuable clinical mentorship and friendly support in developing my theoretical interests, and Cesare Maffei, whose discussions resulted in stimulating new ideas and reflections. The help of Mauro Cavarra has been crucial in carrying out some aspects of the empirical part and the interpretation of the data. Ilaria Carretta has been invaluable in helping to adjust some methodological aspects of the study. I am also indebted to my younger colleagues and trainees at the Clinical Psychology and Psychotherapy Unit, with whom I shared and discussed opinions on the status of psychology as a scientific discipline and a professional practice.

I am very grateful to Michael Strang, Libby Volke, and Katie Hemmings from Psychology Press, who believed in the value of this work and followed the whole editorial process with great competence and respect for my ideas. I want to thank Anne Petrov, whose precious linguistic and stylistic revision helped this work to become a book. I express gratitude to the reviewers of the original work, Adrian C. Brock, independent scholar from Manchester, Geoff Bunn of the Manchester Metropolitan University, as well as an anonymous reviewer, who provided relevant comments on the structure and the contents of the book.

I am profoundly indebted to my family, who ultimately made this book possible. The support of my father Flavio has been beyond the loving help one could expect from a caring father: the passionate discussions regarding the problems concerning the relationship between theory and practice in our disciplines, namely psychology and information technology, helped me to broaden and complete the framework of my reflections. The warm care of my mother, Chiara, and sister, Desirè, now a trainee psychologist, has been significant in carrying out this work. Last, and most importantly, I affectionately thank my wife Erica and my daughters Tatiana and Brenda who, with their care and unconditioned love, made possible the hardest task: to combine my clinical practice and theoretical work with family duties. Thank you. I owe this book to you.

PART 1

1

UNITY OF METHOD

Scientific methodology is a branch between science and philosophy dealing with the criteria the scientific community uses to evaluate the reliability of methods used in science. In general terms, it concerns the application of the principles of reasoning to scientific inquiry. In very broad terms, method is a whole of interconnected and formalized procedures oriented to obtain results. As the eminent psychologist Alan E. Kazdin clearly states, "methodology encompasses the many ways in which these [empirical] observations are made, the arrangements of situations used to obtain the observations, and the means of evaluating the findings and drawing inferences" (2003: 5). Thus, method deals with the justification process, where phenomena are observed and hypotheses are evaluated.

The concept of scientific method has been important in philosophy of science in two respects: not only does it allow for the demarcation of scientific from unscientific knowledge, it allows for the explanation of the historic success of the scientific enterprise, compared with the fate of many pseudo-scientific disciplines (e.g., creationism, astrology, haruspicy) (Bird, 1998).

Regarding the issue of the unity of method, it is worth noting that the debate between the supporters of the existence of a single and reliable scientific method and the supporters of the plurality of methods has its roots in the history of knowledge. Focusing on the twentieth century's development, I will briefly outline the debate,[1] trying to give an idea of the more prominent positions within it. This will be useful in order to better understand the situation of psychology, as part of the sciences.

In general terms, the former position is called methodological monism, and is a core feature of the positivistic and neo-positivistic movements. It maintains that every discipline, in order to obtain the privilege of being called scientific, has to adopt the methodological standards of natural science, that is, the use of empirical procedures and of the hypothetical–deductive method (Hempel, 1942). Science is intrinsically nomothetic, that is, concerned with the postulation of general and universal laws. In this sense, every science is based on positive (empirical) data and explains phenomena through general laws and the specification of the particular circumstances in which they take place. In this perspective, there is only one scientific method, to which all disciplines must conform. On the other hand, supporters of pluralism asserted that the diversity of the objects of inquiry imposes the adoption of different methods: human beings are motivated by reasons and motives and are defined by the historic dimension, which differentiates them from metaphysical entities as well as from physical events or processes. So, the study of human beings requires specific methods.

The core of the debate can be easily traced in the well-known dichotomies that supply the background of twentieth-century and current disputes: nomothetic vs. idiographic approach, explanation vs. comprehension, natural vs. human sciences[2] (Castiglioni and Corradini, 2003). It is clear that the watershed that divides the two opposing fronts is the way by which human beings should be studied, due to their presumed diversity and difference from other kinds of objects. Since psychology deals with human beings, it is clear that this issue is interesting for our aim.

In more detail, the issue of the unity of method doesn't involve unity of the content of science, but unity of its boundaries, that is, the ways we reason and how we should accordingly operate. In this sense, two different meanings can be attributed to the concept of the unity of method:

1. A narrow meaning: method is a general standard of reason (Hacking, 1996: 51) that involves the use of logical tools and formal rigor in inferential procedures (Brunswik, 1952: 1). This meaning deals with the theoretical side of the process of evaluating hypotheses and imposes reasoning according to certain reliable standards: the best way to reason is *via* logic.
2. A broader meaning: method constitutes a summary of the best ways to find out about the world (Hacking, 1996) and involves the use of specific conceptual devices and procedural protocols. This meaning (also) deals with the practical side of the process of evaluating hypotheses. There is one way to best investigate the world: the scientific method.

Although the first, narrow meaning is quite trivial, the second is not. In the narrow meaning, however, science can be comfortably defined as united, and not only the natural science, but also those disciplines called "humanities," such as philosophy, law, literature studies, arts, etc. We expect every human intellectual activity has to follow some basic logical and inferential criteria in order to be accepted as reliable: in this case, unity is a normative precept.[3] These requirements are content free, that is they are independent from the different objects of the scientific inquiry, and constitute the general basic foundations of every scientific (and non-scientific) enterprise. Within the narrow meaning, two scientific requirements have to be considered:

a   Rigor. There must be reasons to accept (or reject) a proposition and the connection between propositions (Agazzi, 2000). For example, a proposition can be accepted on the basis of its analytic status – its truth is based on logical laws and on the meaning of the terms (Alai, 1998: 21) – or on the basis of a comparison with empirical facts. The connection between propositions can be evaluated on the basis of the nature of this connection (causal relation, correlation, mutual exclusion relation, etc.). Rigor deals with the use of explicitly stated logical criteria.

b   Objectivity. Objectivity deals with the intersubjective agreement about knowledge and the ways to obtain it. A fact is objective if different individuals can reach an agreement on the features of the phenomenon they are dealing with in specified circumstances (McBurney and White, 2009: 19). Although the concept of objectivity is strictly linked to the observational procedures (e.g., the reproducibility of observations made by different observers), it also deals with the agreement of the inquirers on the formal criteria of significance used in science: what is considered to be a correct deduction, a successful prediction, a counterexample, etc. (Agazzi, 2000: 13).

The second, broader meaning refers to procedures and policies used in order to obtain reliable knowledge and deals with methodology in its most traditional meaning. So, the broader meaning displays all the complexity of the issue of methodological unity/disunity: this is the battlefield where supporters of monism and dualism have been fought for many years, and still fight.

Thus, considering the broader meaning, I will now illustrate some of the most well-recognized attempts to provide methodological criteria for scientific inquiry in contemporary philosophy of science. I will try to give a sufficiently detailed account of monism as well as dualism, in order to sketch some central features of this complex methodological debate.

On the monist side, one prominent attempt to provide a methodological criterion has been put forward by the neo-positivistic movement. As is well known, one of its main theses was the project of the unification of science, so the issue of method was undoubtedly central. A discipline can be counted as a science only if it embraces the criteria which constitute the basis of the scientific conception of the world, as will be further detailed. Two major aspects of the methodological unity of sciences have to be mentioned because of their importance in the neo-positivistic project of unification. The first states that, notwithstanding the technical differences in the investigational methods, every empirical science supports its statements in the same way: deriving from them empirical implications that can be checked intersubjectively. The second states that for every private (that is, reachable through introspection) fact or event (or observation) there are some "publicly observable symptoms" which constitutes the basis for the intersubjectivity of knowledge (Hempel, 1969). Therefore, the project of unification solidly rests on the grounds of a syntactic view of scientific methodology, which favors an intersubjective agreement on "the logical structure and the rationale of scientific inquiry"

(Hempel, 1979: 357). More precisely, according to such a syntactic perspective, theories' structures are represented in terms of logic–linguistic expressions consisting of an abstract formalism (the language), a set of theoretical postulates (T) and a set of correspondences rules (C) which bridge from data to theory. Thus, a scientific theory consists in the conjunction of T and C (French, 2008: 269–70). I will deal with this issue again later, when considering the philosopher Carl G. Hempel's thought in detail.

There are two building blocks of neo-positivistic methodology, the view which states that reality can be known only by means of mediate or immediate experience and the basis of which is empiricism:

1. Logical analysis. The original formulation maintains that every scientific proposition is logically equivalent to a proposition formulated in a perfect logical language, whose atomic statements refer to aspects of reality (Hahn, Neurath, and Carnap, 1929; Di Francesco, 1994). This can be considered a goal, rather than a matter of fact. The aim of logical analysis is to bring a term or a proposition to its empirical value, assessing its scientific (or non-scientific) status. Only those terms or propositions referable to an empirical, intersubjectively verifiable basis are to be considered scientific (Carnap, 1932).
2. Covering law model. This is the general explanatory device that can be used in every scientific discipline: an event can be explained when it is subsumed under a general law of nature, in conjunction with information about particular facts (Hempel, 1962b: 87; Blackburn, 2005: 175). The first part of the model is called *explanans* and comprises initial conditions (that specify the contingent situation where the explanation takes place) and uniformities expressed in general (universal or statistical) laws. The second part is called *explanandum* and represents the phenomenon that has to be explained, thanks to the *explanans* (Hempel, 1962a: 276–81). A deductive or inductive logical nexus connects the two parts specifying the kind of relation between them: deductive–nomological (*explanans* logically implies *explanandum*) or probabilistic–statistical (*explanans* increases the probability of *explanandum*). The covering law model is the methodological milestone of logical positivism.

These two building blocks clearly display the importance of empiricism, logic and intersubjectivity within the project of a unified science. These are issues that have been cleverly developed by the philosopher Carl G. Hempel, which will be dealt with briefly.

Carl G. Hempel's proposal is as dense as it is exhaustive on the issue of neo-positivistic methodology. We will first consider his remarks on the covering law model. As above mentioned, the deductive–nomological (DN) explanation specifies the cause (or causes) of a specified event, that is to say, for every state of circumstances of the kind in question, an event comes about (same cause, same effect). On the other side, the probabilistic–statistical (PS) form specifies the conditions under which an event occurs with a certain degree of probability. In this case, the occurrence of the event is "practically" certain (as Hempel himself states), even if not in a nomological sense. It is evident that in the DN explanation the focus is on non-pragmatic aspects (Hempel, 1961–62: 82) of the scientific enterprise, the ones mentioned above as syntactic aspects. The DN explanation is objective in the sense that it describes the logical form of scientific procedures, without a reference to pragmatic aspects (i.e., dealing with the objects and the circumstances in which they are found). Hempel maintains that PS is also a non-pragmatic explanation, even if its inductive nature brings it close to a pragmatic conception of explanation, where "practical" aspects are important. However, as the author points out, since non-pragmatic aspects are abstractions from pragmatic aspects, the pragmatic character of PS can only be considered as a matter of degree, in comparison with DN. Thus, the two models of explanation, DN and PS, share the feature of providing good grounds for the explanation of the occurrence of an event in its logical form; that is, non-pragmatic and syntactic (Hempel, 1963: 299). This is the best guarantee for the possibility of intersubjective knowledge (Hempel, 1983: 376). In other words, the more an explanation is based on logic (non-pragmatic and syntactic aspects), the more it can be applied to all kinds of object (i.e., it is object independent) and permit intersubjectivity. To sum up, the main features of the neo-positivistic methodology as illustrated by Hempel are as follows:

- Normativity: "The rules and criteria provided by logical theory can be employed prescriptively or normatively, i.e., as standards for a critical appraisal of particular inferences" (Hempel, 1979: 358).
- Syntactic character: "The methodology of science … is concerned solely with certain logical and systematic aspects of science which form the basis of its soundness and rationality" (Hempel, 1979: 357).
- Non-pragmatic character: "We clearly need a concept of proof which is not subjective in the sense of being relative to, and variable with individuals. Scientific research seeks to give an account … of empirical phenomena which is objective in the sense that its implications and its evidential support do not depend essentially on the individuals" (Hempel, 1961–62: 82).

The syntactic and non-pragmatic characters raise a question about the explanation of human behavior: since in everyday language this kind of explanation is pragmatic and semantic in character, how does Hempel face the issue? The Austrian philosopher formulates an answer on two different grounds. First, as noticed above, the author argues that non-pragmatic aspects are an abstraction from pragmatic aspects, so the problem is inconsistent in these terms; explanations of human behavior might be correctly addressed by Hempel's method. Human beings would be different from other objects only in terms of degree. Second, most of the historical explanations evidently dealing with human beings are nomological in character, although other authors consider them as pragmatic.[4] The point here is that, in Hempel's view, in the particular case of historical explanations, the formulation of nomological links is often left implicit,[5] but can be in principle made explicit (1962a: 286).

Thus, historical explanations (that is, explanations of human-enacted events) share the same normative model of natural events, even if some terms of the explanation are often left implicit, due to the their intrinsic "pragmatic flavor." This flavor derives from a sort of "individuality" people attribute to historic facts: indeed, they are usually considered as individual facts in the sense that their occurrence is unique. Addressing the issue, Hempel objects that every event (*explanandum*), including the physical one, is individual in this sense: the falling of a leaf from a branch is a unique event because it refers to a single and specific occurrence, different from every other events of the same kind. In order to distinguish this meaning of individuality, which associates all events and historic facts to which an individual aspect is usually attributed (as the October Revolution, the Second World War, the September 11 attacks), the author uses the term "concrete events" (Hempel, 1961–62: 302). In Hempel's opinion, concrete events are constituted by individual facts; thus, as already said, even historic (that is, concrete) events can be in principle subsumed under general laws (because they are "made of" individual events, in the sense specified).

On the basis of such arguments, historic events behave exactly in the same way as natural events. Nevertheless, in Hempel's opinion historic explanations have some specific features, at least from a descriptive perspective. Indeed, the deductive–nomological reconstruction of a human event often takes the form of a so-called explanation sketch (1962a: 281), that is an incomplete form of explanation. Hempel suggests two kinds of sketches which are descriptive examples of what historians often do in their practice:[6]

- Elliptical explanations: they "omit to mention certain laws or particular facts which … they tacitly take for granted, and whose explicit citation would yield a complete deductive–nomological argument" (1962a: 282). It is often the case of the explanation of a concrete event (say, the Second World War): many individual events, and the laws governing them, are mentioned, many are left implicit.
- Partial explanations: they provide an incomplete account of the *explanandum*, since not all relevant laws or theoretical principles are specified. Thus, the conclusion is loose.[7]

In conclusion, Hempel tells us that the explanations of events, natural or human, follow the same rules. This constitutes the methodological unity proposed by the neo-positivistic movement, based on the fact that the nature of understanding is basically the same in all areas of scientific inquiry (Hempel, 1962a: 295), being based on logical devices which are object independent. Consequently, the ideal of the unity of science is carried out through the accumulation of scientific knowledge by means of the proper methodology. Method assures the task of scientific knowledge.

The monistic approach has been strongly criticized by those who support a dualistic perspective of knowledge and propose different methods in order to investigate human phenomena. These opponents attribute particular features to the human world and state that those features can be investigated only through distinctive methods. The object (human facts) is considered as different in principle from natural facts. So, different objects means different methods. Let us analyze in more detail these positions, through an overview of the ideas of three of their major proponents. Here, we will only deal with central methodological aspects of their proposals, in an attempt to give an account of the cornerstones of this position.

The first author is the philosopher William Dray. In his book *Laws and explanation in History* (1957), which discusses the peculiarities of historic method, he maintains that the covering law model (CLM) has to be abandoned in order to give a proper account of historical facts. The author highlights two main problems of CLM (Dray, 1957):

- The issue of the generality of laws in history: the alleged general laws that are formulated for historic explanations by CLM theorists are too general to be interesting. Thus, their contribution to the comprehension of the *explanandum* is trivial and their adoption is methodologically pointless. General laws are too general to provide sound explanations of interesting historical details; on the other hand, they turn out to be simply false when they are applied to particular facts. Thus, they comprehensibly end up losing their heuristic power (Dray, 1957: 28–9, 33), failing to be reliable generalizations and useful explanations.
- The issue of connections: CLM theorists maintains that the laws concerned by the model are universal and their connections can be either nomological or probabilistic (Hempel, 1962a). Since historians are interested in explaining the occurrence of that individual event, Dray doubts that probabilistic links (which CLM theorists usually attribute to historic explanations) would guarantee the fact that in this specific case, e.g., A followed B. Rather, the same law can even explain the non-occurrence of that event (i.e., that A didn't follow B) (Dray, 1957: 30–1), so CLM has to be rejected.

For these reasons, in Dray's opinion CLM is methodologically inadequate for the explanation of human events. Moreover, there is a non-methodological motivation to refuse CLM: it concerns the alleged uniqueness of historic facts.[8] The author maintains that natural science deals with abstractions, ideal constructions of the world. On the contrary, history deals with what actually happened in concrete details. Consequently, "it therefore follows *a priori* that since laws govern classes or types of things, and historic events are unique, it is not possible for the historian to explain his subject matter by means of covering laws" (Dray, 1957: 45). The author tries to deepen the meaning of uniqueness, asserting that this notion deals with the fact that every historic event is different from others with which it would be natural to group under a classification term. For example, when a historian sets out to explain the French Revolution, he is certainly not interested in explaining it as a revolution, but as a unique event. In other words, the historian is more interested in the aspects which distinguish the studied event from others belonging to the same category, rather than in the aspects it shares with other categories' members.[9] In Dray's opinion, since historic events can be classified, it doesn't mean that their (proper historic) explanation depends on this classification, which represents them as instances falling under general laws (Dray, 1957: 49). Again, what is interesting here is the uniqueness of historical facts. Coming to the *pars construens* of his proposal, Dray states that proper historical explanations contain three peculiar ingredients:

1. Internal explanation:[10] the historian has to "penetrate behind appearances, achieve insight into the situation, identify sympathetically with the protagonist, project himself imaginatively into his situation" (Dray, 1957: 119). These empathic aspects have a heuristic value, that has to be integrated by a logical analysis (point 3).
2. Purposiveness: this feature is preliminary to point 3. It holds that every action has a purpose, in the sense that one can reconstruct the rational path (conscious or not) which lead to the action at stake.
3. Rational explanation: the historian has to gather all relevant elements in order to understand what considerations (reasons) convinced the subject to act as he or she did. The goal is to grasp the rationale of what was done. The difference between internal explanation and rational explanation is that the latter has an empirical, inductive side that the former doesn't have. The historian asks himself not only (though usefully) "What would I have done in that situation?" (internal explanation), but "What would (for example) Napoleon have done, considering the way he saw the situation, his opinions, his desires, his purposes, etc.?" The attempt to reconstruct the agent's reasons constitutes the peculiar aspect of rational explanation, which is supported by the heuristic value of the internal explanation.

The features briefly described deal with a special kind of explanation, the teleological explanation. The philosopher Charles Taylor, in the first part of his famous book *The Explanation of Behaviour* (1964), discusses its main characteristics. Teleological explanation, based on the notion of purpose and their object, is the goal for the sake of which the *explanandum* occurs (Rosenbleuth, Wiener, and Bigelow, 1943; Taylor, 1964: 6). It answers the question "What is the goal the subject wanted to reach by behaving that way?": clearly, it is an approach devoted to the study of human events. Contrary to most of his behavioristic contemporaries, Taylor thinks that the adoption of a teleological approach stands on empirical, rather than on speculative, grounds. Behavioristic opponents maintain that the notion of purpose, which would lead behavior toward an end, is not open to empirical confirmation, because the only empirical evidence for the operation of the purpose is the same behavior which the purpose would explain. Thus, for behaviorists, "purpose" (P) is not an empirical descriptive term and is considered as an unobservable entity.[11] Nevertheless, Taylor refuses to look at the behavior (B) as a function of an unobservable entity (P). He maintains rather that the condition for B to occur is that the state of the system (S)^{12} and the environment (E) be such that B is required to reach the goal (G), by which the system's purpose is defined. In this sense, the states of the system and its environment can perfectly undergo empirical control, independently of the evidence provided by the occurrence of the behavior itself (Taylor, 1964: 7–10). To cite the effective words of the author:

> The element of "purposiveness" in a given system, the inherent tendency toward a certain end, which is conveyed by saying that the events happen "for the sake of" the end, cannot be identified as a special entity which directs the behavior from within, but consists rather in the fact that in beings with a purpose an event's being required for a given end is a sufficient condition of its occurrence.
>
> *(p. 10)*

Taylor's thesis is firmly based on the irreducible distinction between action and mere movement. Actions are behaviors defined by two prerequisites: they have a goal^{13} and they are intentionally emitted in order to reach that goal (independently from the success of the action itself). The distinction between action and non-action is not only based on the presence of a goal and a purpose, but also on the decisive role of the purpose in the emission of that behavior. This statement expresses the strong link between the agent's intentions and the behavior emitted: the reaching of the goal has to be intrinsically linked with the respective intention (Taylor, 1964: 27–9, 33–9), in order to provide a proper action. To sum up, Taylor's theory of action consists of three elements:

1.   The agent has an intention to reach a goal.
2.   The agent's behavior is directed to the goal.
3.   There is a link between intention (1) and behavior (2): the goal is reached by the emission of a behavior wrought by the agent's intention.

As is evident, the notion of action seems to be central for the teleological perspective just outlined. The philosopher Georg H. von Wright (1971), the last author I'll deal with, distinguishes between results and consequences of an action: for example, if I want to open a window, and I open it, the result is that the window is open. The consequence is, for example, that the room is airing. The teleological explanation deals with the results of a behavior, while the consequences are effects of the results (they are causally linked). In other words, Von Wright wants to emphasize the intrinsic link between the result of an action and the action itself (1971: 112): going back to the window example, if the window didn't open, it would be logically wrong describing that act as opening the window. It is not possible to call an action a behavior that doesn't aim at a goal. He coherently states that the unity of the external aspects of an action is not constituted by the causal nexus between the parts of the action, rather it is constituted by the subsumption of the parts under the same intention. Thus, to teleologically explain a behavior is to identify an object of the agent's intention (von Wright, 1971: 114). In the window example, if the subject finds an obstacle while performing the movements to open it, we can still call those movements "action," because of their intrinsic reference to a goal (i.e., to open the window), independent from the results.

In this analysis of some of the fundamentals of the debate between monists and dualists it is evident that the proponents of the two different methodological approaches do certainly share a narrow meaning of unity of science: knowledge advances by the proper use of logical tools. Nevertheless, it is arguable that for the proponents of a monistic perspective theories can be characterized by what their linguistic formulations refer to, i.e., the approach is syntactic in character. On the other hand, for the dualists, theories are interpreted semantically, because they give priority to the nature and features of those entities to which a theory refers, namely, human beings and historical events. In this perspective, which can be defined as semantic, the laws of a theory serve to delineate the class of models they refer to (French, 2008: 272),[14] where these models are interpreted semantically. This means that there is a one-to-one isomorphism between the data and the substructure of the theory, so theory and data (object) are more strongly embedded than in syntactic approaches, as Hempel proposes.

Thus, the incompatibility between the monistic and dualistic perspectives just outlined concerns the way they approach human beings and their events: the alleged peculiarity of the object of inquiry casts doubts on the methodological uniformity supported by many. It is arguable that the problem of human explanation is the "cause of scandal" of the debate on methodology, based on the difference between monistic (syntactic) and dualistic (semantic) approaches which lies, grossly speaking, in the level of abstraction of a theory. The more the theory is distant from its object, the more it can ignore some of its (alleged peculiar) features; the more it is close to it, the more it has to give an account of them.

In conclusion to this brief description of the debate between monists and dualists, some central general methodological differences between the two approaches can be singled out. They can be understood as aspects of a general perspective from which the scientist looks at the object of inquiry:

- First vs. third person perspective: dualists see human beings as subjects with intentions, goals, desires, opinions, and consider these peculiarities fundamental in order to explain human behavior. Monists consider them as they would every other object of inquiry, that is subject to causes and general laws.
- Internal vs. external approach: human behavior is analyzed in terms of internal states by dualists, whereas monists provides an explanation in terms of observable and quantifiable parameters.
- General vs. particular aspects: monists consider science as an abstraction of the world, so they are interested in a general (syntactic) account of it, whereas dualists are interested in the individuality of an event, not in the properties stating its membership to a class of events.

It is my opinion that the irreconcilability of these positions in many scientific branches dealing with human beings is still current today, notwithstanding a frequent commitment to – more or less – implicit forms of naturalism.[15] The progressively decreasing interest in issues of general scientific methodology and its replacement by philosophical concerns to local areas of science can be read as evidence that the monist–dualist opposition is still open, even if not always in an explicit form. In other words, it seems that the dialectic between these positions substantiates the issue of scientific methodology in those areas of science dealing with human facts and events. The present growing interest in the technical aspects of scientific disciplines and their progressive specialization will not weaken this dialectic. Rather, I think that the importance of the clarification of such an opposition will increasingly and obviously emerge from the practice of science, in a sort of bottom-up way, even if the theoretical questions of the issue do not attract much interest at the present time.

Notes

1 The description will be conceptual and does not pretend to historic completeness.
2 These dichotomies are the modern roots of two different directions of development in psychology: the "mind route," which traced psychology mainly through the reference to mental entities or processes, and the "body route," which traced psychology mainly through the reference to material (i.e., biological) structures (Leahey, 1992; Lundin, 1996).
3 It is worth noting that the "descriptive" turn of post-Popperian philosophy tends to underestimate the systematic and reason-driven aspects of science (i.e., logic) (Kuhn, 1962; Feyerabend, 1975): it gives priority to the incommensurability of different traditions or paradigms of research, their alleged equality in value and the predominance, in the scientific enterprise, of historical, psychological and sociological factors on logical and methodological ones. Following this perspective, no scientific unity or progress can be postulated. Though, we think these aspects cannot be ignored in the debate on the unity of science, where the conceptual framework of inquiry is above all normative (what science/s should or can be) rather than descriptive (how science/s present information).
4 See Collingwood (1946), Dray (1957), Taylor (1964), Von Wright (1971).
5 It is the case of the genetic explanation, a typical historic kind of explanation. It consists in specifying different stages in a sequence of events which lead up to a given phenomenon. Hempel considers it as a nomological explanation because the sequence, by which each stage is linked to the other, is ruled by some general principle (1962a: 288).
6 Hempel maintains that also natural scientists are often guilty of these "sins of imprecision."
7 Hempel considers the Freudian explanation of a slip of the pen as an example of partial explanation: the slip made would express Freud's subconscious wish, but such expression and fulfillment might have been achieved by many other kinds of slip of the pen than the one actually committed (Hempel, 1962a: 283): not all relevant laws are specified in order to explain why that particular slip is emitted.
8 Dray's notion of uniqueness is close to the notion of concreteness proposed by Hempel (Hempel, 1962a: 302).
9 Dray's approach to history is evidently idiographic.
10 The philosopher Robin G. Collingwood (1946: 213) distinguishes between the outside of an historic event (that is, everything that can be described in terms of bodies and movements) and the inside (that is, thoughts, desires, opinions, intentions, etc.).

11 In Taylor's opinion, this idea comes from an implicit behavioristic loyalty to atomistic assumptions, according to which all laws hold between discrete entities. Then, to invoke a purpose means to postulate a new discrete entity as a causal antecedent. But this postulation would violate another requirement: that all entities have to be observable. In this sense, teleological explanations are considered like causal explanations (in that they provide links between separate events), but they would be flawed because of unacceptable features: they postulate unobservable entities (purposes) and the time order is reversed (first the effect – the goal – then the cause – the action).

12 The system (S) refers to all of the states of an organism.

13 There are cases, such as dancing, running, walking, where the aim is simply the emission of the behavior.

14 A model for a set of sentences is an interpretation under which they are all true (Blackburn, 2005: 236).

15 This again is compatible with the so-called post-Popperian turn: the focus shifts from the priority of the normative side of science to the descriptive/sociological side, through the special consideration granted to the discovery context. In other words, historical, psychological, sociological factors (what scientists really do in practice) are more important than prescriptive and logical factors (what scientists should do). Coherently, historians of science are progressively more interested in the details of experiments and in scientific practice rather than in general theoretical aspects (Dupré, 1993: 229).

References

Agazzi, E. (2000). What does "the unity of science" mean? In E. Agazzi, and J. Faye (eds.), *The Problem of the Unity of Science* (pp. 3–14). Singapore: World Scientific Publishing.

Alai, M. (1998). *Filosofia della scienza del Novecento*. Rome: Armando.

Bird, A. (1998). *Philosophy of Science*. Abingdon, UK: Routledge.

Blackburn, S. (2005). *Dictionary of Philosophy, 2nd Edition*. Oxford: Oxford University Press.

Brunswik, E. (1952). *The Conceptual Framework of Psychology*. Chicago, IL: University of Chicago Press.

Carnap, R. (1932). Il superamento della metafisica mediante l'analisi logica del linguaggio, Il neoempirismo, 7: 504–507, 510–520. [reprinted from *Überwindung der Metaphysik durch logische Analyse der Sprache, Erkenntnis*, 2: 219–240]

Castiglioni, M. and Corradini, A. (2003). *Modelli epistemologici in psicologia*. Rome: Carocci.

Collingwood, R. G. (1946). *The Idea of History*. Oxford: Oxford University Press.

Di Francesco, M. (1994). Aspetti logico-linguistici dell'impresa scientifica. In G. Giorello (ed.), *Introduzione alla Filosofia della Scienza* (pp. 79–137). Milan: Bompiani.

Dray, W. (1957). *Laws and Explanation in History*. London: Oxford University Press.

Dupré, J. (1993). *The Disorder of Things. Metaphysical Foundations of the Disunity of Science*. Cambridge, MA: Harvard University Press.

Feyerabend, K. (1975). *Against Method*. London: New Left Books.

French, S. (2008). The structure of theories. In S. Psillos and M. Curd (eds.), *The Routledge Companion to Philosophy of Science*. London and New York: Routledge.

Hacking, I. (1996). The disunities of sciences. In P. Galison and D. J. Stump (eds.), *The Disunity of Science. Boundaries, Contexts and Power* (pp. 37–74). Stanford, CA: Stanford University Press.

Hahn, H., Neurath, O., and Carnap, R. (1929). La concezione scientifica del mondo. In A. Pasquinelli (ed.), 1979, Bari: Laterza. [reprinted from *Wissenschaftliche Weltauffassung*. Wien: Der Wiener Kreis]

Hempel, C. G. (1942). The function of general laws in history. *Journal of Philosophy*, 39: 35–48.

Hempel, C. G. (1961–62). Explanation and prediction by covering laws. In J. H. Fetzer (ed.) (2001), *The Philosophy of Carl G. Hempel* (pp. 69–86). Oxford: Oxford University Press. [reprinted from *Philosophy of Science: the Delaware Seminar*, vol. 1, by B. Baumrin (ed.), New York: Interscience]

Hempel, C. G. (1962a). Explanation in science and history. In J. H. Fetzer (2001), *The Philosophy of Carl G. Hempel* (pp. 276–296). Oxford: Oxford University Press. [reprinted from R. G. Colodny (ed.), *Frontiers of Science and Philosophy* (pp. 9–33). Pittsburgh, PA: University of Pittsburgh Press]

Hempel, C. G. (1962b). Deductive–nomological versus statistical explanation. In J. H. Fetzer (2001), *The Philosophy of Carl G. Hempel* (pp. 87–145). Oxford: Oxford University Press. [reprinted from *Minnesota Studies in the Philosophy of Science* (pp. 98–169), by H. Feigl and G. Maxwell (eds.), Minneapolis, MN: University of Minnesota Press]

Hempel, C. G. (1963). Reasons and covering laws in historical explanation. In J. H. Fetzer (ed.) (2001), *The Philosophy of Carl G. Hempel* (pp. 297–310). Oxford: Oxford University Press. [reprinted from *Philosophy and History*, by S. Hook (ed.), New York: New York University Press]

Hempel, C. G. (1969). Logical positivism and the social sciences. In P. Achinstein and S. F. Barker (eds.), *The Legacy of Logical Positivism*. Baltimore, MD: Johns Hopkins University Press.

Hempel, C. G. (1979). Scientific rationality: Normative vs. descriptive construals. In J. H. Fetzer (ed.) (2001), *The Philosophy of Carl G. Hempel* (pp. 358–371). Oxford: Oxford University Press. [reprinted from *Wittgenstein, the Vienna Circle, and Critical Rationalism. Proceedings of the third International Wittgenstein Symposium*, August 1978, by H. Berghel, A. Huebner, and E. Koehler (eds.), Vienna: Hoelder-Pichler-Tempsky]

Hempel, C. G. (1983). Valuation and objectivity in science. In J. H. Fetzer (ed.) (2001), *The Philosophy of Carl G. Hempel* (pp. 372–395). Oxford: Oxford University Press. [reprinted from *Physics, Philosophy and Psychoanalysis: Essays in Honor of Adolf Grünbaum*, by R. S. Cohen and L. Laudan (eds.), Dordrecht/Boston, MA: Riedel]

Kazdin, E. A. (2003). Methodology: What it is and why it is so important. In A. E. Kazdin (ed.), *Methodological Issues and Strategies in Clinical Research* (3rd edn) (pp. 5–22). Washington, DC: American Psychological Association.

Kuhn, T. (1962). *The Structure of Scientific Revolution*. Chicago, IL: University of Chicago Press.

Leahey, T. H. (1992). *A History of Psychology*. Englewood Cliffs, NJ: Prentice Hall.

Lundin, R. W. (1996). *Theories and Systems of Psychology*. Lexington, MA: Heath.

McBurney, D. H. and White, M. L. (2009). *Research Methods*. Belmont, CA: Wadsworth.

Rosenbleuth, A., Wiener, N., and Bigelow, J. (1943). Behavior, purpose and teleology. *Philosophy of Science*, 10, 1: 18–24.

Taylor, C. (1964). *The Explanation of Behaviour*. London: Routledge & Kegan Paul.

Von Wright, G. H. (1971). *Explanation and Understanding*. London: Routledge & Kegan Paul.

2

UNITY OF LANGUAGE

The issue of unity of science concerns the subject of language in many ways. First, language has a complex relationship with the objects it refers to. Every kind of language, from natural languages to technical ones, has its own vocabulary and its own structure, with the purpose of composing specific meanings: the relationship between concepts and objects is dynamic, and this could be a crucial issue for the unity of science from a methodological point of view. Second, language conveys knowledge; it is the *medium* for communicating what is going on in the world and what an individual, or a group of individuals, thinks. Language, according to this perspective, is the primary tool of every human enterprise, including the science. In fact, and this is the third point, every scientific discipline has its own specific language (technical terms, particular expressions, typical signs), nonetheless every discipline shares huge linguistic areas with other disciplines and/or with natural languages.

While the plurality of languages is a matter of fact, its local (in this case, in the field of science) unity is not. The features just outlined above show why the issue of the unity of scientific language is so fundamental for science and its unification. If science is, somehow, unified, there must be a language that makes science different from any other human task. The unity of scientific language, in other words, would reflect, and guarantee, the alleged unity of science, beside the apparent linguistic diversity that marks every discipline. In order to critically explore this issue, it is possible to consider the positions of two eminent philosophers: on the one hand, Jerry Fodor, dealing with an alleged mental language ("mentalese") supporting the development of our natural languages; on the other hand, Rudolph Carnap, whose proposal is about the general structure of scientific language. Despite the undoubted distance of these proposals, they can shed some light on the issue of the unity of language in science. We will begin with the illustration of some peculiar points of Fodor's theory on the language of thought, then focus on Carnap's proposal as it is specifically concerned with the issue of unity of scientific language.

Jerry Fodor's *Language of Thought*

The philosopher Jerry Fodor approached the issue of mental processes by using the concept of mental representation. In fact, contrary to many opponents, he was persuaded that such kinds of processes really exist and can be explored by means of empirical research as well as by speculation. But assuming the existence of mental representations gave rise to many philosophical problems, among them, the issue of an alleged internal language that permits us to think in complex terms and to learn our natural languages. In Fodor's view, an individual cannot learn a language without knowing the meaning of its predicates, and this involves learning the extension (that is, the rules under which the predicates fall) of its predicates. But, and this is the crucial point, one cannot learn that the predicates (P) falls under specific rules (R) unless one has a language in which P and R can be represented (Fodor, 1975: 64). In other words, Fodor supposed the existence of an internal, private language (internal code or representational system) in order to give an account of our ability to learn and to use languages. This internal code would allow for the carrying out of the computations which govern all human behavior, from mental representations to actions. Two main features can be underscored regarding the internal language:

1. Richness: the width of the functions of this internal code makes Fodor suppose that this internal language must be rich enough to express the extension of any natural language predicate that can be learned. Natural languages' extension, in other words, is contained within the internal language domain. What is denied is that an individual can learn a language that has more expressive power than the original (internal) one. In other words, the extension of every natural language predicate must be in principle expressible in the previously available internal language. This means that the process of learning is to "discover" the predicates' extensions, already contained in the representational system. Simple natural predicates are coded in elaborate formulae, in terms of internal code, and that can explain why learning one part of a natural language is a precondition for learning the rest: the first-learned parts work as abbreviations of complicated formulae that reduce the individual's cognitive engagement, increasing his/her thought skills. This gives an account of the increase in complexity of thought usually associated with the increase in language mastery.

2. Compositionality: complex expressions are derivable from simple expressions properly combined. Compositionality accounts for creativity, while what was just outlined above may convey the idea that everything is already written within us, encoded in the representational system. Instead, propositions and their components can be arranged in different ways, creating a virtually infinite number of possible structures. Learning concepts, in this view, can be reconstructed as a process in which novel complex concepts are composed out of their previously given elements (Fodor, 1975: 96).

Clearly, the machine analogy and the referral to nativism are central points in Fodor's theory. As machines, individuals are provided with an internal language (software) which allows for the processing of information in order to fulfill ordinary tasks of everyday life. Moreover, people are naturally wired with this inner language from birth.

To sum up, individuals have an internal language that processes information and constitutes a representational system, in the sense that it elaborates, composes and connects concepts that lead individuals' behavior. The outputs of the system are propositional attitudes, language, complex behaviors. But what is the structure of this internal language? How does it work? To answer these questions we have to take a brief look at the subject known as folk psychology.

Folk psychology is the perspective according to which the reference to mental states is useful in order to predict and explain behaviors of others and of oneself. In Fodor's view, folk psychology involves the existence of mental causation, that is, the belief that mental states, such as thoughts, desires, etc., have a causal role in behavior. If one asks a man waiting in line at the grocery why he is waiting in that way, he would probably say something like: "I am here because I know that here I can find what I need and the quality of the products is quite high." He would answer by referring to mental states that he considers (causally) relevant in order to explain his behavior. In other words, people usually explain their behaviors in terms of propositional attitudes, which are relational states connecting an individual and a proposition (Fodor, 1985: 84). Folk psychological explanations strongly involve the existence of propositional attitudes and their causal role in our mental functioning: we behave as we do because we have certain thoughts, beliefs, desires, etc. In other words, we are minded (aware of) and engage in behavior that is influenced by our mental states (Cain, 2002: 2). In this way, Fodor welcomes and promotes the relevance of mental life (in a representational form), which characterizes the common sense psychological explanations of everyday life.

Within a folk psychological frame, the author supports a functionalistic point of view; from this perspective, every mental state is identifiable with its own causal role within a virtual network whose knots (intersections) are mental states themselves. The essential feature of each state is the causal and relational position it holds with other states in the network. In other words, every mental state (or predicate) can be localized in the network exclusively specifying its potential or effective causal relations with other mental states (or predicates). Therefore, we have a causal network, where the semantic content of each state doesn't matter; the only aspect that matters is its potential causal effect on the other knots. In addition to this, Fodor maintains that there is another network, that he calls inferential (Fodor, 1985: 85–6), generated by the semantic aspects of the states: every knot of this network contains the semantic content of each state. Thus, we have two independent networks: a causal network, which qualifies each state with its potential or effective causal relations, and an inferential network, which qualifies each state with its semantic content. What is immediately clear is that the semantic content of a statement is manifest and explicit: the man waiting in line at the grocery straightforwardly understands the meaning of the explanation he provides when someone asks why he is there. On the other hand the causal network (that is, the causal relations between mental states) is not directly self-evident to us. At the very least, it requires introspection, but this is a very controversial issue which will not be explored here. Fodor's crucial point is that there is a form of partial isomorphism between the two networks: "the causal role of a propositional attitude mirrors the semantic role of the proposition that is its object" (1985: 86). This isomorphism guarantees that the assignment of semantic contents to a proposition is connected to and constrained by the belonging of the proposition to the casual network of those propositions that exhibit proper patterns of causal relation. In other words, it is possible to "deduce the causal consequences of being in a mental state from the semantic relations of its propositional object" (Fodor, 1985: 87), even if the causal network is directly responsible for the causal effects. To sum up, Fodor distinguishes between causal and semantic properties, maintaining that their connection is guaranteed by the alleged isomorphism between the two networks.

Let's now go back to our original question. The structure of the internal code, which is our mental language, is made by a sort of causal network paired to a semantic one, as mentioned above. The semantic network is explicit, as earlier specified, but what about the causal one? Fodor considers causal properties and syntactic properties in the same way: the syntactic structure embodies and conveys the shape of a symbol (e.g., in geometrical or acoustical terms), and thus the potential or actual relations with other symbols. If this is true, the semantic relations among symbols can be entirely captured by the symbols' syntactic properties and the relations among them (Murat, 2010). Since syntax conveys the functional role of symbols, it is clear why the causal role is equivalent to the syntactic role. On this basis, Fodor, following the machine analogy, supports the priority of syntax over semantic and gives a naturalistic account of thinking: we handle symbols in a syntactic (formal) way, as a computer device, but we are able to preserve the semantic relations in virtue of the networks' mirroring, as outlined. According to this perspective, the author's position seems to subscribe to a sort of unification of any kind of natural language in terms of formal logic, which would also provide solid grounds for the unification of the scientific language, in accordance with the supporters of the neo-positivistic movement (see Chapter 1).

Rudolph Carnap's outlook

The philosopher Rudolph Carnap believed that human knowledge begins with the inquiry into what we experience with our senses. In other words, the basis of knowledge has its roots in subjective data which each individual can detect and explore. One of the major problems is that this data is private, that is, accessible by me and only me: every experience is my experience and no one but me can test it. This would lead to a sort of paradox:

a   if the source of the meaning of knowledge comes from experience,
b   and, if this experience is mine and only mine (is not accessible by others),

c   then, the source of all knowledge is private and intersubjective (scientific) knowledge is impossible.

In other words, the problem of private experience as the basis of all knowledge deals with the issue of intersubjectivity, that is, the eventuality that the opinion about a fact, event, or property of different subjects (whose experiences, as noticed above, are private) can coincide (Blackburn, 2005). In Carnap's view, the possibility of an intersubjective agreement resides in the fact that individuals, in similar circumstances, behave in a similar way (Severino, 1966: 6). According to this perspective, the possibility of an intersubjective knowledge deals with the fact that, in similar circumstances, individuals use their language in similar ways. This is the reason why Carnap believed that the issue of the structure of scientific language was a fundamental problem to be faced.

As I said above, Carnap held that direct experience is strictly individual, different in many ways from that of everyone else. In this sense, the content of experience is evidently not expressible and its meaning is available only for the individual who is directly experiencing it. The use of a proper language is the only feasible way to translate those subjective data into objective (that is, communicable) data. In order to fulfill this task, Carnap relies on the study of language: the reason is that language is made of symbols and only symbols can permit an intersubjective communication. In fact, language is able to condense those aspects of experience, as seen above, that are by definition not expressible. In this perspective, language is a sort of common area that links and intersects the plurality of subjective experiences (Severino, 1966: 14). By means of language, the philosopher's goal is to eliminate possible ambiguities in communication among individuals and, thus, to open up the possibility of an intersubjective science.

From a methodological point of view, Carnap maintains that science only deals with the structure of objects, not with their properties. What does this mean? We need to explore what the author here means by property. The properties of an object refer to its appearance, to its peculiar features (Carnap, 1928). More precisely, properties refer to the subjective experience of the object, to what the individual directly knows about it. Since properties are not intersubjectively expressible, the scientific description of an object cannot be a description of properties. It has to be a description of *formal* properties, that is a description of relations. This kind of description illustrates features that can be specified without mentioning the content and the peculiarities of the object, but, indeed, its relations within a field of objects (Carnap, 1928: 95). An example of a description of properties might be as follows: the objects a, b, c belong to the same field. Each one is a man. A is 20 years old and is tall, b is 21, is short and thin, c is corpulent. On the other hand, an example of a description of relation might be as follows: the objects a, b, c belong to the same field. A is the father of b, b is the mother of c, c is the son of b, a is sixty years older than c (Carnap, 1928: 93). As noted, the second description of properties sets aside superficial, contingent features of the objects, while it considers the formal relations within that field of object and the relations involving those objects. The totality of the formal (relational) features is included in the so-called *structure*. The study of the structure involves the highest level of formalization because it provides the exploration of the totality of an object's relational properties within the considered field.

The structural description unequivocally allows for an object to be singled out from other objects in the same field. In fact, the combination of formal relations that mark an object within a field refers only to that object. In other terms, two objects with the same structure are objectively the same object, though subjectively they can be different. As an example, let's consider a and a'. They are objectively (in terms of structure) the same, in fact they both are fathers. Even so, they are different persons, so they are subjectively (in term of properties) different, e.g., a is 30, tall and thin, a' is 60, short and fat. In principle, every object can be described in terms of structural features and, in Carnap's view, only this kind of description is scientifically valid (1928: 350): scientific propositions exclusively deal with logic relations, without specifying objects' peculiarities. This is true also for language's structure. In *The Logical Syntax of Language* (1934), Carnap maintains that language is a form of calculus, because it deals with symbols assumed to be distributed in different classes. In particular, syntax has to do with that part of language that displays the form of a calculus: indeed, the object of syntax is the formal aspect of words (symbols) combination. Syntax deals with the structure of language, while it ignores the exterior form of symbols. In other words, what is important from a syntactic point of view is the relations between symbols, not their exterior features; in line with Carnap's thought, syntax provides a structural description of language, leaving aside other properties of symbols.

To sum up, it seems that, in Carnap's view, the goal of science is to use language as a tool, a form of calculus whose aim is to discover and describe the relations between objects, that is, to discover their structure (which is detectable objectively), while ignoring objects' superficial features (which can be experienced subjectively) (Carnap, 1928: 103). Carnap's proposal has a clear methodological impact: in order to reach an intersubjective form of science, his method prescribes tracing a phenomena's experience back to expressible propositions, in terms of formal logic. This does not mean that the exterior properties are the structure, but only that they can be precisely *traced back* to the structure, in order to minimize possible communicative ambiguity and permit intersubjective communication. In the author's words, "every scientific statement can be in principle converted into nothing else but a structural statement" (Carnap, 1928: 103). For Carnap, this is the basis for the unification of science: the aim of finding out structural statements allows the scientific enterprise to be organized unitarily, no matter the differences between the variety of scientific branches (and their objects). Thus, formal logic is the language of science and turns out to be its methodological backbone.

Starting from the perspectives thus briefly outlined, we will try to highlight some important aspects regarding the issue of language which deal with the unity of science. First, both Fodor and Carnap seem to consider the importance of a sort of primitive language that would provide the possibility of an intersubjective knowledge. Without that basic tool, the fact that two subjects can reach an agreement on what they are dealing with would be impossible. An intersubjective science has to plunge its roots into the observation statements, that is, statements referring to how things appear to people, beyond the differences connected to the use of different natural languages. Private knowledge, in this way, can be translated into public knowledge as pointed out by Fodor (i.e., the syntactic level provides a general and common framework by which to organize knowledge) and by Carnap (i.e., the structural level allows one to go beyond an account of the object in terms of properties). Scientific language, in general terms, exceeds the barriers of natural languages in order to avoid *multivocalness* (Neurath, 1944: 6), that is, indicating the same object by means of different expressions.

Consequently, translatability can be considered to be the process at the basis of a methodological united science, as Neurath explicitly maintains (1944: 6–10). This point can be explained in terms of different levels of inquiry. At a superficial level we find what Carnap calls properties. They are the object's features, its appearance as the subjective experience portrays it. In Fodor's terms, the superficial level refers to the semantic content of experience. This level is a very rich mess of information, which is not really useful for scientific purposes: on the one hand, because it abounds in information, on the other hand, because its analysis strongly depends upon each observer's subjective perspective. The issue of translatability deals with the need to translate this level to another one, more suitable for scientific goals. This is the syntactic (or structural) level, where only the reciprocal relations between items count. This level of inquiry permits and provides intersubjective reliability, a smaller quantity of information to manage, and applies to virtually every object, no matter its particular feature. These seem to be good reasons to prefer a syntactic approach to science.

In summary, it can be useful to highlight some features that a descriptive language has to fulfill in order to be scientifically reliable. This language has to be public, that is, expressible to others and not private. It has to be intersubjective in that it has to provide the possibility of an agreement when observing the same object. Moreover, it has to be syntactic in character, focusing on structural and relational aspects of the object. Finally, as a consequences of the latter features, it turns out that this language is relatively simple, in the sense that it can reduce a huge amount of information into a relatively small quantity of data, leaving aside information that is considered peripheral or irrelevant for scientific purposes.

References

Blackburn, S. (2005). *Dictionary of Philosophy, 2nd Edition*. Oxford: Oxford University Press.

Cain, M. J. (2002). *Fodor: Language, Mind and Philosophy*. Cambridge, UK: Polity.

Carnap, R. (1928). *Der Logische Aufbau der Welt*. Leipzig: Felix Meiner. [Italian translation *La costruzione logica del mondo*, Milan: Fabbri]

Carnap, R. (1934). *The Logical Syntax of Language*. New York: Humanities Press.

Fodor, J. (1975). *Language of Thought*. Cambridge, MA: Harvard University Press.

Fodor, J. (1985). Fodor's guide to mental representation: The intelligent auntie's vademe-cum. *Mind*, 94: 66–100.

Murat, A. (2010). The language of thought hypothesis. In E. N. Zalta (ed.), *Stanford Encyclopedia of Philosophy* (winter2003 edn), http://plato.stanford.edu/entries/language-thought

Neurath, O. (1944). *Foundations of the Social Sciences*. Chicago, IL: University of Chicago Press.

Severino, E. (ed.) (1966). *La costruzione logica del mondo*. Milan: Fabbri.

3

UNITY OF LAWS

The issue of the reduction between theories

Reflection on the possibility of a unification of science is closely connected to the relation between different theories belonging to the same or to different disciplines. To condense a certain number of theories into a more comprehensive one, or to trace back the study of a specific group of objects to the conceptual and theoretical devices of a more basic theory, is a fundamental epistemic aim for those who support the program of the unity of science. One of the main reasons seems to be that unity is considered to be an indication of rigor, reliability, and truth. Thus, to look for unity means to increase the authority of science in general – or of a scientific discipline – in terms of explanatory and predictive power. In other words, reduction is viewed by its supporters as an epistemological virtue to be pursued, intrinsically linked to the progress of science.

In this chapter, I will try to highlight some primary features of the issue of reduction. Its epistemological version will be treated, while the ontological issues connected to this debate will be the subject of Chapter 4. I will deal with this topic by referring to some of the most relevant influential authors, such as Ernest Nagel and Carl Hempel. In the second part of the chapter, some remarks on the issue will be useful in order to deal with the problem of the non-formal aspects of reduction.

Formal aspects of reduction

In his most influential work, *The Structure of Science*, Ernest Nagel (1961) tried to give a deep account of the problem of reduction. In very general terms, reduction is defined as the explanation of a theory or a set of laws established in one specific area of inquiry (the so-called "secondary science") by means of a theory, or a set of laws, formulated in some other domain (the "primary science") (p. 338). The author distinguishes two kinds of reduction. The first, which is unproblematic and called homogeneous, deals with the broadening of the scope of a theory: once formulated for a type of phenomenon exhibited by a restricted class of objects, now the theory is extended to cover that phenomenon when manifested by a broader class of objects. This kind of reduction turns out to be unproblematic because there are strong similarities between the objects it refers to and the descriptive terms of the primary and secondary sciences are the same. Such a form of reduction, in Nagel's view, is commonly accepted as a sign of scientific development.

The second case of reduction, which the author calls heterogeneous, shows the opposite characteristics: the objects explained by the secondary science are qualitatively different from those explained by the primary science, initially formulated with the aim of dealing with another class of objects. The class of objects of the secondary science is somewhat assimilated to the class of objects of the primary one. Consequently, the primary science doesn't contain the characteristic secondary science's descriptive terms, which are not included in its theoretical arsenal (Nagel, 1961: 339–40). This kind of reduction is quite problematic because, at least *prima facie*, a certain class of objects is treated *as if* it were similar (or identical) to another qualitatively dissimilar class of objects, for which the primary science was originally devised. This is the type of reduction for which Nagel formulates the formal conditions for reduction, which are conditions that have to be satisfied in order to make a reduction possible. Three categories of formal conditions can be distinguished, following Nagel's proposal (pp. 345–58):

1. The first condition asserts that the theories, or sciences, involved in the process of reduction have to fulfill the requirement to be explicitly formulated in all their parts, taking into account axioms, special hypotheses, laws, and other components. As the author clearly points out, this is an ideal demand, rather than a description of the actual state of the theory under consideration. Despite that, this condition of explicitness requires that the content of scientific formulations be carefully classified into definite categories, in order to allow a formal, i.e., logical, analysis of it. The rationale at the basis of this condition is that the classification of the theory constituents into theoretical postulates, experimental laws, observation statements, and "borrowed laws" evidently makes the formal analysis of that theory possible and more clear (Hempel, 1969: 190).

2. The second condition involves the consideration of a particular group of terms called *primitives*. Since the aim of a formal examination of reduction requires the analysis of the linguistic structure of a theory, it is of fundamental importance to distinguish the elementary expressions which give meaning to all of the constituents of the theory. The meaning of these expressions are fixed by their practical use or by explicit norms and can be locutions of formal logic (or mathematical formulae), expressions taken from specialized technical jargon or even taken from ordinary language. The purpose of these primitive expressions is, with the help of purely logical locutions, to form the basis of the meaning of all other descriptive expressions in that scientific

discipline. In other words, they serve as a linguistic frame whose purpose is to shed light on all linguistic expressions within a theory, i.e., to explain all the meanings of its locutions. These expressions constitute the logical core of a theory and can, in short, be divided into observational primitives and theoretical primitives, on the basis of their relying on empirical data or theoretical formulation (Nagel, 1961: 349–51).

3.   The third condition relies on the fact that the relation between two theories (or sciences) is characterized by the existence of both a number of expressions whose meaning is shared, e.g., statements of formal logic, mathematical formulae, and also a usually large number of expressions which are not shared, i.e., expressions that are formulated in the secondary theory but are not in the primary theory. Hence, in order to reduce one theory to another whose relation is similar to that presented, a linkage between the theories must be established. In fact, if the secondary theory does not contain terms that appear in the assumptions made by the primary one, it is *prima facie* impossible to reduce the former to the latter. In order to reduce a theory that contains some term that doesn't appear in the reducing theory, two conditions are necessary: the condition of *connectability* and the condition of *derivability* (1961: 353–4). The former aims to introduce assumptions which permit relations to be established between the two theories involved in reduction. This involves a definition of the concepts of the secondary theory in terms of the primary theory vocabulary, specifying the necessary and sufficient condition for their use within the reducing theory (Hempel, 1969: 198). Examples of this principle are bridge laws, which have the peculiar feature of containing predicates both of the reduced and the reducing theory (Fodor, 1974: 98). This entails a sort of translation of the principles of the secondary theory into principles of the primary theory (Hempel, 1969: 197). The latter condition, the derivability condition, stipulates, with the help of the condition outlined above, that the laws of the secondary theory must be logically derivable from the theoretical assumptions of the primary theory.

These formal aspects apply to virtually every theory and/or scientific discipline, because no empirical content has been considered in their formulation. Depending on the perspective assumed, this can be seen as a virtue or as a limitation. Whether this is a virtue or not will be determined after discussing the relevance of the non-formal issues of reduction, namely the conditions which have empirical or factual character.

Non-formal aspects of reduction

The fact that all, or some, of the conditions just outlined have been met by the theories under scrutiny does not assure the noteworthiness of the reduction under inquiry. Many other considerations must be evaluated in order to test its appropriateness. These considerations deal with pragmatic issues of reduction; in other words, they deal with the assessment of the real instances in which reduction takes place. In what follows, an account will be given of the most interesting aspects that must be considered when evaluating a reduction from a non-formal point of view:

1. First, the primary theory, that is the reducing one, has to prove its probative force. In other words, its theoretical assumptions have to be strongly confirmed by empirical evidence (Nagel, 1961: 358). This condition relates to the degree of justification of the reducing theory within its original field of formulation.

2. Second, the reduction must prove to be fertile. In other words, the reduction has to facilitate the aim to develop the secondary theory, suggesting interesting ways to further or correct the knowledge thus far accepted. Another mark of fertility can be described as follows: the evidence of the secondary theory's laws serves as indirect evidence to support the theoretical postulates of the primary theory (1961: 360–1). Thus, the convergence of evidence belonging to different parts of the secondary science or theory, reciprocally providing probatory material for each other (i.e., toward the justification of the primary science as a whole), can be considered as an important empirical index of the fecundity of the reduction.

3. Third, the appropriateness of the reduction is contingent, that is, it depends on the particular stage of development of the disciplines involved. On the one hand, the reducing theory must contain specific parts (theoretical postulates or descriptive terms) that have a primary role in the reduction process. A certain (primary) theory may have these characteristics at a specific stage of its development while at other stages it may not be distinguished in this way.[1] On the other hand, the reduced theory may be in a stage of active development, whose primary goal is to explore and classify the objects of its domain. In a situation like this, attempts to reduce this theory, even if formally successful, can be self-defeating, as precious energies are diverted from work on crucial questions or problems at that stage of development. In cases like these, the reduction to a primary theory is ineffective and does not provide useful guidance to improve knowledge regarding the secondary theory's object of inquiry. Therefore, the issue of reducibility (or irreducibility) of a theory has to be temporally qualified.

4. The suitability of a reductive explanation depends on the explanatory power of the theory to be (potentially) reduced. When a theory can explain a (macro) regularity with few exceptions, redescribing that phenomenon in terms of micro regularities provides little or no further explanation. The situation is different when the explanation at the macro level shows exceptions or irregularities. These deviant phenomena push scientists to look for micro explanations of such irregularities (Wimsatt, 1976: 679).

5. Even in cases of formally successful reduction (i.e., the classical example of the reduction of the laws of thermodynamics to the kinetic theory of matter), the

disappearance of the secondary theory is not guaranteed. The secondary theory can survive as an independent theory for practical reasons, that is, because its use is particularly useful or heuristically reliable in contexts where the theory is applied.[2] This leads to the consideration that a theory can persist because of its adequateness within the context of use. In fact, its reduction to a reducing theory can result in "irrelevant complexities of descriptions" (Sarkar, 2008: 431).

6.   The reflection on the non-formal aspects of reduction calls for the consideration of two different meanings of "rational" (Wimsatt, 1976: 672). On the one hand, rationality can be seen as the propensity to achieve the aim of science (i.e., in very general terms, explaining phenomena) in the optimal way; on the other hand, rationality can be seen as the propensity to improve the formal rigor in scientific formulations. Within a formal frame, these two meanings have often been considered as overlapping: it is rational to improve the degree of formal rigor of a theory in order to improve its explanatory power. But, on the basis of empirical and practical considerations, the relation between these two functions has to be examined in depth, as will be clear at the end of this chapter.

Supporters of the unification of sciences have always attributed more importance to the formal aspects of reduction, though their awareness of the importance of the non-formal aspects cannot be forgotten (Hempel, 1969: 190, 206). The issue of formal/non-formal aspects of reduction deals, on one hand, with the necessity of maintaining an epistemological outlook on the topic and, on the other hand, with the opportunity to support ontological claims about the subject matter of inquiry.

Reasons for the linguistic turn and its relevance for the issue of the unity of science

As Carl Hempel clearly points out (1969: 189), the debate on the problem of reduction has been taking a linguistic turn for many years, mainly though not exclusively among those who supported the concept of the unity of science in the nineteenth century. In general terms, the linguistic turn consists in the priority examination of the relations between the terms and the laws of the theories (or sciences) involved in the reduction process. Ontological issues – regarding the nature of the objects of inquiry – are left aside in order to highlight the epistemic side of the scientific enterprise. But what are the reasons why a linguistic (that is, epistemic) approach is preferable? I will try to bring to light some of the major aspects that justify a linguistic approach.

An ontological account of reductionism would state that some properties of one subject or event are derivable from (or identical to) the properties of another subject or event (Nagel, 1961: 264; Fodor, 1974: 102), usually physical. But how can the scientist conceptually distinguish between physical and, say, chemical, biological, or psychological events or occurrences? For Hempel (1969), "objects, states, and events cannot be unambiguously divided into mutually exclusive classes of 'physical entities,' 'chemical entities,' 'biological entities'" (p. 190), because any individual event can become an object of inquiry for many different disciplines, depending on the point of view that the observer decides to assume (Agazzi, 2000: 11). In other words, every theory (or scientific discipline) deals with particular aspects of the object, characterizing them as the focus of its investigation. In this sense, no specific physical, chemical, or whatsoever objects exist. These adjectives express different points of view adopted during the scientific inquiry of different aspects of (frequently) the same object.[3] In other words, the distinction between different kinds of objects is "theory-laden": in Hempel's words, "the distinction will concern states-under-a-theoretical-characterization" (1969: 195). Thus, a conception based on the allegedly intrinsic diversity between different kinds of objects would suggest that the possibility to reduce one theory to another depends on the inspection of the properties of the objects, or their "nature", instead of investigating the relations between the theories, that is, of points of view. The crucial point here is that such properties or "natures" are not considered as pre-theoretical entities,[4] but as components of the theory (or scientific discipline) under scrutiny, as Nagel points out (1961: 364–5):

> Whether a given set of "properties" or "behavioral traits" of macroscopic objects can be explained by, or reduce to, the "properties" or "behavioral traits" of atoms and molecules is a function of whatever theory is adopted for specifying the "natures" of these elements.

In other words, for these authors the possibility of reduction is a matter of relations between theories and their components, that is, a matter of syntactic analysis oriented to the purely formal aspects of theoretical terms' combination. Refusing this approach would be to espouse a theory-laden approach before and/or despite the confrontation with the empirical data, which implies the improper holding of unjustified metaphysical assumptions.

In conclusion, does this epistemic, formal, syntactic approach to reduction matter for the issue of the unification of science? At first glance, if unification is understood as the erection of an intricate building (i.e., science) made of different bricks (i.e., the different scientific disciplines or theories) that turn out to be mutually compatible, it is clear that this approach is useful for the construction of the building, because it deals with the possibility of the linkages between bricks. In this sense, a strong ontological commitment about the objects which constitute the topic of the diverse sciences or theories would lead to two critical problems. On the one hand, as seen above, the risk of falling into obscure, unjustified metaphysical assumptions about the world. On the other hand, the focus on the supposed ontological diversity of things would not provide a fertile and strong ground for the unification of sciences: on the contrary, it would be a crucial obstacle on this path. A formal approach, as those briefly outlined above, permits one to clearly analyze the relations between theories and to answer questions such as: how does science develop? Do theories (or scientific disciplines) cumulate or turn out to be included in broader theories? Can the meaning of theoretical terms be compared? Do the reduced theory's terms change their meaning after the reduction? How and in which cases? A linguistic analysis sheds some light on these important topics.

For Hempel (1969: 199–206) theories are seldom (if ever) linked by deductive relations; rather, the reduced ones can be conceived as special applications of the reducing ones, which include the former. Thus, theories (or scientific disciplines) are considered as commensurable entities. In fact, they can be compared on the basis of the common subject matter that they try to explain, even if they don't share a single theoretical term or principle. On the grounds of commensurability, theories can be linked to each other: as seen above, some of them (the reduced ones) will become applicable in limited domains as particular applications of a more general theory (the reducing one), thanks to the above-mentioned conditions. In this perspective, the path to scientific unification is not cumulative: a new theory doesn't simply add to an old one, in the sense of preserving the content of the old theory and adding to it. Rather, the new reducing theory includes the old one, constituting a comprehensive and coherent tool by means of which scientists can read the world from a structural (i.e., formal, syntactic) point of view. According to this view, the issue of reduction is mainly formal. However, non-formal aspects are seen as factors to be considered when evaluating the possibility to carry out effectively a reduction of a theory by means of another one. In other words, non-formal aspects deal with the practical, that is, local viability of reduction.

Notes

1 Ernest Nagel is particularly clear about this point and provides a lucid example: "In particular, though contemporary thermodynamics is undoubtedly reducible to a statistical mechanics postdating 1866 (the year in which Boltzmann succeeded in giving a statistical interpretation for the second law of thermodynamics with the help of certain statistical hypotheses), that secondary science is not reducible to the mechanics of 1700. Similarly, certain parts of nineteenth-century chemistry (and perhaps the whole of this science) is reducible to post-1925 physics, but not to the physics of a hundred years ago" (1961: 362).
2 "The molecular characterization of cell components neither prevents nor is always fully integrated with the continued traditional functional characterization of those components ... The older reduced theories and laws persist because they are adequate in their context" (Sarkar, 2008: 431).
3 For example, water and H_2O can be considered as different points of view of the same object.
4 That is, entities whose existence do not depend upon a theoretical point of view.

References

Agazzi, E. (2000). What does "the unity of science" mean? In E. Agazzi, and J. Faye (eds.), *The Problem of the Unity of Science* (pp. 3–14). Singapore: World Scientific Publishing.
Fodor, J. (1974). Special sciences (Or: The disunity of science as a working hypothesis). *Synthese*, 28(2): 97–115.
Hempel, C. G. (1969). Reduction: Ontological and linguistic facets. In J. H. Fetzer (ed.) (2001), *The Philosophy of Carl G. Hempel* (pp. 189–207). Oxford: Oxford University Press.

[reprinted from *Philosophy. Science and Method. Essays in Honor of Ernest Nagel*, by S. Morgenbesser, P. Suppes, and M. White (eds.), New York: St. Martin's Press]

Nagel, E. (1961). *The Structure of Science. Problems in the Logic of Scientific Explanation.* Cambridge, MA: Hackett.

Sarkar, S. (2008). Reduction. In S. Psillos and M. Curd (eds.), *The Routledge Companion to Philosophy of Science* (pp. 425–434). Abingdon, UK: Routledge.

Wimsatt, W. C. (1976). Reductive explanation: A functional account. In A. C. Michalos, C. A. Hooker, G. Pearce, and R. S. Cohen (eds.), *PSA Boston Studies in the Philosophy of Science* (pp. 671–710). Dordrecht: Riedel.

4

UNITY OF OBJECT

Up to this point the subject of the unity of science has been examined from the standpoint of major theoretical aspects, without considering the topic of the way the world is considered by scientists and philosophers. Since the project of unification of science is directed toward the progressive discovery of the details of nature, a major issue concerns the conception of nature and its structure. Here, "unity of object" refers to the controversial thesis that the object of science displays a sort of internal coherence that has to be discovered. Different theoretical conceptions of the structure of reality suggest different ways to pursue the project of the unification of science or, on the contrary, make it unattainable.

This chapter will first focus on the proposal of Rudolf Carnap, one of the traditional supporters of the project of the unity of science. His suggestions will shed some light on the conception of reality that supports the original proposal of formal unification. Afterwards, the proposal of Brian Ellis about scientific essentialism will be described, a position that corresponds to a unification project based on metaphysical assumptions. In conclusion, some aspects of John Dupré's promiscuous realism will be presented. This original and interesting position suggests a fundamental disunity of human knowledge on the basis of ontological assumptions.

Rudolf Carnap's nominalism

Within the empiricist tradition, abstract entities like properties, classes, etc. have been considered with suspicion. The concept of reality itself is met with the same suspicious attitude. Many empiricists, on the basis of their mistrust toward ontological commitment (Kosso, 1992: 102), tend to avoid the use of terms such as reality, although often is hard not to use them, as Carnap maintains (1950: 20). An empirical account of science implies the possibility of a unified science, based indeed on the investigation of empirical facts. As we saw in the previous chapter, the unification of science is based upon a formal account of it, but still the various scientific disciplines are in the uncomfortable position of using terms referring to reality, including words referring to abstract entities. Thus, the problem is: how is it possible to talk about nature without running into metaphysical (i.e., not empirically justified) obscurities? Keeping in line with the empiricist tradition, Rudolf Carnap tries to show that it is possible to use a language referring to abstract entities without embracing a strong ontological commitment (1950: 20).

For Carnap, if someone wants to speak about a new kind of entity, he has to introduce a linguistic framework (p. 21) for the entity in question. This framework allows for the understanding of the meaning of the linguistic expressions referring to the entity within a context (the framework itself) that talks about the world (Maxwell, 1962: 22). In other words, this framework is a device that provides meaning for the new entity within a system of things that already have meaning. On the basis of the introduction of the linguistic framework, two kinds of questions about the existence of something can be stated: internal questions and external questions. The first kind pertains to the admissibility of the entity within the framework, the second concerns the real existence of the entity (Carnap, 1950: 21). Internal questions can be answered by means of formal logic or empirical investigation, so they apparently don't concern metaphysical assumptions. From this internal perspective, in Carnap's terms:

> To recognize something as a real thing or event means to succeed in incorporating it into the system of things at a particular space–time position so that it fits together with the other things as real, according to the rules of the framework.
>
> *(1950: 21)*

Therefore, the linguistic framework is the guarantee of the (temporary) existence of the entity under scrutiny. Since we assume a linguistic framework, the "thing language," as Carnap calls it, one that talks about everyday objects, questions about the (internal) existence of various things can be raised and answered. But the acceptance of a linguistic framework for a certain kind of entity only means that the admissibility of the entity as a possible *designatum* is accepted. Moreover, the admissibility of the entity is not fixed independently from the categories of space and time, rather it is contingent, in a sort of agnostic-like ontological position, leaving open and unanswered the question about its real existence. Thus, according to a position that gives priority to the formal and syntactic aspects of the scientific inquiry, accepting the "thing world," that is, the world as described by the terms and statements of the linguistic framework, means no more than accepting a form of language, i.e., the rules for forming statements and for testing, accepting, or rejecting them (1950: 22).

On the basis of these considerations, internal questions are not problematic, while external ones are, in Carnap's opinion. In fact, the thesis of the reality of the world, to which external questions refer, cannot be formulated in the "thing language," or any other language. The "thing language" is used for practical reasons because it is useful and efficient for everyday purposes, and the decision to adopt it is based on our everyday experience. The acceptance and the consistency of the "thing language," in other words, doesn't give evidence in favor of the reality of things. Rather, its reliability "makes it advisable to accept this language" (1950: 22). Thus, the problematic nature of external questions lays in the fact that they cannot receive proper answers on the basis of the appropriateness of the internal language: in other words, the existence or reality of a thing cannot be inferred on the basis of the expedience and usefulness of the linguistic term that refers to it.

In Carnap's view, the acceptance of a linguistic framework is a practical (that is, based on considerations of usefulness and appropriateness), rather than a theoretical, question (1950: 27). Nevertheless, embracing a linguistic framework involves *de facto* the adoption of theoretical assumptions: various rules, procedures, confirmation rules, law-like sentences, etc. In other words, the author seems to underestimate the theoretical significance of the adoption of a linguistic framework, that is, a (theoretical) device assumed by the speaker/inquirer in order to achieve certain goals (e.g., to speak about abstract entities).

Clearly, the practical considerations that lead to the adoption of a linguistic framework entail the acceptance of a certain point of view, and that necessarily entails some theoretical considerations. According to Grover Maxwell (1962: 11), what is observable, and consequently what can be spoken about, is determined by science itself; therefore it is determined by specific theoretical assumptions. In other words, every kind of knowledge is bounded by the perspective assumed by the scientist, who espouses some primary theoretical considerations concerning aspects of the world that interest him or her. Without those assumptions, no inquiry can be initiated. From this it follows that there are no *a priori* or a-theoretical criteria for separating the observable from the unobservable (Maxwell, 1962: 11): that which is observable, or which it is possible to speak about, is established by precise theoretical choices which can be espoused on the basis of practical considerations (as Carnap highlighted) or considerations of other kinds. The main point, here, is that Maxwell explicitly maintains that everything we observe or speak about is a function of some theoretical assumption linked to our physiological structure, our current state of knowledge and the instruments (logical as well as practical) that we happen to have available (1962: 14–15). Therefore, this leads to a position of ontological abstentionism, because the line that divides what is observational and what is theoretical is not sharply drawn (depending on the factors outlined above) and has "no ontological significance" (Maxwell, 1962: 15).

The proposals put forward by Carnap and Maxwell are consistent with a formal account of the scientific enterprise (see the previous chapters): science sets the rules that permit one to speak about the world without an ontological commitment. In this way, science can pronounce on the features of nature, but tells nothing about their reality.

Brian Ellis' essentialism

Since science deals with the gradual understanding of reality, some thinkers consider that a central issue is to discover the essential characteristics of reality. Here, I will focus mainly on the proposal of Brian Ellis, which can be considered a fine example of essentialism. In contrast to a nominalistic position, essentialists believe that there are some kinds of things in nature whose existence is objective and mind independent (Ellis, 2001: 17; 2008: 139) and, therefore, that one can distinguish those properties of a thing that are essential to it and those that are accidental (Blackburn, 2005). The things that share the same essential properties form kinds, or sets of things whose existence would be impossible without the essential properties that characterize them.

Natural kind essentialism claims that natural kinds have essential properties. We can illustrate this as follows: to say that the possession of property P is part of the essence of the kind K necessarily implies that every member or sample of the kind K possesses P (Bird, 2009: 497). These essential properties characterize a particular kind and distinguish it from others: they constitute its essence, identity, or nature. Essential properties are fixed in nature, i.e., they are not bound by spatio-temporal constraints. In other words, it is postulated that substances that form natural kinds, e.g., chemical substances, have always shown their structure as we can observe them now. In other words, they are immutable. For example, "There is no species of chlorine existing now or at any other time that could possibly be a species of any other element than chlorine" (Ellis, 2008: 140). In contrast, this is clearly not so, for example, in the case of biological taxonomy for which evolutionary considerations would clearly violate the criterion of immutability, whose violation is considered to be a symptom that the existence of the entity at stake is not rooted in the structure of nature, but is mind dependent.

From this perspective, the world turns out to be made of things included in natural kinds, whose components share essential properties that constitute their peculiarity and differentiate them from other kinds of things.[1] These essential differences are not conventions, nor are they pragmatically chosen in order to disentangle the intrinsic disorder of nature. Rather, as we saw above, their existence is independent of the inquirer or observer; all he has to do is to discover this predetermined order. In other words, nature is not a continuous *spectrum* of substances that has to be categorized, rather it is constituted by discrete entities, precisely called natural kinds (Ellis, 2008: 140).

In more detail, according to Ellis' theory, the world is composed of things belonging to three natural kinds, whose relations are strictly hierarchical (2008: 142):

1. Substantive natural kinds include all of the natural kinds of substances.
2. Dynamic natural kinds include all of the natural kinds of events and processes.
3. Tropic natural kinds include all of the natural properties and relations.

The hierarchical relations between natural kinds are developed by Ellis' basic structural hypothesis. It assumes that at the summit of each category there is a global kind, which includes all other natural kinds in its category. It is ontologically more fundamental than any other of its species and involves, indeed, the existence of subspecies. For example, the global substantive kind would be the class of all physical systems such as fundamental particles, which evidently contains subspecies, such as electrons or quarks, for example. At the base of each hierarchy are the infimic species of the global kinds, whose main feature is that they don't have natural subspecies; in other words, they are primary constituents of their including global kind. In the middle, there are all of the kinds of greater or lesser generality composed of the infimic species and subspecies of the global kinds (for example, chemical substances). According to this hypothesis, physical nature turns out to be highly structured and characterized by distinctive real essences for each natural kind, at every level of generality. This means that every natural kind is provided with "intrinsic properties or structures in virtue of which things are of the kinds they are" (pp. 142–3).

To sum up, these are the main features enumerated by Ellis concerning natural kinds in an essentialistic frame (2001: 19–21):

1. Their existence does not depend on human interests, psychologies, perceptual apparatus, languages, practices, or choices. The distinction between natural kinds is based on facts about their essential nature.
2. They must be categorically distinct. They form discrete entities whose borders are sharp.
3. The distinction between them is based on intrinsic differences. In other words, natural kinds' members cannot differ only extrinsically, that is, depending on how things in the world happen to be arranged or happen to be related to one another.
4. If two members of a given natural kind differ intrinsically from each other, and these intrinsic differences are not ones that can be either acquired or lost by members of the kind, then they must be members of different species of the kind.
5. Natural kinds are characterized by essential properties and real essences.
6. Their qualities are immutable, time independent.

In particular, the substantive kinds are essentially defined by causal powers, rather than by structural aspects, since at the most elementary level there is no structure at all (understood as relations between parts). However, causal powers are defined in terms of dispositions, the full description of which will tell us what things having this property should be expected to do in various circumstances. For this reason, an essentialistic metaphysics like that of Ellis seems to postulate two fundamental properties in nature: dispositional properties (causal powers, capacities, propensities, which tell us what things of that kinds are supposed to do) and categorical properties (spatio-temporal and numerical relations, which provide for a proper descriptions of the diverse circumstances in which dispositional powers may act).

The centrality of dispositional properties in Ellis' proposal is supported by his thesis of *dispositionalism*, which postulates that the laws of natures describe the essences of natural kinds. At every level, laws of different hierarchical positions describe the behaviors of things which correspond to their essences. This claim, in Ellis' opinion, has two important theoretical consequences (Ellis, 2008: 143): on the one hand, he claims that the hierarchy of laws of nature is intrinsically correlated with the hierarchy of the natural kinds. Laws are solidly grounded in the world's natural kind structure (Bird, 2011). On the other hand, the laws of nature turn out to express metaphysical necessities: for example, electrons are necessarily negatively charged, physical processes are necessarily intrinsically conservative of energy, and so on.

In conclusion, scientific essentialism, as Ellis calls his own proposal, entails a well-structured world, whose properties and laws intrinsically define reality. Therefore, the proper description of the world involves the discovery of properties and laws of nature that really exist in the present and which will always exist. Theoretical assumptions such as the reduction of the complexity and multiplicity of reality to a simpler conception of it, the real existence of natural components, their stability in time, the hierarchical structure of nature, seem to provide good grounds for a project of scientific unification from a metaphysical point of view. As Ellis clearly states, "ontologies typically try to explain the overall structure of the world … The test of an ontology is how well it achieves its aim of global unification" (2001: 62).

John Dupré's promiscuous realism

In contrast to the proposal just outlined, Dupré's perspective of promiscuous realism is based on what he calls ontology of common sense, one which is strongly pluralistic. According to this perspective, common sense tends to classify things not by unifying them under a simple and unified structure of concepts, but rather by the individuation of fragmentary and diverse categories (Dupré, 1993: 19). In his opinion, one should not ignore this spontaneous, pragmatic, and pluralistic view when dealing with metaphysical issues concerning the scientific enterprise. Such an outlook may turn out to be very important when considering the ontological status of reality. Reflecting on biological classification, Dupré notes how scientific and common sense terms referring to natural kinds[2] are intrinsically different and maintains that "such divergence … often occurs for good reasons that preclude any reasonable expectation of eventual convergence between the two" (p. 27). In other words, the common-sense way of classifying things can be very different from, and even incompatible with, scientific categorization. Examples come from the vegetable as well as from the animal kingdom, as this quotation shows:

> A particularly interesting example is provided by the moths. The order Lepidoptera includes the suborders Jugatae and Frenatae. It appears that all the Jugatae are moths. The Frenatae, on the other hand, are further subdivided into the Macrolepidoptera and the Microlepidoptera. The latter seem again to be all moths. But the former include not only some moths but (all) skippers

and butterflies. The trouble here is not that we cannot give a reasonably plausible account of the extension of the English term moth, but rather that the grouping so derived is, from a biological point of view, quite meaningless.

(Dupré, 1993: 28–9)

Is there any possibility for the convergence of the two languages? The case for cladism seems to be a fine example of the intrinsic improbability that this will happen. Cladism is a biological theory affirming that taxonomic distinctions should reflect evolutionary events of lineage bifurcation, ignoring any other available criterion (for example, morphological or reproductive criteria). If there is a case for such a revision in the professional biological context, for which cladism may represent a sound theoretical perspective, it is nevertheless unlikely that ordinary, common-sense language would ever espouse such quirks of evolutionary theory, and thereby adopt this way of classifying living things.

What is at the basis of the big differences between the common-sense and the scientific way of organizing the world? Dupré is convinced that the key point is in the different functions they serve. Ordinary language has many aims in distinguishing kinds of organisms. Organisms may acquire recognition for a variety of reasons: they are economically or sociologically important, are intellectually intriguing, are furry and appealing, etc. This is true also for scientific language, where organisms may acquire recognition, and consequently become classified on the basis of morphological similarities, reproductive similarities, evolutionary considerations, etc. Moreover, such reflections show the likelihood that there may be other plausible specialized ways of classifying things, which are neither coincident with scientific nor with ordinary language: the vocabularies of the timber merchant, the furrier, the herbalist, just to borrow some of Dupré's examples. From this argument it follows that there are many grounds for classification, in ordinary language as well scientific practice. This pluralistic attitude is deemed "promiscuity" by the author, who maintains that nothing in his proposal suggests that the kinds so recognized are in any sense illusory or unreal: this is the reason why he considers himself a realist. In other words, different ways of classifying things can be conceived and each one really exists, on the grounds of the adoption of specific, and diverse, theoretical positions (Dupré, 1993: 43).

Dupré affirms that there is no general criteria for individuating kinds (within the animal world as well as within the inanimate world). Rather, questions about the breadth and borders of kinds should be considered locally, taking into account the specific features of the object and the particular problems or questions that the classifier has in mind. Consequently, classifications made on the basis of the specific features of the object can really differ from classifications made according to the particular problem at hand and this reflects, for Dupré, distinct ontological statuses (1993: 50–1). Dupré insists that this does not reflect a methodological point of view, but rather an ontological one: only a pluralistic vision of reality can take into account its incredible complexity and is likely to prove adequate for its investigation. The existence of many overlapping and intersecting kinds is not evidence for their unreality (Dupré, 1996: 105), in biology as well as in any other domain of reality:

> There is no God-given, unique way to classify the innumerable and diverse products of evolutionary process. There are many plausible and defensible ways of doing so, and the best way of doing so will depend on both the purposes of the classification and the peculiarities of the organism in question, whether those purposes belong to what is traditionally considered part of science or ordinary life … Realism about biological kinds has nothing to do with insisting that there should be some unitary cause of biological distinctions.
>
> *(Dupré, 1993: 57)*

In other words, there cannot be natural kinds from an essentialistic point of view. As was noted above, essentialism states that natural kinds are immutable, have always existed, that their members don't change in time. On the contrary, promiscuous realism affirms that natural kinds are strongly bounded to space and time. But, from this point of view, how can we define a natural kind, if the existence of its essence is denied? The naturalness of kinds is such because they represent differences in nature that, though overlapping and intersecting, really exist. To quote a previous example, there is no reason to deny that a particular subclass of Lepidoptera is recognized ordinarily as moths and that this class might exist even independently from our recognition. Discovering kinds doesn't involve discovering essences; rather, its purpose is to identify interesting (from different points of view), real discontinuities in the world (Dupré, 1993: 64–7; Cartwright, 1994).

Dupré's argument against essentialism is based on empiricist grounds, for which the evaluation of the explanatory potential and the existence of specific kinds has to be achieved by means of empirical research. In other words, the existence and usefulness of kinds is assessed *a posteriori*: the commitment to real essences (in an essentialistic frame) either is vacuous or violates this demand (Dupré, 1993: 80). In his view, what makes a kind useful in explanatory terms is that its instances share some properties or dispositions and are susceptible to the same forces. The discovery of these properties or dispositions, however, does not provide a justification for attributing the status of essentiality to some of them. For Dupré, the "naturalness" of kinds only consists in the singling out of discontinuities in nature, whose instances share common properties and dispositions, and which are susceptible to the same forces. Naturalness doesn't entail the attribution of essentiality to some of the kind's properties, since it would be a highly arbitrary and non-empirical assumption. Dupré called this position categorical empiricism (1993: 80–3).

Presuming the availability of different ways to categorize objects and the legitimacy of diverse classifications of natural kinds, Dupré supports the idea that there is room for various properly grounded scientific projects, each one describing only one of the many properties of things. In particular, there is no reason to expect a convergence of these projects onto one grand theoretical system (Dupré, 1996: 105–6). There are as many appropriate scientific projects as there are empirically grounded ways to categorize the world, therefore the flourishing of new (or non-"traditional") scientific disciplines is welcomed. As a result, the main question about the scientific enterprise becomes as follows: on which grounds do we justify the pursuit of a particular project of inquiry rather than any of the many possible alternatives? Dupré maintains that we should select those projects that best serve the goals that motivate our inquiry (1996) by means of a proper account of the features of the inquired-about object (1993: 34–57). According to such an approach, the birth and development of the special sciences are not only theoretically justified, but also desirable in order to best achieve the goals of those disciplines and to give proper and sound answers to the questions they legitimately raise.

In conclusion, the way of conceptualizing the variety of the entities in the world strongly influences the practicability of a unification project. If the world is, at some level, composed of the same kinds of properties, dispositions, and forces, the convergence of the branches of science dealing with apparently different objects would be possible and desirable. On the contrary, if the existence of real essences is denied, a unification of science according to metaphysical claims would be unjustified. Candidates other than metaphysics should come forward in order to make this enterprise feasible.

Notes

1 Most authors, as Ellis (2008: 140) maintains, would accept essentialism regarding physics or chemistry, but would be skeptical of essentialistic claims about the existence of natural kinds at higher (for example, biological or psychological) levels of complexity, mainly, but not only, because of the violation of the criterion of immutability.
2 Here the term is used in a very broad and liberal way, referring to classes of objects defined by the common possession of some important theoretical properties.

References

Bird, A. (2009). Essences and natural kinds. In R. Le Poidevin et al. (eds), *Routledge Companion to Metaphysics* (pp. 497–506). Abingdon, UK: Routledge.
Bird, A. (2011). Natural kinds. In *Stanford Encyclopedia of Philosophy*, http://plato.stanford.edu/entries/natural-kinds
Blackburn, S. (2005). *Dictionary of Philosophy, 2nd Edition*. Oxford: Oxford University Press.
Carnap, R. (1950). Empiricism, semantics, and ontology. *Revue Internationale de Philosophie*, 4: 20–40.
Cartwright, N. (1994). The metaphysics of the disunified world. *PSA: Proceedings of the Biennial Meeting of Philosophy of Science Association*, 2: 357–364.
Dupré, J. (1993). *The Disorder of Things. Metaphysical Foundations of the Disunity of Science*. Cambridge, MA: Harvard University Press.
Dupré, J. (1996). Metaphysical disorder and scientific disunity. In P. Galison, and D. Stump (eds.), *The Disunity of Science. Boundaries, Contexts and Power* (pp. 101–117). Stanford, CA: Stanford University Press.
Ellis, B. (2001). *Scientific Essentialism*. Cambridge, UK: Cambridge University Press.
Ellis, B. (2008). Essentialism and natural kinds. In S. Psillos, and M. Curd (Eds.), *The Routledge Companion to Philosophy of Science* (pp. 139–148). London and New York: Routledge.

Kosso, P. (1992). *Reading the Book of Nature. An Introduction to the Philosophy of Science.* Cambridge, MA: Cambridge University Press.

Maxwell, G. (1962). The ontological status of theoretical entities. In H. Feigl, and G. Maxwell, *Scientific Explanation, Space and Time*, vol. 3, (pp. 3–27). Minneapolis, MN: University of Minnesota Press.

PART 2

5

EVIDENCE OF FRAGMENTATION IN PSYCHOLOGY

The assumption that psychology as a science is somehow fragmented is well known among professionals and researchers and has been so since the early years of the discipline. As an example, Karl Bühler's *Die Krise der Psychologie* appeared in 1927, the same year that Lev Vygotsky's *Historical Meaning of the Crisis in Psychology: A Methodological Investigation* was published. Almost from the beginning of the success of psychology as a science and as a socially relevant discipline, an awareness (often considered uncomfortable) of psychology's disunity occupied the hearts and minds of a large number of practitioners who devoted their lives to it. Therefore, the desire to explore psychology's boundaries, limits, and structure has long been cultivated by those psychologists sensitive to these kinds of philosophical problems.

But what does *disunity* mean? Does it refer to the plurality of methods used by psychologists? Does it refer to the plethora of diverse theories that fall under the big umbrella of psychology? Or does it refer to the enormous gap that differentiates, for example, the practice of the experimentalist from that of the psychoanalyst? Does the fragmentation stem from the huge number of specialized areas within psychology, a manifestation of which includes the existence of fifty-six divisions within the American Psychological Association? These and other questions are still debated between psychologists and philosophers.

A sizeable literature dealing with fragmentation has been produced in the last thirty years, but its vastness ironically tends to mirror the very nature of the issue under investigation, showing fragmentation and disunity in contents and methodological approaches. In other words, authors writing about fragmentation, disunity and the crisis of psychology, have been facing the problem from perspectives ranging from political viewpoints (for example, Sternberg, 2005) to rhetorical (Katzko, 2002), via theoretical–methodological (Henriques, 2004; Staats, 1996), historical (Richards, 2002), educational (McGovern and Brewer, 2005) and meta-theoretical (Rychlak, 1993; Fenici, 2009) levels of inquiry. Taken as a whole, the literature on fragmentation in psychology is a sort of Tower of Babel that strives to explore the discipline's disunity, leaving the reader with the strange impression that there is no prior level of inquiry and that the task of attaining commensurability, if possible, is too hard even to be imagined.

In accordance with de Groot (1990) and Goertzen (2008), a necessary precondition for properly facing the issue of fragmentation is to put some order into the different levels of discourse in a provisional taxonomy that individuates the grounds and the features of the supposed fragmentation of psychology. In other words, it is necessary to ascertain the diversity of levels of inquiry and the priorities in the analysis of the fragmentation of our discipline. Therefore, in the following analysis, I will try to focus on the main topics of fragmentation from professional and philosophical perspectives. In fact, it will be seen that the two often intertwine over the course of development of our discipline.

The development of psychology and grounds of fragmentation

In order to begin to explore the subject of fragmentation, it is fundamental to view psychology as a human enterprise, hence as a sociocultural phenomenon. In particular, I will deal with the process that brought to life the professional role of the psychologist in Western societies, trying to discover the assumptions and conditions that constituted the basis for his/her existence as a social actor. In this brief review, many aspects of fragmentation of the discipline will be presented, though an uncontroversial definition of fragmentation is difficult to provide. In psychology it can be understood as the general tendency to tolerate and foster differences and to mistrust integration. Herein, I discuss how aspects of fragmentation emerge, for example, from the way the discipline developed, from the different sources of knowledge that merged into psychology, from the idiosyncratic approaches stemming from theoretical weaknesses regarding the application of knowledge, from the different contexts wherein psychologists are asked to intervene. These are aspects which fostered the development of psychology and substantiate its original fragmentation.

The profession of the psychologist has been a sort of crossroads where diverse professional roles converged and condensed into this new professional role. From the origin of the discipline (end of the nineteenth, beginning of the twentieth century), the role of psychologists has been primarily identified with that of the scientist (Richards, 2002: 11), whose main aim is to explore passive, "third person," objects using objective, i.e., reproducible and intersubjectively assessable, methods. The identification with the scientist is understandable, as psychology was a new discipline freshly derived from philosophy and many of the efforts of those who practiced it were directed toward providing scientific credentials for their discipline (Reisman, 1991). In other words, the role of the scientist embodied the hopes for a recognized status (hence scientific) for psychology. A second discipline which contributed to the development of the role of the psychologist was the medical profession. Many psychology practitioners originally were physicians with philosophical interests (Reisman, 1991: 21) about behavior and mind. Interrogating people about their mental conditions is readily recognized as part of the physician's roles, where the expert and the client are bound by an asymmetric relationship (Carli, Paniccia, and Lancia, 1988: 67–8; Richards, 2002: 12) based on the gap between the mastery of specific (medical) knowledge and the lack of it. In other words, the patient needs the physician in order to solve problems she/he is not able to face alone. Related to this role of physician are those of the philosopher and the teacher, which incarnate the concern for issues relating to mind, relationships, therapy, rehabilitation, education. These roles, and possibly others, fulfilled two different and complementary functions in the development of professional psychology:

1. They served as role models for "giving psychology a shape." At the beginning, psychologists didn't have a specific role, with precise boundaries and a definite field of action, at least from a social point of view. As an emerging profession, they may have felt that they required an "anchoring" to well-known professions and social roles, in order to attain a proper social legitimacy and establish a professional identity.
2. They provided people with a social representation of what psychologists were and did. The interests, field of action, objects of inquiry and methodologies of those who practiced psychology were understood by analogy and/or contrast to other well-known professions.

In a sense that will be made explicit in what follows, these role models may be considered as still active and somehow helpful today in psychological practice. This plurality of references, though useful, inevitably poses some problems relating to the identity and practice of psychologists: who are psychologists as a whole? What do they usually do as a professional community? What are their goals? What are their methods? The analogy with other professions might well provide some clues, but the core of these questions still remains open. An interesting interpretation of this peculiarity of the psychological profession is suggested by the Italian psychologists Carli et al. (1988). The authors maintain that those who benefit from a psychological intervention (for example, counseling, psychotherapy, education, assessment) don't know the nature and the modes of that intervention. In other words, they don't know how the psychologist will operate in his/her professional practice. Though, this is evidently not the case in other kinds of professions. An example may clarify this issue. The potential client of a lawyer has a relatively clear idea of what will happen during the professional relationship, even though it is the first time he/she needs a lawyer. For example, the aim of the intervention of a lawyer may be to support the client who has been involved in a lawsuit. In order to be effective, the lawyer needs to know all the information the client is able to provide about the issue of the inquiry. Moreover, the lawyer is required to use all of his/her knowledge and technical devices in order to fulfill the client's expectations, namely, to achieve the aims for which they have agreed at the beginning of their professional relationship. In sum, this kind of professional relationship is based on three assumptions:

1. The professional intervention requires a specific pattern of actions that both the client and the practitioner know and agree upon.
2. The relation is motivated by the achievement of an explicit goal.
3. The practitioner is required to accept the goal that the client proposes. If not, the relation has no longer reason to exist.

This clarity about the goal and the pattern of actions required in such a relation doesn't characterize the intervention of a psychologist (Gaj, 2009: 84–5). As already noted, the client asks for psychological intervention with specific expectations, but those expectations are strongly influenced by the various professional functions that are socially attributed to the psychologist (for example, counselor, psychotherapist, trainer, diagnostician). These so-called "social representations" of the psychological role may be very different from the "real" professional practice, i.e., what psychologists really do in their practice. In other words, between those socially influenced functions, as perceived by the client, and the real professional offer there is a gap. Psychologists are somehow called upon to fill this gap. In other words, what people think about psychological practice is often quite different from what psychologists really do.

Although the diverse social models attributed to the psychological practice may represent a hindrance to the social recognition of the discipline, they also represent opportunities. Indeed, these models may be used as means through which the methodology of intervention becomes explicit, gaining visibility to the psychological work within the social context (Carli et al., 1988: 29; Salvatore and Pamplomatas, 1993: 95–6). This issue requires further exploration.

In the relationship with a psychologist, the client adopts specific representations, choosing from those at his/her disposal (as we saw above). Moreover, the selected relational model is somehow connected to the reason the client is asking for a psychological intervention. In other words, the relational model about psychology and its practice presented by a client is consistent with the problem he/she is presenting to the psychologist. For example, two parents concerned about the explosive behaviors of their child will probably approach a psychologist thinking of his/her intervention as "educational," where the practitioner is a sort of "teacher" who will return their child's behavior to a supposed normality or acceptability. In this sense, the image of the psychological practice is somehow connected to (and influenced by) the problem presented by the client. Such a representation encourages the parents to consult a psychologist, so from this perspective it somehow promotes psychology and psychologists. Nevertheless, this representation and the consequent relationship may be distorted compared with the actual professional practice of an average psychologist. Therefore, a psychologist consulted for such a problem cannot ignore the representations of his/her clients in the process of setting up and designing his/her professional intervention. In fact, in recognizing the distorted representations of the psychological intervention, a psychologist may use them as informative material relevant for the design of his/her intervention: the relational model provides data for the assessment. In this sense, the plurality of the social representations concerning the psychological practice somehow allows for the deployment of its technical tools, thanks to the analysis of the representations displayed by the client when approaching the practitioner.

However, the question about which theory, technique, or methodology constitutes the core of the intervention remains open, since "the unclear professional boundaries are not only apparent between professional psychology and other health care disciplines but also are seen within the field itself" (Henriques and Sternberg, 2004: 1053). In conclusion, the plurality of representations which made up the role of psychologist is not only a historical aspect of the development of our discipline, but also a present feature of psychological practice. This kind of plurality doesn't deal with the institutional organization of psychologists as a professional community; rather, it is particularly evident in the various ways the psychological practice is represented by the potential beneficiaries of psychology, namely the clients.

In order to describe the framework in which psychology has developed and still expands, expressions like social representation, social role, social model, and the like have been used. The importance of such terms in the definition of the psychological practice is connected to the fact that those who practice psychology deliver a particular kind of service, that is, a process which deals with the relation between an expert and a customer. Put simply, what psychologists do is to deliver psychological services: psychology *is* a service. Now the question is, what is a service? It may first be defined as an immaterial process that is achieved within a relational and communicative process between a producer and a consumer (Olivetti Manoukian, 1998: 52). Delivering a service means managing particular aspects that characterize many elements of the process of the delivery itself (Normann, 1984). In the case of a service, the product (the service itself) cannot be previously displayed and it doesn't exist before its delivery. In other words, the service is a sort of "tip of an iceberg": the client may appreciate the whole nature of the service only after its delivery, while before its delivery what he/she may appreciate are only some partial clues about it (this is particularly true of psychological services, as shown by the examples above).

Thus, to pursue the notion of service, the difference between the production and the sale is vague and tends to disappear, not only in the case of a psychological service: producing a service is to sell it, and selling it means to produce it. Moreover, the client takes an active role in the process of delivery of the service. In other words, the client is more than a consumer because every kind of service (be it a lesson, a haircut, or a psychotherapy session) cannot take form without a certain degree of participation, depending on the kind of service. In fact, those who deliver a service do not merely interact with the consumers: rather, they must be able to join together with consumers as an important part of the productive process. Indeed, as argued, the consumption of a service is not completely separable from the production and it involves a direct connection and cooperation between the deliverer and the consumer. Another point to take into account is that the delivery of a service is strongly influenced by the social and cultural features of the context wherein it takes place and its modes heavily depend upon the local features of the place where the service is delivered. In other words, the provision of a service is an expression of the sociocultural referents in which it takes place: for example, we cannot imagine a professional haircut that is independent from the fashion of the time and society where it is performed. Moreover, beyond the sociocultural referents, the specific circumstances where the service takes place are particularly salient: there won't be a haircut without proper tools, specific places devoted to it and competent stylistic and technical knowledge of the hairdresser. All these features are time-and-place dependent and are responsible for different kinds of haircuts for different places and times.

That being said, the interplay between the social dimension and the modes of the provision of a specific kind of service is a basilar topic in the understanding of psychology's fragmentation. As Valsiner (2006: 601–8) claims, the main accepted themes and discourses within society have strongly influenced, and defined, some important features of our discipline. Under the influence of historical and social factors, different kinds and modes of psychological inquiry temporarily gained or lost in importance: for example, the focus on private vs. public life or the focus on pragmatism and social utility selectively directs and guides psychologists toward different modes of interpreting their discipline, creating, *de facto*, different kinds of disciplines. This strong dependence on social factors somehow limited the scope of psychology, fragmenting it into many different expressions, bound to specific aspects of their social frames of reference. As a result, "science becomes swallowed by society," in Jaan Valsiner's words (2006: 609).

The psychologist Graham Richards shares the same basic ideas on the subject of the fragmentation in psychology. He maintains that psychology serves as an arena within which different groups of power negotiate different ways of "doing" psychology, each one including specific concerns about the nature and the resolution of psychological problems (Richards, 2002: 28). Here the focus is on the weakness of psychology as a science: instead of being a science, in fact, it is described as a discipline in service of and subservient to the societies wherein it develops, with poor coherence or little common concern about the objects of inquiry and the methodologies. This is specifically due to the strong influence of society on psychology's development: "psychologists will tend to wield a level of power within the discipline proportionate to that exercised in society by the constituencies they represent" (p. 29). In this scenario, there is not much room for scientific and philosophical considerations. Even though this position is clearly questionable in its entirety, it is evident that within the discipline "the diversity directly relates to just such issues as what psychologists consider its [psychology's] aims to be, the methods appropriate to pursuing them, and even how they conceptualize its subject matter" (2002: 28).

In accordance with these authors, Cahan and White (1992) claim that the fragmentation of psychology has been a consequence of its application. When societies, American as well as European, repeatedly consulted psychologists on questions of social interest, a heterogeneous set of individuals tried to give appropriate answers. The resulting heterogeneous set of psychological interventions has become the cradle of applied psychology, whose aim is to answer socially relevant questions. The contents of this cradle are heterogeneous in character because of different coexisting approaches and the relatively rudimentary paraphernalia supplied by psychologists who, in turn, belong to a professional community that is (not always) familiar with the application of theoretical knowledge in service of varied social needs. Unfortunately, the work of many psychologists is scattered, fragmented, often speculative, as will be evident later. As the questions were understandably ill-formed – this often happens when dealing with questions coming from psychology's consumers, as seen above – the answers were sketchy and superficial. This scenario led to a growing and fragmented body of research and practices that did not comfortably fit with traditional experimental methodology and, in one way or another, constantly challenged it (Cahan and White, 1992: 231). In conclusion, there is consistent evidence to maintain that, for a long time, psychologists have been working in different contexts, trying to answer questions of social interest with different models and approaches, often applied in an extemporary way.

The psychologist Sergio Salvatore (2006: 123) provides an interesting viewpoint by which to analyze psychologists' attempts to apply their knowledge to the real problems they are asked to solve in different contexts. He maintains that there is a tendency in the discipline to take its objects of interest directly from reality or, complementarily, to reify psychological constructs (see also Katzko, 2002: 264–5).

An example of reification of psychological constructs involves the subdivision of psychology into different branches. These branches display the general tendency of the discipline to ground itself on specific real contexts of intervention, with consequent progressive sectorialization. Here, the term sectorialization does not refer to a conventional agreement about the features of a group of professionals that share a specific field of intervention. Rather, still following Salvatore, sectorialization refers to the different psychological fields (school psychology, organization psychology, sport psychology, etc.) as autonomous areas of psychology based on the adoption of particular objects and methods of inquiry (see also Sternberg and Grigorenko, 2003). Again, psychological branches so understood are based on real objects according to common sense, rather than on psychological constructs, intended as aspects of the object defined in theoretical terms. In other words, organizations, schools, or sport fields are not realms of phenomena characterized by any psychological specificity (Salvatore, 2006: 124); rather, the author says that what happens in those contexts is obviously of psychological interest, but does not acquire psychological meaning because of the specific context.

Considering the example of school psychology, learning processes observed in schools are not different from the same kind of processes observed elsewhere, though some particularities may be detected. In addition, the organization of a school may not follow particular rules due to the fact that it pertains to a school, but may be understood rather as a special case of a wider category of phenomena, e.g., organizational processes. This is an example of reification based on the object of inquiry, where an allegedly different area of psychology is merely justified by the reference to a real context, without a strong theoretical justification. Contrary to this approach, it may be reasonably asserted that the psychological relevance of a context is not grounded in the context itself, but in certain psychological processes *observable* in that context and *relevant* to that context, whose study often crosses the boundaries of real contexts (i.e., is not context specific).

On the other hand, many branches of psychology are defined on the basis of the real object on which they ground their inquiry. Some kind of social psychology, just to pick an example from Salvatore, deals with objects as they are defined in everyday language: for example, the way political leaders influence their audience. However, the psychological models used to describe and explain these objects refer to general psychological models, such as cognitivism. In other words, there is a gap between the object – which is conceptualized in common-sense terms – and the theoretical devices used to explain the object. In this case, the object is "taken literally," conceived as the layman would conceive it, without considering that the object of scientific inquiry must be a construct, an abstract and theoretically informed concept used to indicate aspects of the real object. This might be a problem, since the process of deriving constructs from common-sense objects is fundamental to the scientific enterprise. Indeed, this process allows one to operationalize the object – making explicit the links between the real object and the construct itself – and to make legitimate and clear the theoretical maneuvers undergone by the object. Without the reference to constructs, the scientific explanation of a phenomenon is likely to be heuristically empty and theoretically inconsistent.

Salvatore describes another instance, the tendency to reify psychological construct. This tendency may be noticed in the case of developmental psychology. In the international literature, the concept of developmental psychology refers to the branch of psychology that deals with the construction of models that describe and explain psychological dimensions as processes.[1] Contrary to that, for example, the object of developmental psychology is commonly considered to be a real phenomenon: the different phases of life. In this case, development is not considered as a construct that specifies a point of view through which some aspects of a real object may be analyzed, rather it is considered *as a real object*, as intended by common sense.

From the point of view of fragmentation, the definition of psychology on the grounds of real objects as they are commonly understood, and not on the grounds of theoretical constructs, is problematic for two reasons. One is theoretical: psychology and its concepts tend to be similar to everyday language and this may be a hindrance to the construction of an autonomous and fertile discipline. Psychology may turn out to appear theoretically empty, grounding its knowledge on common sense. The second reason is pragmatic: the dependence on the contexts where psychology operates constrains the psychological applications to common sense. In other words, applied psychology runs the risk of losing its transformative potential by conceptualizing its means of intervention as the layperson would conceptualize them. No divergent thinking or noticeably improved competent behavior is fostered if the conceptual tools that are used by psychologists are isomorphous with, or directly derived from (Richards, 2002: 10), the concepts used by laypersons. As a consequence, the fruitfulness and appropriateness of psychological interventions may be poor or little valued.

In conclusion, the direct encounter of psychology with social, real problems had a crucial role in initiating the fragmentation process of the discipline, and still has, moving psychology away from the supposedly safe terrain of experimental methods, common to the scientific disciplines and the academic approach to psychology. At the beginning of applied psychology, new and unknown phenomena called for psychological intervention. The trust in psychological practice grew progressively, producing social expectations that needed to be satisfied, in order to create and strengthen the credibility of psychology as a science. However, the demands for psychological consultations were often vague and ill-conceived and needed to be reformulated. The need for reformulation left room for a growing set of different theoretical and methodological means of facing the problems to be solved. Though this phenomenon may be seen as an opportunity, one of the most important tendencies within psychology has been the conceptualization of its objects as commonly understood, real objects, in absence of pronounced theoretical perspectives. This approach progressively impoverished the social and scientific status of the discipline and hindered the development of strong cross-contextual and theoretical outlooks. Another tendency, as highlighted by Richards, has been to export to the new fields of intervention techniques borrowed from other stronger similar professions, or techniques used in other contexts. However, the blind transfer to various social contexts of techniques or theories sharpened in different settings or based on different competencies revealed, once again, the theoretical and methodological weakness of psychology in facing socially relevant problems.

In other words, two different routes have been followed in order to answer to the growing demand for a pragmatic and socially relevant discipline of psychology: one which faces new problems with old theories and the other facing new problems with no theories. In both cases, the outcome has been the same: fragmentation.

Psychology's two cultures

The scenario briefly sketched may be considered as just one of the most evident expressions of the long-standing schism between an objective approach and an interpretative, humanistic approach to psychology. Driver-Linn maintains that the two ways to study human beings have been developed for the reason that humans, on one hand, are inherently social beings and thus need to be considered in their subjectivity and, on the other hand, are still part of nature and consequently their study may profitably gain from an objective approach (2003: 270). In other words, the situation highlighted by Driver-Linn is but a reflection of the old dispute between those supporting a monistic methodology, claiming the legitimacy of an objective outlook on human beings, and those supporting a dualistic methodology, claiming the peculiarity of humans among other natural objects.

Thus, psychology has developed with the two different traditions, each carrying different assumptions about what constitutes progress. This can be considered the first macro-level where fragmentation takes place in the discipline. This internal disjunction can be understood as the first step to fragmentation at the very basis of psychological science. The original schism was perpetuated as psychological demand progressively grew (see previous paragraph). Gradually, two clusters of activity crystallized: experimental psychology, which mainly developed and performed in academic settings, and problem-centered psychology, which was developed in order to deal with social matters (Bagnara et al., 1975: 52–3; Cahan and White, 1992: 229). These two main branches of psychology were historically divided by at least two central methodological issues: the issue of the relevant data to be considered in psychological inquiries (subjectivism *versus* objectivism) and the issue of the way to treat those data (quantification *versus* qualification) (Lundin, 1996: 10–12). The objective and quantificational approaches, strongly favored by experimentalists and academics, prioritize observable and directly measurable data whose detection can be achieved precisely and intersubjectively, that is, in a way that can be shared by different subjects. The subjective and qualificational approaches, favored by those working in problem-centered settings, prioritize the inner, private experience of people which may be detected and studied preferably through verbal reports. These two banks of the psychological river turn out to be so distant today that the psychologist Gregory Kimble refers to them as "psychology's two cultures," an expression that gave the title to his famous 1984 article in the *American Psychologist*. The author assumes that these conflicting cultures, understood as different ways of conceptualizing the discipline, its values and its methods, exist even among scholars of a single field, not only among those who deal with distinct areas of the discipline. Thus, the schism seems to be widespread among psychologists. The relevance of Kimble's contribution is the empirical attitude of his proposal: after a review of the dimensions previous writers suggested as being at the core of the schism, the author identified twelve clusters of dimensions, each with distinctly opposing viewpoints. In general terms, it is evident that the clusters highlighted deal with the debate between a monistic *versus* a pluralistic account of psychological practice. Therefore, the value of Kimble's work is the attempt to empirically inquire into a matter which until then received only theoretical and speculative attention. Going into details, the clusters which he identified were the following (Kimble, 1984: 834):

1. Most important values (scientific vs. human). Related opposing ideas: increasing knowledge vs. improving human condition; methodological strength vs. relevance; obligation to apply psychological knowledge vs. no such obligation.
2. Degree of lawfulness of behavior (determinism vs. indeterminism). Related opposing ideas: lawful vs. without law; understandable vs. incomprehensible; predictable vs. unpredictable; controllable vs. uncontrollable.
3. Source of basic knowledge (objectivism vs. intuitionism). Related opposing ideas: sense data vs. empathy; observation vs. self-report; operational definition vs. linguistic analysis; investigation vs. common sense.

4. Methodological strategy (data vs. theory). Related opposing ideas: investigation vs. interpretation; deduction vs. induction; evidence vs. argument.
5. Setting for discovery (laboratory vs. field). Related opposing ideas: experimentation vs. survey/case study; manipulation vs. naturalistic observation; hypothesis testing vs. correlation; control vs. realism; precision vs. ecological validity.
6. Temporal aspects of lawfulness (historical vs. ahistorical). Relating opposing ideas: developmental vs. descriptive approach; longitudinal vs. cross-sectional study.
7. Position on nature/nurture issue (heredity vs. environment). Relating opposing ideas: physiology vs. situation; biological vs. social science.
8. Generality of laws (nomothetic vs. idiographic). Relating opposing ideas: species general vs. species specificity; 'standard man' vs. individual uniqueness; universalism vs. contextualism.
9. Concreteness of concepts (hypothetical constructs vs. intervening variables). Relating opposing ideas: biological reality vs. abstract conception.
10. Level of analysis (elementism vs. holism). Relating opposing ideas: molecular vs. molar; part vs. whole.
11. Factor leading to action (cognition vs. affect). Relating opposing ideas: reason vs. emotion; thinking vs. motivation; intellect vs. impulse; rational vs. irrational.
12. Conception of organisms (reactivity vs. creativity). Relating opposing ideas: automaticity vs. voluntary control; associationism vs. constructivism.

For each dimension, Kimble made a ten-point differential scale. Each item consists of two parts: a pair of opposed statements followed by a summary of the conflicting ideas contained in the statements (see the twelve dimensions above). Subjects made their responses on a ten-point Likert scale indicating their personal degrees of endorsement of the position at stake. Three groups of subjects were considered by the author: undergraduate students ($N=100$) without previous training in psychology (interestingly, no clues of psychology's two cultures is detected within this group), officers of the American Psychological Association divisions ($N=81$), which were psychologists with important roles in the American psychological community, and general members of the American Psychological Association ($N=164$) who belonged to one of the considered divisions (3, Experimental; 9, Society for Psychological Study of Social Issues; 29, Psychotherapy; 32, Humanistic). The goal of the author was to obtain data that would give a description of the two ways of understanding the discipline from the perspective of those who practice different kinds of psychology. The results of Kimble's study are very interesting: psychologists have significantly dissimilar opinions about the considered dimensions, contrary to untrained people (undergraduate students). In particular, as was expected, the author concludes that professionals with different opinions about central issues in psychology find their way into organizations and fields where those values are somehow dominant. More precisely, for example, experimentalists prioritize the objective side of the *continuum*, while psychotherapists value the subjective side. In other terms, the fields of psychology "receive" or attract those individuals who support a vision of the discipline which turns out to be coherent with the field itself. Or, conversely, those who are interested in specific psychological issues tend to espouse positions which are somehow coherent with the tradition that has been dealing with that issue. In this sense, fields look rather closed and self-sufficient, dedicated to perpetuating and feeding their own vision of the discipline. One of the most impressive outcomes concerns the agreement of all psychologists in considering determinism the common ground of the discipline (the differences are in terms of extremeness of the position). On the other hand, the opinions about other issues vary greatly. From these results, psychology seems to be even more fragmented than expected:

> In the case of objectivism versus intuitionism, members of Division 9 [Social Issues], who usually side with the humanists, are on the scientist end of the scale. In still another, data versus theory, the psychotherapists (Division 29) join the psychologists interested in social issues (Division 9) and take a stand opposed to that of experimentalists (Division 3), who are now in the same camp of the humanistic psychologists (Division 32).
>
> *(Kimble, 1984: 838)*

This picture shows an image of contemporary psychology as being composed of different communities which work under different, often conflicting, conceptions of the science (Yanchar, 1997: 151–2; Yanchar and Slife, 1997: 236). In fact, the dimensions considered, though a simplification of important general issues in the philosophy of science, can effectively illustrate the opinions about the foundations and features of psychology as envisaged by the practitioners. As seen above, it is reasonable to consider those dimensions to be expressions of long-standing issues – central and still unsolved – at the basis of the conception of psychology. These are topics that have existed throughout the development of psychological theorizing and are still current today (Lundin, 1996: 9). But the schism doesn't deal only with the beginning and development of psychology; as was hinted at in Chapter 1, it has deep roots in the controversial debate over the monist vs. pluralist views in the social sciences themselves. The crucial point is represented by those fundamental conceptual concerns that generated the schism and still feeds the fragmentation of psychology (Goertzen, 2008: 833–42). Thus, the displays of fragmentation highlighted above concerning psychology and its applications may be considered a consequence of a primary, original issue on which psychologists are still in disagreement about the nature and methods of psychology itself, i.e., the opposition between methodological monism and dualism.

Different kinds of fragmentation

Using an expression by Henderikus Stam (2004: 1259–60), the existence of psychology's two cultures may be considered a disciplinary maneuver as well as an epistemological act. While the latter option is a methodological claim, from the perspective of the former option, the schism results from the expression of different groups of power (see also Richards, 2002) whereas the striving for unification is basically oriented to the preservation of the institutional health of psychology. In fact, many authors are worried that the fragmentation detectable in the discipline would cause the loss of its status as an independent discipline (Sternberg, 2005: 3; Yanchar and Slife, 1997: 237) and the consequent institutional dissolution (Yanchar, 1997: 152–3). This concern is effectively illustrated by the psychologist Stephen C. Yanchar:

> Psychology is in a unique position … because it not only consists of many competing theoretical perspectives and research programs, but also because it possesses no common definition or purpose that all psychologists may rally around. Rather, research programs and discourse communities have become increasingly insular and parochial; they have begun to drift away from psychology proper to affiliate more closely to sciences or scholarly enterprises that seem more similar to themselves than do other communities of psychologists.
>
> *(1997: 153)*

Such a perspective on the fragmentation of psychology, which may be called institutional, highlights some interesting aspects of the fragmentation process. These aspects are also relevant when considering the phenomenon from a proper epistemological standpoint. In what follows, I will try to draw attention to those disciplinary or institutional aspects of fragmentation in psychology that I believe have some epistemological significance, and I will try to highlight why.

To this aim, a primary perspective is that of the psychologist Robert J. Sternberg, whose role as former President of the American Psychological Association pushed him to face the problem of fragmentation from a professional and institutional angle. For Sternberg and Grigorenko (2003: 23–4) there are three bad habits among psychologists which are responsible for the institutional fragmentation of psychology. The first one is the exclusive or almost exclusive reliance on a single methodology: psychologists are trained largely in the use of one or two methods. The training in a specific method involves a lot of time and money and researchers or professionals may seek to maximize the return on their investment (Sternberg and Grigorenko, 2003: 29), even when they come to see the flaws of their preferred methodology, or inadequacy in respect to the object of inquiry. This may foster misuse of methodological tools. For example, mathematical methods may be used to fit data, rather than to test theories. In other words, methods and parameters used in psychological research are not always determined by theoretical considerations, but they may be chosen *post hoc* so as to maximize the fit to data (Gigerenzer, 1998: 198). This misuse, together with the tendency to rely on a single method, may discourage learning and moreover the selection of the objects of interest may be based on the method that is known, rather than on the specific requirements of the object itself. Consequently, psychologists may come to consider a single method as the best way to study an entire set of problems or phenomena.

This approach obviously involves methodological flaws in that each method has its disadvantages and permits the understanding of certain features of the objects from a specific, but limited, perspective. In fact, every method provides a sort of biased knowledge, whose biases are determined by the method itself (see also Gigerenzer, 1998). From an institutional point of view, this approach creates and feeds fragmentation and incommunicability among psychologists using different methods: in other words, the use of a method becomes a norm that seems perfectly reasonable and unquestioned by those who share it, but the norm may be considered otherwise by other psychologists working in other areas. In other terms, the use of a method may create sub-groups in the discipline which focuses their activity on the use of the method itself, rather than on the progressive study of an object of inquiry. In short, the importance of the method threatens to overwhelm the relevance of the features of the object itself.

The second bad habit described by Sternberg and Grigorenko concerns the way the discipline and its scholars are identified and self-identified more in terms of psychological sub-disciplines (e.g., social, clinical, experimental psychology) rather than in terms of the psychological phenomena they are meant to study. The point, here, is that dividing the discipline into traditional fields prevents its unification around a common interest and specific objects of inquiry. The authors, in other words, think that psychology would be better organized around interesting phenomena of study using a variety of methodological devices, rather than on arbitrary fields of psychology (see also Robinson, 2007: 196). The implicit aim of the present situation, in Sternberg and Grigorenko's opinion (2003: 32), is to preserve the academic or professional traditional organization, a sort of *status quo* bounded to economic and didactic matters. In the present situation, the organization of psychology is somehow suitable for economic and training reasons. The preservation of a disciplinary organization based on methods (e.g., experimental psychology) or broad and vague fields (e.g., clinical, developmental, evolutionary psychology) leads to the fragmentation of psychology and to a progressive isolation of its internal communities (Gigerenzer, 1998: 199–200; Yanchar and Slife, 1997: 238), with the risk of degrading the study of important subject matters, around which the authors hope a new psychology will arise. To summarize, current psychology fields may be seen as being designed around something other than their objects of interests.

The third and final psychologists' bad habit proposed by the authors is the tendency to adhere to a single paradigm, or frame theory, when investigating psychological phenomena, e.g., behaviorism, cognitivism, psychoanalysis (Sternberg and Grigorenko, 2003: 24). These theories are considered to be basic assumptions to which all feasible objects of inquiry are subject, including the legitimate methods that can be used and which also involve a general account of the aspects of the world that are interesting for psychology, as understood through the lens of that frame theory. Again, the existence of several incommensurable frame theories produces fragmentation within the community of psychologists.

In another article, Sternberg evokes an additional source of disciplinary fragmentation: the science–practice split (2005: 5) or bifurcation (Yanchar and Slife, 1997:

239–40). As we saw above, the aims of the two components have often been conflicting, since from the origin of psychology, those who were interested in experimental questions about mental functioning and those who were interested in clinical questions concerning psychopathology and therapeutic interventions (p. 240) or social issues found themselves on different sides of the same river. Interests, methods, theories and background assumptions about the discipline were often very different. Thus, although science (understood as academic psychology) and practice (understood as applied psychology) should naturally be linked, they exhibit ideological and methodological differences that threaten to undermine the unity of the discipline with respect to its scientific status and social utility. As Berdini et al. (1992) and Grasso, Conese, and Fucilli (1997) highlighted in two interesting studies about the cultural representations of clinical psychologists in Italy, the practitioners' points of view significantly differ from their academic colleagues in three main areas. First, practitioners usually define their practice around the context (schools, companies, hospitals, etc.) where they operate, or around their typical users (students, patients, workers, etc.) (see also Salvatore's proposal above for a critical remark). The reference to the theories or methods is secondary, unlike those who devote themselves to science, for which the specification of the theoretical references and the methodological procedures have priority. Second, the practitioners see themselves as professionals whose aim is to operate in accordance with the – more or less explicit – targets provided by the contexts wherein they operate. Doing so, they tend to attribute priority to the "action," often disconnected from a specific theory, whose aim would be to reliably lead the practitioner's inquiry to desired goals. Hence, their work may take on a general and nonspecific flavor, unlike scientific settings where every undertaking should have its theoretical and methodological framework as clear as possible, with the aim of intersubjectivity and reproducibility. Third, psychologists do not have a strong attitude toward the testing of their professional interventions: there is little agreement upon the standards and relevance of verifying a psychological intervention's outcome, such as the use of structured tests, determination of client satisfaction, symptoms remission. This is dissimilar to those scientific settings where the testing of hypotheses is a central concern.

The situation outlined is similar to the one described by the study proposed by Wilson et al. (2009). The authors' aim was to qualitatively explore practitioners' attitude toward evidence-based practice in psychology (EBPP). I omit the details of this interesting study in order to focus on the outcomes relevant for the issue of science–practice split. Although some participants responded that informing practice with research is their "ethical responsibility," they also said that it is "difficult to keep up with existing research" and that "empirical research has limitations" (p. 406). Moreover, many participants expressed difficulties in properly applying research to a given client. Finally, almost all participants referred to the existence of a "gap between research and practice" (p. 406). Some participants hoped for a better understanding of the researchers' world in order to foster cooperation and practical usefulness for research's outcomes.

Roughly, it might be said that the split between science and practice reflects the opposition of the two cultures identified by Gregory Kimble (1984). On the scientific side, the main attitude involves the emphasis on objectivity, on the use of quantitative methods and on the priority attributed to the research activity over its possible application. On the practical side, the main attitude involves the emphasis on subjectivity, on the use of qualitative methods and on the priority attributed to pragmatic application over research (i.e., research is justified by its possible or potential applications). These remarks seem to be coherent with Sternberg's recognition of a science–practice split in psychology.

It is possible to sum up Sternberg's views in terms of four main disciplinary sources of fragmentation. They not only have institutional relevance, namely, consequences for the organization of psychology as a social endeavor, but they also play a relevant epistemological role in the search for unity in psychology. These may be summed up as follows:

- The exclusive or almost exclusive reliance on a single methodology.
- The identification of the discipline and its scholars more in terms of psychological sub-disciplines rather than in terms of psychological phenomena of interest.
- The adherence to a single paradigm, or frame theory, when investigating psychological phenomena.
- The science–practice split.

The above line of investigation mainly points to the broader aspects of fragmentation in psychology, those that account for the disciplinary disunity of the psychologists' professional community. But this state of affairs has epistemological consequences of course, or, in other words, the two cultures in psychology also have epistemological manifestations. In what follows we will take into account other relevant epistemological issues which are potentially significant sources of fragmentation.

Going deeper in an attempt to analyze and to make sense of the diverse forms of psychology, the psychologist Joseph Rychlak evokes a principle of complementarity, in analogy with the famous Niels Bohr's double explanation of light's phenomena.[2] Rychlak maintains that in physics the principle of complementarity provides for two coexisting explanations of findings that are valid, i.e., predictably reproducible in experimental settings. In other words, the principle is conjured up and operates *after* the experimental evidence has been found and is useful in order to provide a complementary account of facts that are paradoxical (1993: 934), and that require two different explanations. The case for psychology is not exactly the same, though it is similar in some respects. In our discipline, there are not valid experimental findings (or data) that are so different as to require a complementary account, that is, the presence of coexisting and non-reducible explanations of the same phenomenon. Rather, if psychology is to have a principle of complementarity, it operates *before* the proven fact occurs, as an aspect of the theorizing aimed at explaining the phenomenon at hand. In other words, in Rychlak's view (1993: 935), the complementarity in psychology would refer to the existence of different theoretical frames that are not (apparently) reducible to each other but do indeed complement each other. These frames are theoretical assumptions or backgrounds that lead to and set the modes of empirical testing: in fact, "When psychologists conduct an experiment, they are necessarily making a preliminary selection as to which grounding they will be using to conceptualize their findings" (p. 935). In any case, the theoretical grounds that are rejected are not invalid or illegitimate, but indeed somehow complementary, yet irreducible to each other in principle. With the aim of grounding his proposal on a historical analysis, Rychlak advances four broad theoretical levels of explanation on which to ground psychological explanations. They are not to be ranked, as they are not reconcilable or capable of solitary application:

1. *Physikos.* The level of explanation which is grounded on material processes and which doesn't recognize a difference between animate or inanimate objects.
2. *Bios.* The level of explanation which is grounded on processes like genetics and organic systems. As the author himself maintains, it is difficult to distinguish this level from the previous level.
3. *Socius.* The level of explanation which is grounded on the analysis of subjects in terms of group relations and cultural influences.
4. *Logos.* The level of explanation which is grounded on concepts such as mental acts or cognitive organization.

As may be evident, the distinction between these different theoretical levels doesn't have definite boundaries and the content of each is vague. Consequently, it is not clear whether they deal with one or more specific theory/ies, have a specific methodological approach, or a definite anthropological view of human beings and their functioning. More conceptual work seems required in order to adequately define these levels. However, this approach may be useful because it gives priority to a theoretical evaluation in any kind of psychological research ambit over the relevance of the specific contexts where psychological knowledge may be used. In fact, at an intuitive level, the analysis of the fragmentation suggested by Rychlak is able to encompass the different limbs animating the multifaceted body of psychology, beyond the two cultures considered above. Rychlak therefore seems to further Kimble's work. The relevance of his proposal consists of the emphasis on the need for a mutual consistency between theory and research: it suggests the need to critically evaluate the coherence of the theoretical grounds at stake with the hypotheses to test and the ways the constructs proposed are operationalized (Rychlak, 1993: 938). Every aspect must be coherent with the theoretical assumption that has been adopted. This would compel scholars and professionals to stay within one theoretical assumption and to make it explicit, making their discoveries available in a more intersubjective manner, and more strongly connected to theoretical grounds.

Another interesting analysis of disunity in psychology comes from the Dutch psychologist Michael W. Katzko, who attributes a central role to the way most psychological research is conducted and interpreted (2002: 262). More specifically, the manner in which scientific discoveries are illustrated in psychology papers may provide interesting insight into the issue at stake. In Katzko's opinion, a critical proliferation of theoretical terms is one of the main causes of fragmentation in psychology. In particular, he considers that the rhetorical means used in scientific publications and the way in which scientific results are communicated may reflect sets of values and implicit conceptualizations regarding the discipline (p. 263). In other words, these regularities in the way research is expounded entail patterns of implicit beliefs, goals, and values that may contribute to the apparent lack of unity of psychology. For Katzko the problem has to be faced carefully, but it does not constitute a substantial crisis for the discipline, as it does not necessarily imply a non-rigorous process of hypotheses testing.

Nevertheless, it will be clear that this problem may hide a more substantial topic of vast epistemic relevance. This problem, in Katzko's terminology, is called the *uniqueness assumption* (p. 263). The uniqueness assumption establishes a terminological equivalence between the experimental design language and the theoretical language (p. 264). The difference between the two levels of language is removed. Such an implicit assumption may be detected in many psychological studies, as Katzko illustrates with some examples[3] and involves an interpretation of the values of the dependent variables as if they were "caused by one and only one psychological factor" (p. 263). In such cases, the theory is not conceived of as a *possible interpretation* of the gathered data. Rather, it is conceived of as *the evidence* of the correctness of the theory itself. In such cases, Katzko remarked that "The actual data – the relations between dependent and independent variables – were transformed into a terminology specific to the variables in question and then rhetorically presented as a theory that explained the data" (p. 264). The empirical regularity, ascertained through observation, is thus reified into an independent theoretical language (see also Robinson, 2007: 191): the distinction between observational language and theoretical language disappears and the two are considered to be equivalent.

The problem, as Salvatore (2006) already noticed, stems from the distinction between the data, which may be considered as measures of specific aspects of reality, and the theoretical constructs, which are non-observable abstract concepts describing organized psychological units (Pedon and Gnisci, 2004: 139). In other words, for Katzko, researchers tend to reify their observations into theoretical entities or relations (1993: 265; Robinson, 2007: 191). The consequence is that for every observation a new theory is required to explain that observation. Researchers should be reminded that the distinction between data and theory has to be rigorously respected, otherwise any data gathering by experimental, clinical or other research devices may push the psychologist to introduce a new theory without sufficient justification (Goertzen, 2008: 836): "Another experimenter, manipulating a different set of variables and using the uniqueness assumption to explain the data, will by definition create a theory different from the first. The seed is now sown for a proliferation of mutually exclusive theoretical terminologies" (Katzko, 1993: 265; see also Henriques and Sternberg, 2004: 1052). The problematic nature of the uniqueness assumption stems from the fact that the empirical data become part of the theory to be tested rather than simply being objective, independent evidence. Data must be considered as empirical evidence which could justify a theory, not as components of a theory: they are not part of the theory which is grounded on them. As the philosopher Peter Kosso (1992) asserts, the relationship between data and theory should not be circular, as is implied by the uniqueness assumption. Thus, the data should not be observed by the same theory that has to be tested. In other words, the theory used to convey information about a piece of scientific evidence must be different from the theory to be justified. For example, in a laboratory where scientists are working on DNA, the laws of optics which govern the operation of a microscope are not under scrutiny; the biological theory/ies on which the scientists are working are. In that circumstance, the laws of optics are taken for granted, i.e., are not the objects of the process of justification.

> This "circle-blocking" independence [of theories from a circular relationship] is a measure of objectivity of the evidence and of the process of justification. Independent evidence is outside of the influence of the *particular* theory it serves, though it is still within the theoretical system of science. It is internal, as it must be, in the latter sense, though external of the particular claims it tests.
>
> *(Kosso, 1992: 158)*

In other words, the circularity between the data (gathered with the aim of testing the theory at stake) and the theory to be tested is only apparent. In fact, the solution is that the theory to be tested *be different* from the theory used to examine and ascertain the empirical data:

> The benefits of independence can be further appreciated by considering our own human perceptual system. We consider our senses to be independent to some degree when we use one of them to check another. If I am uncertain whether what I see is a hallucination or real fire, it is a less convincing test simply to look again than it is to hold out my hand and feel the heat. The independent account is the more reliable because it is less likely that a systematic error will infect both systems than that one system will be flawed.
>
> *(Kosso, 1992: 156)*

Therefore, the uniqueness assumption seems to express a substantial epistemic flaw to which psychologists are often subject, not only a rhetoric flaw. The fact that the data and the corresponding theory are considered as equivalent has obviously serious consequences: first, whenever a theory is rejected for some reason, the data are dismissed along with the associated theory or method. But if the data are dismissed, so are important links between variables which may need alternative theoretical interpretations. Second, and consequently, in this way psychological research may progressively lose access to phenomena which might ultimately be properly explained and so are worthy of further scientific inquiry. Third, incommensurable theoretical

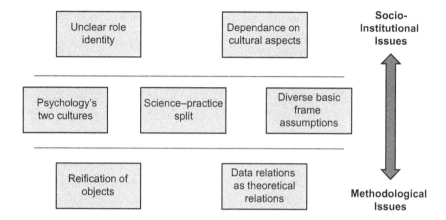

FIGURE 5.1 The fragmentation of psychology: a continuum from socio–institutional to methodological aspects

claims proliferate. There are as many different research designs as one may imagine, and this phenomenon does nothing but feed the process of fragmentation in psychology.

In conclusion, there seem to be several aspects of disunity in psychology, depending on the perspective one takes. The model presented in Figure 5.1 summarizes the topics illustrated in the previous analysis, setting them at different levels in the structure of psychology. A certain amount of fragmentation at every level may be ascertained, from socio-institutional issues – related to the shape and the functions of psychology in the society – to methodological issues – related to the way the discipline develops its knowledge in a scientifically sound way. All of these aspects contribute to a lack of unity, or fragmentation, in the field of psychology, both on a socio–institutional level, as a discipline with social aims, and on a methodological level as a scientific discipline.

Notes

1 According to the dictionary of the American Psychological Association, developmental psychology is the branch of psychology that studies the change – physical, mental, and behavioral – that occurs from conception to old age (VandeBos, 2007).
2 Briefly, the need for a double explanation of light phenomena, which have a particle nature *and* a wave nature, whose importance depend on the type of measurement under consideration.
3 I refer readers interested in examining the examples to Katzko's work. Here is just a sketch (Katzko, 2002: 264):

>   Rosch (1975) examined the same problem (as Paivio, 1971) – how to account for the internal mediators (representations) of certain observed phenomena – from a slightly different angle. Response latency was again used as a dependent measure, now interpreted as a distance between semantic categories, with distance being along a dimension of category similarity. The uniqueness assumption was again used to interpret a specific finding as being caused by a single psychological parameter. In

this case, the distance similarity was interpreted as evidence for the prototype structure of the categories themselves. This prototype, or concrete exemplar, view of a category made no reference to Paivio's image interpretation of his data, but the similarity of the data is striking.

Another display of the uniqueness assumption is "when each of several so-called theories of emotion are built on a specific kind of data" (p. 264).

References

Bagnara, S., Castelfranchi, C., Legrenzi, P., Minguzzi, G., Misiti, R., and Parisi, D. (1975). Per una discussione sulla situazione della psicologia in Italia. *Giornale Italiano di Psicologia*, 3: 285–305.

Berdini, G., De Berardinis, D., Masina, E., Mazzotta, M., Orgiana, C., Rubino, A., and Tavazza, G. (1992). Immagine del lavoro dello psicologo clinico. *Rivista di Psicologia Clinica*, 2: 212–237.

Bühler, K. (1927). *Die Krise der Psychologie*. Jena: Fischer.

Cahan, E. D. and White, S. H. (1992). Proposals for a second psychology. *American Psychologist*, 47(2): 224–235.

Carli, R., Paniccia, R. M., and Lancia, F. (1988). *Il gruppo in psicologia clinica*. Rome: Carocci.

De Groot, A. D. (1990). Unifying psychology: Its preconditions. In W. J. Baker, M. E. Hyland, R. van Hezewik, and S. Terwee (eds.), *Recent Trends in Theoretical Psychology, Vol. 2* (pp. 1–25). New York: Springer.

Driver-Linn, E. (2003). Where is psychology going? Structural fault lines revealed by psychologists' use of Kuhn. *American Psychologist*, 58(4): 269–278.

Fenici, M. (2009). Psychology and psychologies: Which epistemology? *Humana-mente*, 11: 5–15.

Gaj, N. (2009). Towards a unified model in clinical psychology. A historical and epistemological analysis of its development. *Ricerche di Psicologia*, 2: 73–93.

Gigerenzer, G. (1998). Surrogates for theories. *Theory and Psychology*, 8(2): 195–204.

Goertzen, J. R. (2008). On the possibility of unification. The reality and nature of the crisis in psychology. *Theory and Psychology*, 18(6): 829–852.

Grasso, M., Conese, P., and Fucilli, G. (1997). Competenze psicologico cliniche e contesti operativi nei servizi socio-sanitari. un'indagine sulla rappresentazione della cultura professionale degli psicologi clinici del territorio di Bari. *Rivista di Psicologia Clinica*, 1: 87–132.

Henriques, G. R. (2004). Psychology defined. *Journal of Clinical Psychology*, 60(12): 1207–1221.

Henriques, G. R. and Sternberg, R. J. (2004). Unified professional psychology: Implications for the combined-integrated model of doctoral training. *Journal of Clinical Psychology*, 60(12): 1051–1063.

Katzko, M. W. (2002). The rhetoric of psychological research and the problem of unification in psychology. *American Psychologist*, 57(4): 262–270.

Kimble, G. A. (1984). Psychology's two cultures. *American Psychologist*, 39(8): 833–839.

Kosso, P. (1992). *Reading the Book of Nature. An Introduction to the Philosophy of Science*. Cambridge, MA: Cambridge University Press.

Lundin, R. W. (1996). *Theories and Systems of Psychology*. Lexington, MA: Heath.

McGovern, T. V. and Brewer, C. L. (2005). Paradigms, narratives, and pluralism in undergraduate psychology. In R. J. Sternberg (ed.), *Unity in Psychology. Possibility or Pipedreams?* (pp. 125–143). Washington, DC: American Psychological Association.

Normann, R. (1984). *Service Management. Strategy and Leadership in Service Business*. New York: Wiley.

Olivetti Manoukian, F. (1998). *Produrre servizi. Lavorare con oggetti immateriali*. Bologna: Il Mulino.

Pedon, A. and Gnisci, A. (2004). *Metodologia della ricerca psicologica*. Bologna: Il Mulino.

Reisman, J. M. (1991). *A History of Clinical Psychology*. Philadelphia, PA: Hemisphere Publishing Corporation.

Richards, G. (2002). The psychology of psychology. A historically grounded sketch. *Theory and Psychology*, 12(1): 7–36.

Robinson, D. N. (2007). Theoretical psychology: What is it and who needs it? *Theory and Psychology*, 17: 187–198.

Rychlak, J. F. (1993). A suggested principle of complementarity for psychology. *American Psychologist*, 48(9): 933–942.

Salvatore, S. (2006). Modelli di conoscenza ed agire psicologico. *Rivista di Psicologia Clinica*, 2–3: 121–134.

Salvatore, S. and Pamplomatas, A. (1993). Il prodotto in psicologia clinica. Considerazioni sulla capacità di domanda del mercato. *Rivista di Psicologia Clinica*, 2–3: 92–122.

Staats, A. W. (1996). *Behavior and Personality. Psychological Behaviorism*. New York: Springer.

Stam, H. J. (2004). Unifying psychology: Epistemological act or disciplinary maneuver? *Journal of Clinical Psychology*, 60(12): 1259–1262.

Sternberg, R. J. (2005). Unifying the field of psychology. In R. J. Sternberg (ed.), *Unity in Psychology. Possibility or Pipedream?* (pp. 3–14). Washington, DC: American Psychological Association.

Sternberg, R. J. and Grigorenko, E. L. (2003). Unified psychology. In A. E. Kazdin (ed.), *Methodological Issues and Strategies in Clinical Research* (3rd edn) (pp. 23–47). Washington, DC: American Psychological Association.

Valsiner, J. (2006). Dangerous curves in knowledge within psychology: Fragmentation of methodology. *Theory and Psychology*, 16(5): 597–612.

VandenBos, G. R. (2007). *APA Dictionary of Psychology*. Washington, DC: American Psychological Association.

Vygotsky, L. S. (1927/1997). The historical meaning of the crisis in psychology: A Methodological investigation. *Collected Works of Vygotsky*, vol. 3, New York: Plenum.

Wilson, J. L., Armoutliev, E., Yakunina, E., and Werth, Jr., J. L. (2009). Practicing psychologists' reflections on evidence-based practice in psychology. *Professional Psychology: Research and Practice*, 40(4): 403–409.

Yanchar, S. C. (1997). Fragmentation in focus: History, integration, and project of evaluation. *Journal of Theoretical and Philosophical Psychology*, 17(2): 150–170.

Yanchar, S. C. and Slife, B. D. (1997). Pursuing unity in a fragmented psychology: Problems and prospects. *Review of General Psychology*, 1(3): 235–255.

PART 3

6

FIVE PROPOSALS OF UNIFICATION FOR PSYCHOLOGY

In view of the situation that has been described in Chapter 5, the need for a unified frame in psychology has been felt among some philosophically oriented psychologists. Beyond the issues already considered, there are a variety of reasons for giving psychology a more coherent shape. Some of the authors whose proposals will be considered here maintain that fragmentation involves the impossibility of communicating between scientists (Kimble, 1996; Staats, 1996) and creates confusion and disagreement about fundamental issues (Henriques, 2011). Moreover, the current content of psychological science is considered to be organized in a way that turns out not to be functional in the development of new knowledge (Staats, 1996), creating problems among those practicing the professional as well as the scientific side of the discipline (Sternberg, 2005). These and others reasons which will be analyzed later in more detail brought some psychologists to set themselves the task of proposing a unified approach to psychology. In this section, I will take into account five attempts to develop a unified outlook for psychology whose roots and approaches are very different, as will become evident.

Gregory Kimble's functional behaviorism (1996) and Arthur Staats' psychological behaviorism (1996) both ground on the behavioristic tradition. Norman Anderson's information integration theory (IIT) (2008) is derived from the cognitive psychology tradition and the information processing theory. Gregg Henriques' unified theory of psychology (2011) is a sort of meta-theory that eclectically frames concepts from different theories and research programs. Finally, Robert Sternberg and colleagues' proposal of unified psychology (2003), starting from methodological and theoretical issues, deals with practical and institutional problems of organization in psychology, which is considered both as a science and as a profession.

Each proposal will be first discussed according to its descriptive characteristics, then some critical remarks will be added at the end of each discussion.

Gregory Kimble's functional behaviorism

In his 1996 book, *Psychology: The Hope of a Science*, Gregory Kimble intends to reach the goal of the unification of psychology from a radical behavioristic perspective. On the trail of Newton's laws of motion (Kimble, 1996: ix), Kimble tries to portray psychology's contour on the basis of relatively few theoretical principles. These principles have the aim of holding the field together (Kimble, 1996: 39) and of dealing with the fragmentation that plagues psychology and divides it into different areas. These very general principles, which have the virtue of being able to be applied across the boundaries of psychology's traditionally narrow specialties, share some crucial assumptions (Kimble, 1996: x). First of all, the behavior of organisms is considered to be the product of evolution. This hypothesis requires that psychology's laws apply across a range of animal species, considering psychology a scientific discipline whose aim is to explain different animal and human phenomena which share very general features. Second, the evolution of behavior is considered part of the organic evolution; consequently, the laws of psychology must be compatible with those of biology. Third, behavior evolves in a consistent manner with biological facts, so it has to aim at adaptation to the surrounding environment, as biological evolution also does. The approach consisting of these assumptions is called functional behaviorism (Kimble, 1996: 39). The term behaviorism is necessary because it recognizes the criteria that psychology must meet in order to be considered an empirical science.[1] The functionalist perspective acknowledges that behavior is the product of evolution through interaction with the environment. As those general features suggest, the object of psychology is animal and human behavior and its goal is to maximize the orderliness of the knowledge concerning the object. Scientific laws are the primary means with which to achieve this order, by describing the connection between the independent and the dependents variables (Kimble, 1996: 10, 11). The first kind of psychological law Kimble takes into account is the Type-1 law, which has the following general form:

Independent variable $\longrightarrow$ L1 $\longrightarrow$ Dependent variable

L1 refers to Type-1 laws, which take two different forms. The first kind of laws, Type-S[2] laws, relates responses (dependent variables) to the stimulus or stimuli (independent variable) that triggered them:

Stimulus/i $\longrightarrow$ Type-S law (L1) $\longrightarrow$ Response

The second kind of Type-1 laws are Type-P[3] laws, which relate behavior (response, dependent variable) with properties, characteristics, or attributes of organisms:

Property of an organism $\longrightarrow$ Type-P law (L1) $\longrightarrow$ Response

If Type-S laws are described as stimulus–response laws, Type-P laws can be qualified as response–response laws, because they describe the connection between two measures of behavior. For example, looking at the statement above, we can consider as an independent variable the performance on an intelligence test (say, the WAIS-IV), which is a form of behavior.[4] On the dependent-variable side, we can consider the performance on a given subject at school, which is also a behavior. In this sense, this kind of law connects behaviors to other behaviors.

These two Type-1 laws display different outlooks on the subject's behavior. Type-S laws deal with the experimental manipulation of variables in order to explore the relationships of behavior to conditions which can be changed by the experimenter's will. This approach seeks commonalities in behavior, searching for those aspects that are universally shared. On the other hand, by connecting behaviors with other kinds of behavior and establishing a correlation between them, Type-P laws concentrate on individual differences (Kimble, 1996: 12).

The other two kinds of laws postulated by Kimble are Type-2 and Type-3 laws, which concern intervening variables, that is to say, variables which are positioned between the independent and the dependent variable. In particular, Type-2 laws (L2) connect intervening variables to independent variables, while Type-3 laws (L3) connect intervening variables to dependent variables, according to the following statement:

Independent variable ⟶ L2 ⟶ Intervening variable ⟶ L3 ⟶ Dependent variable

As noted before, the independent variable in the statement can be an environmental stimulus (as in Type-S laws) or a measure of the subject's behavior (as in Type-P laws). Through a William James quotation, Kimble seems to identify intervening variables with mental life and mentalistic concepts (1996: 21). Intervening variables, in his view, are mentalistic concepts such as intelligence, style of parenting, stress, or imagery, just to quote some of the author's examples (Kimble, 1996: 20). In fact, he maintains that these kinds of concepts can be considered acceptable only if they are somehow linked to observable events. In other terms, in order to be considered worthy of scientific consideration, these concepts need operational definitions which give them a meaning that is based on public observation (Kimble, 1996: 23). This is clear from the following statement, which is a variation of the former:

Environmental conditions/

Property of an organism ⟶ L2 ⟶ Concept ⟶ L3 ⟶ Behavior

In this perspective, concepts assume scientific acceptability according to a "bottom-line criterion," which means that they acquire their scientific meaning in virtue of their traceability to "thing-level operations" (Kimble, 1996: 25).

Within the framework provided by the Type-1, 2, and 3 laws, the core of Kimble's proposal is represented by the five hypotheses that he presents as "psychology's equivalent of Newton's laws of motion" (1996: 42). In Kimble's view, these hypotheses are "common and time-honored Western ways of thinking – the salient landmarks of the intellectual environment in which the sciences have been evolving for millennia" 1996: 43).

Now, let us consider the main features of Kimble's proposal. Hypothesis 1 states that behavior is the joint product of potentials and instigations. Potentials are characteristics of individuals that may or may not gain expression, depending on the situation. Instigations are internal or external factors that trigger or suppress potentials. In other words, there are potentials that can be activated or suppressed on the basis of environmental contingent circumstances. This is a very general principle that can be applied "from action potential of the single neuron to pathological reactions brought on by stress" (Kimble, 1996: 54).

Hypothesis 2 describes the two ways of dealing with different kinds of environmental events. Behavior is a blend of adaptation and coping. Adaptation happens when the organism faces events that cannot be controlled or modified. In this sort of situation, individuals try to change themselves to meet the demands of the environment. Conversely, when environmental control is possible, individuals try to change their outside conditions ("world") in order to satisfy their own needs; this form of adjustment is called coping. As in the case of hypothesis 1, examples of these two adjustment strategies can be pointed out from a variety of topics in psychology[5] (Kimble, 1996: 70).

Hypothesis 3 asserts that behavior happens when instigation raises a potential (see hypothesis 1) to a specific threshold. The concept of threshold expresses the non-linear character of biological organisms' behavior: lesser instigations may have effects in order to produce the behavior, but they stay latent until the "fatal" instigation brings them to a threshold. This would explain why most of the times a potential is apparently triggered by a certain instigation in an on/off mode. This hypothesis accounts for those behaviors that happen as a result of the gradual accumulation of smaller factors (Kimble, 1996: 104), which are very common in the psychological literature.

Hypothesis 4 maintains that behavior is under the control of two opposing processes, excitation and inhibition. These processes are bound in a mutual relationship, because excitation elicits inhibition, while inhibition involves excitation. Moreover, their interaction is adjusted in a subtractive way: inhibition lessens excitation, and vice versa. In Kimble's view, excitation and inhibition occur in contexts that cover the entire spectrum of psychological adjustment, from attentional processes, reflexes, sensory processes, and perception to conditioning affects and the functioning of civilized societies (Kimble, 1996: 43, 74, 75).

In conclusion, hypothesis 5 assumes that behavior is operated through a hierarchical organization. This means that the majority of psychological events, from neural processes to verbal or social phenomena, are organized in elementary chunks methodically included in an arranged structure.

As mentioned before, Kimble's hypotheses have a general scope allowing his concepts to be applied through the variety of psychological fields, covering the domains of cognition, affects and reaction tendencies (1996: x), from which he provides many examples. As Newton's laws of motion, Kimble hypothesizes the outline of Type 1, 2, and 3 laws should provide a general frame when considering psychology as a scientific endeavor.

What kind of psychology is suited to Kimble's functional behaviorism?

Gregory Kimble's hope, as expressed in the title of his book, is that the principles he proposes may offer the basis upon which psychology may finally be unified and considered a science. From his perspective, psychology is a natural science and, as every natural science, it "must obey rules of science: it must be deterministic, empirical, and analytic" (1996: ix). It must also be a behavioral psychology, because sciences "are about observable reality" (1996: ix). From this point of view, psychology has to espouse the hallmarks of the scientific inquiry: first, it must be empirical, in the sense that it advances through observations rather than through intuition or authority. This leads Kimble to exclude from the psychological inquiry the analysis of subjective data, which are considered to be misleading as they "mistakes private truth for public truth" (1996: 2). In other words, in order to consider psychological knowledge as scientific – and Kimble admits that there are other available methods, with different criteria of truth, to understand behavior – it must be traced back to public observable facts. This approach is evidently rooted in the monistic tradition, which states that every discipline must support its statements in the same way: deriving from them empirical implications that can be checked intersubjectively, and tracing back private facts to public observable facts (see Chapter 1; Hempel, 1969: 269).

This methodological option is explicitly aimed at earning scientific credentials for psychology, as the author thinks that the consideration of private, or subjective, phenomena necessarily brings psychology to drift due to the confusion of psychology with common sense (Kimble, 1996: 3). Considering what Hempel said, this is a quite puzzling position, because the methodological core of monism asserts that the nature of understanding is basically the same in all areas of science (Hempel, 1962: 295), therefore private phenomena can be in principle objects of psychological inquiry, providing that knowledge be intersubjective and traceable to empirical facts. Here, Kimble seems to connect the use of the empirical method to the sole analysis of public facts, excluding the possibility of studying private facts by means of procedures which permit operationalism, that is, the individuation of empirically reliable (observable and measurable) data that can be intersubjectively checked and that empirically define the private fact at stake.[6] This can be seen as a limit of the author's approach, which involves the exclusion of interesting psychological issues, which are not in principle out of the methodological realm in which functional behaviorism developed.[7]

Another requirement that allows psychology to be considered as a science is elementism, the principle by which phenomena are to be reduced to components, instead of accepting them at face value as wholes. This position is coherent with the previous assertion that psychology is different from common sense and supports an analytical approach to the world. This is consistent with the syntactic perspective adopted by the neo-positivistic tradition and Hempel (1962), who maintains that in principle the contents of experience, which he called "pragmatic aspects," are non-pragmatic in character, because they are considered to be solely concerned with the logical and systematic aspects of experience (see Chapter 1). In other words, reality can be resolved into its elements, whose analytic consideration is a fundamental aspect of the scientific method. The level of psychological explanation is highly abstract: for Kimble, psychology is distant from the content of experience (i.e., the content of behavior), which it ignores, and is interested in the general, systematic aspects of human conduct. This is consistent with the position of Rudolf Carnap (1928), who maintains that science must deal with the description of the structure of an event, which is the whole of formal relations that constitute the event itself. Accordingly, the language Kimble uses is focused on the relation between the constituents of the considered psychological field, while ignoring those properties of the field that can be considered superficial or contingent (see Chapter 3).

But how do those elements, considered in their syntactic, formal features, turn out to be mutually linked? The answer is in the principle of determinism supported by Kimble, which "requires a treatment of behavior and experience as events with natural causes, instead of manifestations of God's purposes or individual free will" (Kimble, 1996: 1). Also this principle is consistent with a monistic view of science, which depicts a world governed by general laws, to which both humans and material objects obey. According to the general outlook of functional behaviorism, there is no room for purposiveness or concepts such as intentions, goals, desires, or opinions. Despite his rather formal adherence to a monistic, i.e., deterministic perspective, Kimble's proposal explicitly tries to bridge the rift between the so-called nomothetic and idiographic traditions. As already considered, he maintains that individuals' behavior obeys a set of common general laws, whose existence permits human behavior to be treated in a scientific way. On the other hand, the author attributes great importance to the role of the environment (as is clear from his five hypotheses) in modeling individual behaviors, in line with the behavioristic tradition. In particular, he affirms that the inevitable uniqueness of behaviors is due to the variety of contexts in which the general laws operate: this variety is responsible for the observable diversity of individual behaviors, in spite of the limitedness of the set of laws which govern them.[8]

The picture that emerges from Kimble's proposal offers an image of psychology as a means to study human and animal behavior – between which there is continuity – via the methodological devices of traditional sciences, in particular physics.[9] As we saw above, the reason for this is to obtain scientific credentials for psychology through its methodological identification with more "mature" and solid sciences. This leads to the focus on methodological issues, while neglecting issues about the problem of the object of psychology. In fact, in Kimble's view, psychology generically deals with behavior, both human and animal. But there is another scientific discipline that deals with human and animal behavior, namely biology, with which psychology must be compatible, in Kimble's opinion. The author says that this would not lead to reductionism, i.e., the claim that the laws of psychology must be translatable into those of biology. Yet, the two kinds of laws must not mutually conflict (Kimble, 1996: 40). In the light of these claims, however, it is not clear why "the most comfortable concepts for psychology are grounded in biology" (1996: 31), referring to color vision processes, chromosomal processes, and language disorders caused by brain injuries. Does this sort of assertion form a prelude to the possibility of reducing psychological concepts into "most comfortable" biological concepts and mechanisms? The search for scientific methodological credentials seems to obscure the problem of the existence of a proper and autonomous psychological level of explanation. Moreover, Kimble is not explicit in affirming whether the relation between psychology and biology is understood on linguistic grounds (a matter of relations between components of different theoretical perspectives, connected by syntactic and formal aspects) or on ontological grounds (a matter of existence of qualitatively different or identical kinds of entities). However, it can be inferred that the relationship between the two scientific disciplines is understood to be grounded on linguistic, rather than on ontological, elements, according to the theoretical and methodological background of functional behaviorism (see Chapter 4 for more details).

In conclusion, it is worth noting that the author, in line with other interpretations, views the state of fragmentation of psychology as a consequence of its rough and sketchy application in different and narrow contexts (see Chapter 5; Cahan and White, 1992). This kind of application historically hindered serious theoretical remarks about the relationships between theory and practice, i.e., the ways psychological knowledge can be applied to practical, real problems. Even though he considers this to be the primary cause of psychological fragmentation, Kimble excludes from his proposal the professional, applied side of the discipline. In this way, a picture of psychology as a scientific, academic discipline emerges, whose only aim is to properly explain human and animal behavior in its general features. The modes of application of psychological knowledge are left to the professional, as a direct and unproblematic derivation of this knowledge itself. In other words, while Kimble recognizes the importance of the connection between theoretical knowledge and professional practice for the issue of the fragmentation in psychology, his proposal seems to forget the problematic character of the issue, confining it to the common sense of professional psychologists.

Notes

1 More about this issue will be discussed in the next paragraph.
2 S stands for "stimulus."
3 P stands for "properties."
4 In a broad sense, behavior can be defined as an organism's activities in response to external or internal stimuli (VandenBos, 2007).
5 Is it interesting to note that Kimble maintains that experiments on classical and operant conditioning are laboratory realizations of this principle. In fact, in classical conditioning, the

organism learns to adapt (adaptation). In operant conditioning, conversely, the organism acquire strategies that favor the positive and diminish the negative (coping) (1996: 57).

6 Private facts cannot be ignored, at least because they are observable (verbal) reports. The problem, as indicated by the Italian philosopher Umberto Curi (1973) in his comment on Bridgman's operationalism, is the choice of the method by which to reliably analyze those facts.

7 It must be said that often the behavioristic tradition, just because it is rightly considered to be derived from the positivistic tradition, supported the idea that psychology must exclude subjective facts because they are not observable and measurable. Psychology, as an empirical science, must deal with observable behaviors. Though, in the light of a deeper look into the neo-positivistic position (see Hempel in Chapter 1), this assumption is not completely justified: human and natural events can be treated as if they were basically the same. The study of the former is less problematic because the inquirer can directly observe the phenomena; the study of the latter imposes the detection of observable data which provide information about private (i.e., non directly observable) phenomena. Thus, the method doesn't impose a specific kind of objects: it proposes to solely consider the empirical and operational aspects of the object at stake.

8 This position seems to be different from Hempel's which maintains that, despite appearances, every event can be in principle reconstructed on the basis of general laws and that uniqueness is only apparent (1962: 281; see also Chapter 1).

9 This seems to be quite evident at the very beginning of the author's work, where he declares that he modeled his scientific psychology on Newton's laws of motion. Further, he noticed that "one of the ambitions of the science of psychology is to express its … laws numerically" (Kimble, 1996: 22), without providing any explicit argument that justifies this kind of ambition.

References

Anderson, H. N. (2008). *Unified Social Cognition*. New York: Psychology Press.

Cahan, E. D. and White, S. H. (1992). Proposals for a second psychology. *American Psychologist*, 47(2): 224–235.

Carnap, R. (1928). *Der Logische Aufbau der Welt*. Leipzig: Felix Meiner. [Italian translation *La costruzione logica del mondo*, Milan: Fabbri]

Curi, U. (ed.) (1973). Introduzione. In *L'Analisi operazionale della psicologia*. Milan: Franco Angeli.

Hempel, C. G. (1962). Explanation in science and history. In J. H. Fetzer (2001), *The Philosophy of Carl G. Hempel* (pp. 276–296). Oxford: Oxford University Press. [reprinted from R. G. Colodny (ed.), *Frontiers of Science and Philosophy* (pp. 9–33). Pittsburgh, PA: University of Pittsburgh Press]

Hempel, C. G. (1969). Logical positivism and the social sciences. In P. Achinstein and S. F. Barker (eds.), *The Legacy of Logical Positivism*. Baltimore, MD: Johns Hopkins University Press.

Henriques, G. R. (2011). *A New Unified Theory of Psychology*. New York: Springer.

Kimble, G. A. (1996). *Psychology: The Hope of a Science*. Cambridge, MA: MIT Press.

Staats, A. W. (1996). *Behavior and Personality. Psychological Behaviorism*. New York: Springer.

Sternberg, R. J. (2005). Unifying the field of psychology. In R. J. Sternberg (ed.), *Unity in Psychology. Possibility or Pipedream?* (pp. 3–14). Washington, DC: American Psychological Association.

Sternberg, R. J. and Grigorenko, E. L. (2003). Unified psychology. In A. E. Kazdin (ed.), *Methodological Issues and Strategies in Clinical Research* (3rd edn) (pp. 23–47). Washington, DC: American Psychological Association.

VandenBos, G. R. (2007). *APA Dictionary of Psychology*. Washington, DC: American Psychological Association.

7

ARTHUR STAATS' PSYCHOLOGICAL BEHAVIORISM

In the words of the Arthur Staats, the aim of psychological behaviorism is to behaviorize psychology, on the one hand, and to psychologize behaviorism (Staats, 1996: 13), on the other. More specifically, the aim is to unify psychology under the methodological approach of a modified behaviorism. In other terms, the project entails the explanation of phenomena of psychological interest in a rather sophisticated behavioristic way. The methodological landmark of this proposal consists in making behavior analyses of those phenomena.[1] Psychological behaviorism (PB), whose features are systematically illustrated in Staats' book *Behavior and Personality. Psychological Behaviorism* (1996), attributes great importance to the process of learning in human behavior explanation. In order to do that, PB prescribes analyzing behaviors in a detailed manner and to focus not only on the principles of learning, but also on the conditions under which learning takes place. PB considers the principles of learning as basic to the acquisition of complex human behaviors (Staats, 1996: 37); though, for a comprehensive understanding of it, we need to move from the study of elementary principles in artificial simple situations to the study of more elaborate behaviors carried out in naturalistic situations (1996: 75).

The theoretical device that is at the core of PB and that permits the explanation of human behaviors is the three-function learning theory, which is centered on the nature of the different functions of a stimulus. The basic conception is that stimuli can have multiple functions, depending on the kind of reaction they elicit. In this frame, PB defines what are traditionally called "reinforcer stimuli" as those stimuli that are able to elicit an emotional response, contrary to traditional behaviorism.[2] The emotional function is the first function that Staats individuates. Emotional responses are elicited, through classical conditioning, by stimuli that are biologically important to the organism, namely functional for its survival. This is "the essential behavioral reason why emotions are important" (Staats, 1996: 41). As we will soon see, the reason why we feel emotions is that they permit us to learn adaptive behaviors in different circumstances. In fact, if a stimulus is able to elicit an emotional response, positive or negative, it will also strengthen or weaken the ensuing behavior, serving as a reinforcer: the stronger the emotional response elicited by a stimulus, the stronger the reinforcing function of that very stimulus. Thus, the emotional value of a stimulus is logically different from its reinforcing value, though the two are deeply related. The two functions (emotional and reinforcing) are conceptually distinct for Staats. The third function of a stimulus, beside the emotional function and the reinforcing function, is the incentive function. This function entails that when a positive emotional stimulus is presented, the organism will approach the stimulus; when a negative emotional stimulus is presented, it will avoid the stimulus. The incentive function indicates which kind of basic behavior, approach, or avoidance[3], will be elicited by the nature of the stimulus. In the author's words:

> It is important that incentive … power be distinguished from reinforcing power. In reinforcement, the stimulus is presented following any motor behavior, and has a strengthening effect on the behavior for future occasion. The incentive function, in contrast, occurs when the stimulus is presented first and then elicits or brings on a particular behavior in that situation.
>
> *(Staats, 1996: 42)*

To sum up, every stimulus which has an emotional aspect has three functions:

1. It elicits an emotional response, positive or negative (emotional function).
2. It can act as a reinforcer for future behavior, when presented as being contingent on a behavior (reinforcing function).
3. It is able to direct the organism's behavior (incentive function), producing approach (positive emotional stimulus) or avoidance behaviors (negative emotional stimulus).

It is evident that the emotional dimension of the stimulus is fundamental in Staats' proposal. The connection between this function – which is connected to the biological relevance of the stimulus itself – and the reinforcing function is determined by biological needs, in the author's view. In contrast, the third function – stimuli elicit approach or avoidance behavior – is learned. To illustrate this point:

> Suppose that the sight of an apple on a table elicits a positive emotional response in a hungry child. It is also the case that approaching, grasping, and biting the apple will yield reinforcement to the child … When the child is reinforced for approaching the apple, the child has also been reinforced for approaching a stimulus that elicits a positive emotional response. Through this experience the child will learn an association between the stimulus of the positive emotional response and an approach behavior.
>
> *(Staats, 1996: 48)*

Once generalized, this mechanism will be applied to any stimulus that elicits a positive, or negative, emotional response. But what may happen if the stimulus doesn't possess biological relevance, that is, it doesn't initially elicit an emotional response? Indeed, only a few stimuli have biological relevance (for example, those relating to food, danger, sex). Biologically (and hence emotionally) neutral stimuli acquire an emotional relevance through high-order classical conditioning. High-order classical conditioning is when a conditioned stimulus – which is a stimulus that previously acquired an emotional value – is used as the unconditioned stimulus in order to produce conditioning to a new stimulus[4] (Staats, 1996: 76–7). This can be defined as a kind of vicarious learning, not dependent upon the occurrence of biologically significant stimuli. This is the procedure through which any environmental stimulus can acquire an emotional relevance and consequently can be considered through the lens of the three-function learning theory. In this perspective, the theory can be considered as a general frame where classical and operant conditioning are linked together and account for different aspects of learning processes. In particular, classical conditioning accounts for the emotional function (a stimulus elicits a response), while operant conditioning for the reinforcing function (a stimulus presented after a specific behavior will strengthen or weaken that behavior). Together they account for the generalization of the emotional value to neutral stimuli and the learning of the incentive values of the stimuli. Moreover, the three-function learning theory operates consistently with a set of secondary principles such as extinction, generalization, discrimination, intermitting conditioning, motivation, which are consistent with the traditional research on behavioral and learning processes (see Staats, 1996: 54–7). Thus, this framework is presented as sufficient for explaining all basic learning processes that occur in human behavior.

In the author's view, the three-function learning theory not only explains behavioral processes but it is the fundamental basis by which to understand the primary level of cognitive processes through the notion of image (Staats, 1996: 65). In a nutshell, sensations – what individuals experience – are considered to be responses to stimuli that produce sensory processes in the organism. Considering sensations as responses means that they can be learned and that an organism can be conditioned to have a sensory response, even in the absence of a sensory stimulus. These sort of sensory responses which are elicited through conditioning, in the absence of a sensory stimulus, can be called images. Images are the basic level of human cognition and their formation can be explained through classical and operant conditioning within the framework of the three-function learning theory.

In general, through the processes of classical and operant conditioning, human beings learn complex combinations of stimuli and response, and only rarely a stimulus is able to elicit multiple responses. If the responses are mutually compatible, they all can occur, but if they don't, one will be more strongly learned in that specific situation. This consideration leads to the principle of cumulative hierarchical learning, the notion according to which the available responses to environmental situations are hierarchically organized through continuous learning.[5] The author maintains that humans acquire multiple basic response repertoires, which are the bricks that constitute human cognition. In other words, the proper development of each repertoire permits other repertoires to be acquired whose learning can be properly achieved only on the basis of the development of the former. This general architecture of human cognition is hierarchical and is based on the notion of basic behavioral repertoire (BBR); as the author highlights, this notion was conceived through the detailed study of three BBRs, those dealing with language, emotion, and sensory-motor skills (Staats, 1996: 81–94), which are considered to be central aspects in the adequate development of individuals. A BBR is a complex system of stimuli that are able to elicit emotional responses, and will also serve as reinforcing and incentive stimuli (consistently with the three-function learning theory). Not every behavioral repertoire is basic; to be a BBR, a repertoire must have some features, such as being the foundation for learning other repertoires, which widely affects the individual's experience or provides him/her with elements that are useful in a variety of life situations[6] (Staats, 1996: 156). At first, a child's BBRs are simple and composed of relatively few elements; subsequently, development consists in learning additional elements in previously acquired BBRs, in order to develop higher-order BBRs. In this perspective, BBRs can be considered as the universe of potential behaviors an individual has learned and they provide continuity and consistency in the individual's experience. In fact, the behavior displayed in a specific situation is a function of those potential behaviors at the disposal of the individual and the characteristics of the present situation. More precisely, the distal environment accounts for the learning, in the past, of the potential behaviors at disposal (BBRs), while the proximal environment, the one that causes a specific behavior, constitutes the present eliciting factor for the behavior that is displayed (Staats, 1996: 187–8). From this point of view, individual differences – under the form of BBRs and previous learning – are preserved, as is the importance of the environment in eliciting behaviors, in accordance with the behavioristic tradition.

As we have already seen, one central point in Staats' theory is that an individual's behavior has its determinants in the emotional reactions that have been learned. One important class of stimuli in everyday social interaction is obviously represented by people: their physical and behavioral characteristics have emotional value for us and can be properly understood through the three-function learning theory (Staats, 1996: 119). This leads to the unification of the explanation of social phenomena under the aegis of the same methodological umbrella: the three-function learning theory not only accounts for basic behaviors; rather, it also accounts for complex social phenomena. According to the author, the general principle is that individuals ordinarily learn repertoires of responses with respect to classes of social stimuli. This is important for understanding both social interaction and child development, which are both processes occurring within a relational frame. In particular, child development occurs within a specific social situation where the parents and child interact, and thus can be considered a special form of social interaction. In this context, children usually learn a strong positive emotional response to their parents, so they become strong sources of reinforcement in the training of their children and in the acquisition of BBRs. The repetition of positive conditioning trials produces a very strong positive emotional response to each other, attracting approaching behavior and developing what we ordinarily call love bonds (Staats, 1996: 163). This is an example of how human beings can be considered as emotional stimuli within social interactions and thus have reinforcing and incentive values, in addition to other less complex stimuli.

In its task to behaviorize psychology, PB doesn't refuse to analyze the notion of personality – as behaviorism did – as it is one of the most important constructs in traditional psychology. In the PB frame, personality features are constituted by the individual BBRs, that is, by the learned individual modes to address different kinds of environment (Staats, 1996: 176). In other words, the subject's environment up to the present results in the learning of individual BBRs and present behavior turns out to be a function of the specific circumstance (life situation) and the individual BBRs. Therefore, there are two sources of individual variability: personality (the acquired BBRs) and environment. In this perspective, personality is evidently composed of specifiable BBRs. Thus, personality is formed by potential stimulus–responses constellations (Staats, 1996: 193) that cannot be conceived as intervening variables. Rather, they can be considered as dependent as well as independent variables. They are the result of learning, so they are dependent variables, but they also are independent variables as they act as causes of human behavior. In Staats' perspective, this double soul of personality (as a system of BBRs) is able to resolve, in a unified manner, the schism between those refusing the concept of personality – considering it only as a bunch of behaviors, thus as a dependent variable – and those supporting a view of personality as a cause of behavior, hence as an independent variable.

Within this frame, what is the role of biology with respect to personality? For Staats, the mechanisms responsible for sensing, learning, and performing behavior are biologically determined, but they do not play a role in explaining particular behaviors or traits of behaviors (Staats, 1996: 181). Rather, biological factors mediate in many ways the learning processes and the production of present behavior. In greater detail, the biological state of an individual can affect BBRs' development, fostering or hindering it. Then, the biological state of the individual can also have an effect after the BBRs are acquired, fostering or hindering their use in a specific situation. Finally, the biological system may affect the way in which the individual interacts with the specific situation under review, thus affecting the present behavior. In short, organic conditions affect behavior only through the above-mentioned ways, i.e., influencing the learning and/or behavior implementation. Organic conditions are not responsible for the mechanisms that account for behavioral production: thus, biology is an instrument by which behavior are learned or produced, not a "creator" of behavior (Staats, 1996: 184).

The issue of personality involves also the consideration of what we subjectively feel, what we experience from our first person perspective. Concerning this issue, Staats believes that what we experience as our self, or our being, are the operations of our BBRs (p. 197). Our thinking, planning, wanting and the way we purposively behave is the subjective side of the BBRs in operation. This is the reason why we believe we have power over our actions and will. And we are right, in Staats' opinion, even if "it is not necessary to go outside scientific causality to provide an explanatory account" (1996: 198). The cumulative processes of hierarchical learning are too complex to be recognized as the causes of behavior. Also the BBRs share the same properties, and this is a reason why the individuals will not recognize the causes of their behavior. To this classical behavioristic account of free will, Staats adds that, in addition to the action of the environment on the individual, the individual also acts on the environment. In more detail:

> The individual learns BBRs which determine how the individual will act in the situation met. But that behavior will affect others, importantly acting upon the world. Moreover, those effects on the world will, in return, act back upon the person. In this way the individual determines the environment she meets, and she determines her own behavior, because that environment will affect her.
>
> *(Staats, 1996: 198)*

Again, the author tries to unify two traditionally separate outlooks on free will within the frame of the PB's personality theory: the behavioristic perspective (which excludes the possibility of free will) and the folk psychological perspective (which supports its existence).

As should now be clear, the appropriate development of BBRs leads to the structuring of a normal, that is functional, personality. However, something can go wrong in the process and this can entail the emergence of abnormal, that is, non-functional, behaviors. The simplest version of the PB model of abnormal behavior and its causes is the following. An individual's past environment, which is responsible for the development of the BBRs, may be either deficient or inappropriate. This leads to the development of deficient or inappropriate BBRs, which means that the repertoires contains potentially necessary behaviors that are not completely functional or behaviors whose occurrence is inappropriate, both of which situations are abnormal. In addition, the PB model indicates that the individual's current environment is a possible source of abnormal behavior: if it is deficient or inappropriate, other things being equal, the present behavior can be abnormal, not functional.

In sum, there are three possible causal sites of dysfunctional behavior: past environment, BBRs, and current environment. Also, abnormal biological conditions can contribute to producing abnormal behavior, in accordance with the principles considered above for personality development. Abnormal biological conditions can occur during the learning process of BBRs (resulting in deficient or inappropriate BBRs; e.g., a case of microcephaly or Down's syndrome), after proper BBRs have been learned (causing a deficiency or inappropriate expression of the BBRs, e.g., a brain injury occurring in adulthood) or during the process of sensing and responding to the present environment (e.g., an episode of alcohol abuse) (Staats, 1996: 258–9). From this perspective, each abnormal behavior or pathological disorder can be profitably analyzed in a unified and related manner, through the lens of PB. Therefore, PB provides a general frame for the explanation of dysfunctional behaviors, which is strongly based on the concepts and principles of the theory of personality above mentioned. Abnormal and normal development are conceptualized on the basis of the same basic principles.

In conclusion, it is evident that Staats tries to give an account of diverse psychological phenomena by means of the same set of concepts, those referring to PB. In this framework, the processes giving rise to basic learning, cognition, human development, social interaction, personality, and abnormal behavior turn out to be unified, based on the essential notions of stimulus functions and of BBRs. Staats' model envisages a rather small number of concepts which the author uses in the explanation of a variety of psychological phenomena, connecting psychological areas which are rarely connected theoretically.

What kind of psychology is suited to Staats' psychological behaviorism?

Staats' psychological behaviorism is grounded on a philosophical approach called unified positivism (Staats, 1996: 2) by the author himself. This philosophical stance is monistic in character, as it asserts that traditional scientific methods must be applied to psychology's phenomena (Staats, 1996: 373). In particular, unified positivism is based on observation (i.e., experimentation, naturalistic, clinical observation) and systematic construction of theory, which involves consistency, empirical definition, generality, and parsimony. This is the traditional philosophical frame of unified positivism. However, observation is recognized as a procedure where objective and subjective aspects intersect: on one hand, it is objective because it permits an intersubjective agreement; on the other hand, it is subjective because every scientific endeavor has to be considered as a social construction, that is, a relative (i.e., not absolute) undertaking (Staats, 1996: 2). Thus, unified positivism seems to acknowledge the validity of a traditional conception of science, while admitting the contingent nature of it. The reference to positivism seems to justify the use of behavioristic procedures in order to study those phenomena that belong to different fields of psychology: "Behavior principles are part of a unified set. Whatever is analyzed in terms of those principles is placed into a unified framework" (Staats, 1996: 14).

Thus, behavioral analysis provides a strong methodological reference for psychology, on the grounds of a basically traditional conception of science. Moreover, unified positivism, in its essentially monistic aspects, also justifies Staats' interest in unification. The project of unification, for those who supported the neo-positivistic movement, was based mainly on two features (see Chapter 1): the common way by which each scientific discipline justifies its statements (deriving from them empirical implications that can be intersubjectively acknowledged), and the individuation of public facts which can be considered as "observable symptoms" of private facts (Hempel, 1969: 269). On this conceptual basis, which Staats seems to share, the author asserts that unified positivism has the aim of producing reliable psychological knowledge and to make "the search for relationships a primary endeavor" (Staats,

1996: 373), making psychological unification as its main goal. In fact, "It has not been generally recognized that a central task of the science is to organize, relate, unify, and simplify its diversity, and that unrelatedness of its many phenomena provides an inexhaustible set of problems" (Staats, 1996: 5). Unified positivism is no doubt directed toward unification, even though it is not clear why unification is so important, and whether the problem of unification is an absolute *desideratum* or something that is contingently desirable, on the grounds of the present features of science in general, and of psychology in particular; the latter would be in line with the constructionist aspects of Staats' proposal. Assertions like "The prolific nature of the modern disunified science itself becomes a handicap" or "The content of psychology is disorganized in a way that is not scientific" (Staats, 1996: 4) do not help to lessen the doubt.

The author's position, in my opinion, only considers basic aspects of the traditional monistic approach in order to integrate them with a surface constructionist view of science. This integration doesn't seem to be properly justified, since methodological monism and social constructionism are incompatible in many respects. In fact, monism is grounded on a syntactic, logical view of scientific methodology (see Chapter 1), while considering science as a social construction means to prioritize those semantic aspects which contingently direct science toward its ever changing goals. Moreover, the monistic approach supports the concept of scientific progress through the progressive validation of reliable theories, on the grounds of their methodological credentials. The constructionist view sees all scientific endeavors as contingent and immeasurable; scientific progress is not possible in principle, since science is mostly moved by extra scientific (i.e., social, psychological) aspects. Lastly, as noticed above, the issue of unification is understandable and desirable from the viewpoint of the monistic stance; it is hardly justifiable from a constructionistic outlook, but as a contingent requirement of the present state of psychology on the basis of practical and contingent considerations. Though, in this case the extent of Staats' proposal would be smaller and less revolutionary than promised in his intentions. In the end, it is to be noted that while the monistic aspects of PB permeate most features of the author's proposal, the constructionist aspects do not seem to be clearly noticeable or justifiable in the general framework: the connection between monism and constructionism remains obscure.

PB's refusal of mentalistic concepts (i.e., concepts referring to mental states) is a feature that strongly connects Staats' philosophical background to the neo-positivistic tradition. This means that psychological (i.e., mentalistic) concepts have to be "translated" into empirically justifiable concepts, which permits an intersubjective, therefore scientific, knowledge of them. In other words, concepts like thinking, purpose, reasoning and so on are conceptualized in behavioral terms (Staats, 1996: 71), acknowledging behavior analysis as the common methodological stance through which psychology can get its scientific credentials, as we saw above. PB recognizes that there are internal behavioral processes which cannot be directly observable, but nevertheless give rise to behaviors. Their analysis can be accomplished by making observable what originally is not, finding out those "publicly observable symptoms"

(Hempel, 1969: 269) that make mentalistic concepts acceptable on the basis of their empirical translation. This means to identify those aspects of mentalistic concepts that can be behaviorally explained through the application of the three-function learning theory, as in the case of what is commonly called "intention":

> Most people discard behavioristic explanations of human behavior because they make people into automatons. Present the stimulus and the person responds. That seems to belie our common experience, which is that we do things because of our intentions, which are experienced before we do something. That experience suggest our feelings determine our behavior. The PB analysis provides an explanation of "intentions." That is, if the individual has a strong positive emotional response to the words "Super Bowl ticket," then she has the experience of "wanting" the ticket. And that emotional response will mediate the behaviors to get the ticket. In a sense the subject determines her behavior by how she feels, but that feeling itself depends upon past learning. This account behaviorizes the mentalistic concept of intention and also makes the approach cognitive.
>
> *(Staats, 1996: 95)*

In other words, traditional psychological concepts, which are mentalistic, are taken into account for their heuristic value although for a proper scientific consideration they are traced back to their empirical (i.e., behavioral) counterparts. In the case illustrated above, intentions are considered as feelings ("the experience of wanting") due to a learned positive emotional response to a bunch of words (Super Bowl ticket). Those feelings are not considered as intervening variables nor as epiphe-nomena,[7] but as internal behavioral processes that cause other behaviors. In this case, an internal, not directly observable behavior (the experience of wanting) is the stimulus that elicits the emission of directly observable behaviors (the actions needed to buy the ticket). As a matter of fact, internal behavioral events – as well as all kinds of behavior – have stimulus properties that can contribute to determining the individual's behavior (Staats, 1996: 367). Human behavior is thus considered a train of internal and external events which hold stimulus as well as response properties. The connections between those events seem to be causal, that is, regulated by deterministic links. The processes underlying those connections can be properly explained by the behavioristic principles, as they are described in the PB approach.

According to a monistic position, PB holds a syntactic view of psychological knowledge. All statements about human behavior can be traced back to the basic principles of Staats' theory. The core processes through which behavior learning occurs are those described in the three-function learning theory: PB provides for a language where a set of theoretical postulates (the laws of learning) meets a set of correspondences rules (based on observation), through which data (the observed behaviors) are bridged to the theory (see Chapter 1). From this perspective, the explanation of human behavior is traced back to those principles regarding learning processes which provide a sort of syntax through which the development of scientific psychological knowledge occurs. Staats asserts that traditional learning principles – those that are applied and studied in animal learning settings – are the basis of human learning processes (1996: 103), but that human learning processes cannot be completely traced back to those working in the animal kingdom. Accordingly, PB claims as follows:

> Humans learn via the basic principles, as do species lower in the phylogenetic scale. But human learning involves much more than the basic principles. Human learning involves principles and concepts that do not apply to lower animals.
>
> *(1996: 34)*

Hence, PB's syntactic approach does not directly rest upon the principles of general (i.e., animal) learning, rather it rests upon those principles that constitute the *proprium* of human learning. In turn, these principles illustrated in PB rest upon animal learning principles, even if they are qualitatively different when compared with them. Hence, while recognizing the autonomy of the explanation of human behavior, PB's main core is the centrality of the learning principles which are acknowledged as common aspects both of the animal kingdom as well as of the human world.[8] The connection between animal and human learning is controversial: claiming that animal behavior is the basis of human learning and at the same time claiming that human learning is qualitatively different from animal learning leaves open many questions about the nature of this connection which Staats does not answer.

However, PB provides a sort of primitive language through which the large mess of information coming from the world can be properly analyzed for scientific purposes (see Chapter 2). The language proposed by PB allows us to translate that large mess of information into statements that are able to specify those features of the data which are relevant for scientific purposes. These features can be called structural, as Carnap has (1961: 95): they account for a process (in this case, learning) only by referring to the relations between the parts involved in the process (the behaviors of the learner and the contingencies in her environment), without mentioning its semantic contents (for example, cycling, eating, or bathing).

The issue about the connection between animal and human learning principles discussed above is connected to the issue relating to reduction and to the existence of different levels of psychological inquiry. In this regard, PB claims that all traditional psychological fields represent different levels of study, arranged on a dimension that is defined by simplicity–complexity or basic–advanced:

> There is a generally advancing progression, from the more basic fields to the more advanced; the basic principles and concepts at one level serve as the starting point for analyses at the next level of advancing complexity.
>
> *(Staats, 1996: 18–19)*

In the author's model, at the basis there is the biological level, which seems to provide for the general architecture of human beings (i.e., their propensity to interact with the environment and to learn from the experience). Then, basic animal learning, human learning, social interaction, child development, personality, psychological measurement, abnormal psychology and behavior therapy (behavior restructuration) come one after the other. Each level has its own methods, problems, and objects of investigation, and has the task to relate these materials to the level below it and to the level above it (Staats, 1996: 19–20). Such a position suggests an interdependence between the levels, none of which is dominant over the others. However, each level seems to maintain its autonomy, at least on the basis of its methods, problems and objects of investigation. It is not easy to say if the existence of those levels reflects an ontological commitment or an epistemic necessity (i.e., linguistic, see Chapter 3): the alleged peculiarity of each level seems to witness an ontological diversity, while the assumption that each level provides principles and concepts to be used in the following level – starting from the basic animal learning level – seems to witness an epistemic hierarchy whose aim is to better explain phenomena of the same ontological kind which turn out to be different only on the surface. As we saw above, the controversy regarding the centrality of animal learning or the autonomy of human learning still remains: the question is whether PB is a reductionistic model based on the animal level – and this would mean the attribution of an epistemic value to the levels – or whether PB claims a real autonomy of human levels from the animal level. However, the following quotations seem to suggest an epistemic interpretation of the existence of the levels:

> A level theory begins with the principles and concepts of the overarching theory and elaborates them by applying them to the phenomena, concepts and principles of the field.
>
> *(Staats, 1996: 372)*

> Psychological behaviorism takes the position that animal behavior principles are basic and that these principles must be elaborated in additional levels of study.
>
> *(Staats, 1996: 103)*

Here, what seems to be the core are the principles and concepts of the overarching theory, which can be applied contingently to different objects and contexts. In this case, the levels are only fields of application of a general set of laws which was established in one specific area of inquiry (Nagel, 1961: 338), i.e., animal or human behavior learning research. From this perspective, PB is reductionistic in character, even if the above-mentioned problems remain open: it is not clear what the "principles and concepts of the overarching theory" are. Do they refer to animal learning, as the second quotation above suggests, or do they refer to human learning, as the previous quotation seems to suggest? Is there an autonomy of the latter from the former, or is human learning just a version of animal learning? If PB is a reductionist model, does this reduction rest upon animal learning principles or upon human learning principles? In other words, while Staats' proposal appears to be reductionistic – in the sense that unification is accomplished via common

principles underlying different areas of inquiry – it does not make a definite ontological commitment regarding the object, or objects, with which psychology deals.

Lastly, with regard to the relationship between theory and practice, Staats claims
that PB allows for a strong connection between these two often split aspects of
psychology (see Chapter 5 for more detail). In fact, the account of human behaviors
within the PB framework, mainly through the use of the concept of BBR and the
three-function learning theory, provides an explanatory continuity between the
processes involved in basic psychology, child development, social life, personality
development, abnormal personality development, and psychological treatment. In
other words, the consideration of human life as the result of complex learning
processes also suggests those intervention methods which can be used in case
something goes wrong in normal human development. Such intervention methods
are based on a diagnosis in terms of BBRs, which involve questions such as: which
BBR(s) is/(are) damaged? What is – or has been – the role of the distal and/or
proximal environment regarding those BBR deficiencies? Is it possible to correct
these deficiencies? In what way? More precisely, a diagnosis in terms of PB will
suggest or specify the etiology and treatment of the disorder (Staats, 1996: 346),
identifying what is – or has been – the problem regarding the observable dysfunctional behavior at stake. Once the behavior has been analyzed in this way, the PB
treatment so devised aims at creating or restoring the conditions wherein learning
of proper (i.e., adaptive) behavior may be accomplished. Therefore, within the PB
framework, the psychologist is able to identify the behavioral problem and to
intervene in it with the use of the same theoretical tools. Thus, PB strongly connects the theoretical aspects to the practical aspects; the common element is that
the two share the same conceptual framework, based on the essential principle that
human behavior is learned and consequently can be modified if it turns out not to
be functional in the achievement of desired goals.

As a whole, PB is a rather coherent system where a small amount of concepts
and principles are used in order to give an integrated account of a variety of
psychological phenomena. The task of conceptual unity is prescribed by the author
as desirable *per se*; though, in the quest for unity some aspects still remain
controversial and should deserve further study.

Notes

1 More on this issue will be discussed in the next paragraph.
2 In operant conditioning, the reinforcement is the process in which the frequency or the
   probability of a response is increased by a dependent relationship, or contingency, with a
   stimulus or circumstance (the reinforcer) (VandenBos, 2007).
3 These two basic behaviors are considered to be the main modes of human behavior.
4 High-order conditioning is essentially human and is a central differentiation of the species
   from lower animal (Staats, 1996: 77).
5 In Staats' view, this process also accounts for individual differences between subjects
   (1996: 78, 158).
6 The child's world changes as a function of age, and whether the child will become
   adjusted or not depends on whether the child has the relevant BBRs (Staats, 1996: 157).

7 They are neither intervening variables because they aren't hypothetical entities influenced by the independent variable and that in turn influence the dependent variable, nor epiphenomena because they aren't incidental products of some higher-level process.
8 In line with the behavioristic tradition, Staats acknowledges the existence of an essential continuity between the animal and the human world.

References

Hempel, C. G. (1969). Reduction: Ontological and linguistic facets. In J. H. Fetzer (ed.) (2001), *The Philosophy of Carl G. Hempel* (pp. 189–207). Oxford: Oxford University Press. [reprinted from *Philosophy. Science and Method. Essays in Honor of Ernest Nagel*, by S. Morgenbesser, P. Suppes, and M. White (eds.), New York: St. Martin's Press]

Nagel, E. (1961). *The Structure of Science. Problems in the Logic of Scientific Explanation.* Cambridge, MA: Hackett.

Staats, A. W. (1996). *Behavior and Personality. Psychological Behaviorism.* New York: Springer.

VandenBos, G. R. (2007). *APA Dictionary of Psychology.* Washington, DC: American Psychological Association.

8

GREGG HENRIQUES' UNIFIED THEORY OF PSYCHOLOGY

The intent of Henriques is to propose a model of unified psychology that is compatible with both scientific psychology and folk psychology. The consequence of this approach is that the image of psychology that emerges from his book, *A New Unified Theory of Psychology* (2011), meshes reasonably well with common-sense notions about mind and behavior, though it is deeply grounded in science, as displayed by the great number of examples that the author draws from scientific research. The model provided is a sort of meta-theoretical system that organizes in a systematic manner the empirical findings of the different isolated branches or theories of psychology. The principal aims of this framework are to clearly distinguish psychology's subject matter, to show psychology's relationship with other sciences, and to integrate key insights from different psychological traditions or lines of research (Henriques, 2011: 5, 8). The framework provided is different from existing psychological paradigms (for example, psychodynamic theories or cognitive sciences), as will become evident in what follows, in that it has the aim of integrating all of these theoretical needs described above, while attempting to include the main objects of interest of animal and human psychologies in a unified and coherent framework. The model provides four main components that trace psychology's boundaries and contents: the behavioral investment theory, the influence matrix, the justification hypothesis, and the tree of knowledge system. The aim of the present chapter is to investigate each component in more detail.

The first component of Henriques' model is the behavioral investment theory (BIT) which considers human and animal behavior in terms of invested work effort, specifically in terms of relationship between costs and benefits (Henriques, 2011: 45). BIT creates bridges between extant theoretical perspectives of behavioral functioning, outlining an integrated and coherent approach to animal and human behavior. There are six principles that underlie BIT (Henriques, 2011: 48–55):

1. Principle of energy economics: the organism must acquire, on the whole, more energy than the amount of energy its behavioral investment costs. In other words, the behavior is organized so that the energy obtained is more than the energy that has been spent, given the organism's knowledge and capacities.
2. Evolutionary principle: this principle states that the processes that regulate behavior investment are built across generations. In virtue of evolutionary forces, the organism is predisposed to respond to certain stimuli in a certain way (for example, visceral responses or reflexes).
3. Principle of genetics: this is the ontogenetic variation of the former principle (which refers to phylogenetic aspects). This principle says that the individual's genetic make-up influences its behavior.
4. Computational control principle: this principle involves the way the organ that is supposed to control behavior, the nervous system, functions as an information-processing system. This means that it translates "physical and chemical changes in both environment and in the body into neuronal patterns of information that represent the animal–environment relationship" (Henriques, 2011: 53) upon which behavior is organized.
5. Learning principle: it describes how the organism manages its behavior during its lifetime. Behavioral investments are allocated depending on the contingencies to which the organism responds. Here Henriques quotes the three-function learning theory (Staats, 1996) as the theoretical device that most usefully describes these processes in detail (see Chapter 7 in this volume).
6. Developmental principle: this principle supports the idea that each developmental stage requires different behavioral investment strategies, depending on the specific needs (genetically, hormonally, or culturally determined) of that particular stage.

These principles describe the general structure of an organism's behavioral investment system, the way it works, the factors by which it is influenced, and the forces that drive it. The BIT has the scope to describe very general and basic aspects of behavior and deals with animal as well as human functioning. When considering the applications of the BIT to human behavior, Henriques provides a general framework composed of four levels which describe how humans behave in their species-specific way. We will consider them one by one.

The basic level of behavior is called sensory-motor and involves automatic, reactive stimulus–response connections. This level includes every elementary form of learning, from instinctual reflexes to habitual motor patterns, like walking.

The second level is called operant–experiential and refers to voluntary, dynamic, seek-and-approach behavior. The general formulation which organizes the behavior states that the perception (P)[1] of a motivated state (M)[2] leads to an emotion (E), which works as an organizing principle that selects the proper behaviors. These can be broadly divided into approach behavior and avoidance behavior (see also Staats, 1996).

The third level deals with imaginative thought, which consists of the human ability to manipulate mental representations and to treat them as simulations of behavioral investment patterns, whose outcomes can be anticipated and evaluated. This is a very important function: the predictive validity of mental simulations and the fact that they require a small amount of resources make them very useful in order to experiment and evaluate different behavioral patterns, without the costs associated with their actual production (Henriques, 2011: 77).

The fourth level regards the linguistic justification and the human capacity to symbolically label perceived objects. Details about this level will be presented when dealing with the justification hypothesis. As a whole, all of these levels refer to aspects of human behavior that can be understood through the principles outlined by the BIT in a broad and systematic general framework.

Let us now turn to the second component of Henriques' model of unified psychology, the IM (influence matrix), which is an extension of the BIT to the domain of human social motivation and emotion (2011: 84). The theoretical basis of the IM is that the social dimension is primary for humans; in fact, the ability to influence the actions of others in accordance with one's interest, which can be called social influence, is considered to be a resource that humans are motivated to acquire as a primary need. The IM can be understood as a representation of the "self–other" dialectic, where individuals reciprocally negotiate the acquisition of social influence; the balance between independency, which is the capacity to self-assert and to be a differentiated individual, and dependency, which is the ability to be interpersonally involved and interconnected, is associated with higher social influence and better psychosocial adjustment (Henriques, 2011: 91, 94, 104).

For IM, the interpersonal processes involved in the acquisition of social influence can be grouped into three broad categories. The first category concerns *care elicitation*, which is the first way to elicit positive social responses from the caretaker by means of the expression of dependency needs; this is the basis of the ability to gain social influence. The second category concerns *competition*. Direct competition is when two or more individuals are overtly in opposition for the achievement of a limited resource, this being a more primitive way to obtain social influence. In direct competition there are clear winners and losers. In contrast, indirect competition does not involve clear winners and losers, but social ranking and comparison. Thus, it is an evolved way to obtain social influence. Finally, the third IM category concerns *altruism*. Henriques conceives altruism in behavioristic terms: "By being giving and deferential an individual can become a rewarding stimulus and that, in turn, can translate into social influence for the altruist" (2011: 88).

In the IM framework, emotions are associated with the process of gaining (positive emotions) or losing (negative emotions) social influence. In this way, emotions give feedback about this process, orienting the individual toward corrective actions, if needed.

As already stated, the author's model provides four main components that trace psychology's boundaries and contents. We already investigated the BIT, which is composed of six principles that outline an integrated approach to the fundamentals of human and animal behavior, and the IM, which is an extension of the BIT to the primary social dimension of human relations. Let's now turn to the third component, the justification hypothesis (JH). While the BIT represents the foundation for the understanding of animal as well as human behavior on a common ground, JH provides the framework to understand what is unique about human beings. The problem it addresses is that of social justification, which is the human tendency to explain the legitimacy of one's thought or action to others. For their entire life, indeed, individuals try to build justification narratives that provide sound reasons for their behavioral and thought patterns, specifying what is happening, why it is happening, and why one is doing what in that context (Henriques, 2011: 115). The existence of this species-specific device supports a two-domains view of the human mind, which includes two systems of information processing (Henriques, 2011: 122). The first system is a nonverbal, perceptual–motivational–emotional, parallel information-processing guidance system that analyzes resource availability and organizes action, according to the BIT. This system can be compared to sentience and it refers to nonverbal conscious experiences, such as feeling pain, seeing colors, being hungry, remembering an event. The second system of the JH is uniquely human and is a verbal, reflective, sequential information-processing system. In Henriques' opinion, this is a relatively new evolutionarily product that can be called a self-consciousness system, and which involves the language-based portion of our mind which provides narratives of the kind specified above. This system, in contrast to the former which involves experience, involves self-awareness and verbal-making meaning about the experience: thus, the role of language is central for self-consciousness. The hypothesis is that as language sophistication advanced during evolution beyond simple descriptions and commands, it became a useful tool to more directly access and assess the thoughts and intentions of other human beings (Henriques, 2011: 119). The clashing interests between individuals made self-consciousness key in human interactions, putting pressure on them to create socially justifiable explanations in order to support their own interests and goals.[3]

The self-consciousness system split in turn into two broad domains: the private self and the public self. On the one hand, the private self is the center of self-reflective awareness, where self-dialogues take form and produce a private narrative of what is happening and why. The public self, on the other hand, is the interface with the external social environment and involves the explicit articulation to others of the portion of our thinking that we want to share with them.[4]

The JH is important for the emergence of another species-specific feature of human beings: culture. In fact, in Henriques' opinion, the result of language evolution, which allowed access to others' thoughts by means of the capacity to ask questions, was the emergence of justification systems at the individual and small group level. Progressively, these systems got networked together to coordinate populations groups, giving rise to cultural phenomena. In fact, culture provides the borders to the acceptability of one's conduct in a specific cultural context: to perform in concert with others is to perform in a justified fashion, while the contrary is associated with an experience of discomfort and is considered unjustifiable (Henriques, 2011: 146–8).

To summarize, the JH provides a framework in which to understand the evolutionary problem faced by a unique human feature, self-consciousness, which is a language-based device whose aim is to socially justify our conduct or thoughts. The sharing of such a capacity gives rise to complex and networked justification systems that constitute culture.

The fourth and final piece of Henriques' model of unified psychology is the tree of knowledge (ToK) system, which provides a macro-level framework where psychology is interrelated with other branches of science and where its subject matter is identified. This part of the model establishes links between the natural domains (the structure of reality, as described by the author) and the scientific disciplines which has the aim to investigate those domains: the system entails the correspondence between the existence of different "so-called" natural domains and the sciences. According to Henriques, there are four broad, hierarchically arranged natural domains, whose origin stems loosely from the notion of energy: matter, life, mind, culture. More precisely, nature itself is viewed by Henriques as a nested hierarchy, where wholes at one level are parts of wholes at another, superior level (2011: 158). To each level corresponds an equivalent scientific discipline, namely physics (whose object is matter), biology (whose object is life), psychology (whose object is mind), and the social sciences (whose object is culture) (Henriques, 2011: 154). Henriques identifies some joint points, which are theories that link the domains and specify their reciprocal connections. Quantum gravity theory is the first joint point between energy and matter, representing a merger between the two pillars in physics: quantum mechanics and Einstein's general theory of relativity. The modern evolutionary synthesis is the joint point between matter and life, because it represents a general framework explaining how complex, self-replicating molecules evolved into organisms. BIT turns out to be the joint point between life and mind, through the understanding of basic behavioral principles, while the JH is the joint point between mind and culture, connecting the human capacity for self-consciousness to language skills and cultural development (Henriques, 2011: 153). From this perspective, the ToK system is able to descriptively fill the gap between different natural domains and areas of knowledge, integrating them into a coherent system.[5] The ToK system is a valuable framework which permits human behavior to be considered as a complex phenomenon with multiple and different aspects: the argument here is that "human behavior is made up of processes that operate on different behavioral frequencies that can be separated according to the dimensions of informational complexity represented by the ToK System" (Henriques, 2011: 156). To make this principle clear, the author illustrates the case for self-consciousness, which is a phenomenon that involves all four of the dimensions of complexity in the ToK system. Indeed, every self-reflective action entails physical, biological, psychological, and sociocultural aspects, which can be understood through the lens of the scientific disciplines pertaining to each of the four dimensions. This means that every complex human phenomenon must be studied from different yet integrated perspectives, each one providing information that turns out to be necessary, but not sufficient, to completely understand the next level according to the notion of nested hierarchy described above. For example, information about matter, provided by physics, is key to understanding life phenomena (the subsequent level in the ToK system hierarchy), but this information is not enough to grasp the specificity of biological systems, for which we need biology and its principles. In conclusion, the ToK system specifies the relationship between different levels of knowledge and their reciprocal connections, in order to give psychology its place among sciences.

Concerning the discipline of psychology and its formal organization, Henriques proposes to divide it into three great branches. Psychological formalism, which is the first branch, is the basic science of psychology, whose object is mental behavior (mind in the ToK system). Here, the term mental refers to "the distinctive manner in which animals behave relative to material objects like rocks or organic objects like plants or cells" (Henriques, 2011: 186). Psychological formalism is a "purely natural science discipline" (2011: 192), and represents the foundation of the other two psychological branches.

Human psychology, the second branch, focuses on human mind and behavior. While psychological formalism – through the BIT – shows how animal behavior is continuous with human behavior, human psychology – through the JH – deals with the qualitative shift that characterizes humans and that justifies the separation of human psychology from the basic science of psychology (psychological formalism). In fact, human behavior has unique features such as being mediated by symbolic language, being self-reflective, and being embedded in cultural contexts. These are the landmarks that make human psychology qualitatively distinct from psychological formalism. It is worth noting that human psychology doesn't deal with the mind dimension in the ToK system (which pertains to psychological formalism), rather it deals with human behavior, which is considered the smallest unit of analysis in the social sciences, thus in the culture dimension. In other words, human psychology must be considered as the basis of the social sciences[6] and as a subset of psychology in general, because humans are a subset of animals (Henriques, 2011: 196).

The third branch in psychology is professional psychology, which is considered distinct from the previous two branches. Professional psychology uses knowledge produced by the other two branches in order to improve the human condition. Thus, it aims to prescriptively reach professional goals and turns out to be more value-laden than the other branches, whose main target is to describe animal as well as human conduct with the ultimate aim of expanding knowledge. From this perspective, professional psychology responds to different needs and operates with different aims, as compared with psychological formalism or human psychology.[7]

What kind of psychology is suited to Henriques' unified theory of psychology?

The complexity of Gregg Henriques' multifaceted proposal makes the description of its philosophical stances a hard task. First of all, it is not easy to say whether this unified theory has its roots in the monistic or in the dualistic vision of science. On one hand, the ToK system, which deals with the general architecture of the world, is defined as monistic in the sense that everything has a common source, that is energy, which provides an ontological base for science. However, each level – matter, life, mind, culture – is described as autonomous and corresponds to a different scientific discipline which seems to require different kinds of methods in order to grasp the specificity of the objects which are "fundamentally different dimensions of complexity" (Henriques, 2011: 15). Thus, from a methodological perspective Henriques' unified theory seems to suggest a dualistic stance, because it considers human facts as different, in principle, from natural (material or biological) facts (see Chapter 1), and this would lead to the adoption of different methods, even if this is not explicitly claimed: "An integrated pluralism is where there are differences in emphasis that stem from separate needs, goals, and other idiographic factors" (2011: 26). Hence, the theory seems to be somewhat dualistic when it claims that science is made by broad, separable domains (Henriques, 2011: 154) and that psychology, as all the other sciences, cannot be reduced to physics and can be "crisply defined" (2011: 15, 155) as an autonomous discipline.

Nevertheless, other features may be noticed which can be traced back to a monistic source: first, objectivity and coherence are considered as important *desiderata* of the scientific enterprise (Henriques, 2011: 27). Second, the model is foundationalist to the core and proclaims universal truths about the universe and the human condition (2011: 4). Third, the need for unity in psychology expresses the need for an extensive theoretical system that suggests an underlying common scientific methodology (2011: 5). In other words, Henriques seems to feel close to what he calls a *modernist conception* (Henriques, 2011: 253), a basically monistic stance, which provides a foundationalist vision of science, where science is considered as a particular kind of justification system whose features are shared by all its branches: systematic observation and measurement, theoretical explanation, prediction, and testing leading back to measurement (2011: 154). However, this monistic position seems to be rather weak and refers to a narrow meaning (Hacking, 1996: 51) of the unity of science (see Chapter 1): the unity of method seems to be guaranteed by the general standards of reasoning that involve the use of logical tools in order to obtain accuracy and rigor in inferential procedures. No specificity seems to be attributed to the scientific enterprise, compared with other human methods of knowledge. Thus, from a methodological point of view, Henriques' unified theory seems to oscillate between a weak monism and a proper dualism, while it seems to espouse an apparent dualistic perspective from an ontological point of view. Later in this chapter, his position should become clearer to the reader.

The methodological issue gets even harder to unravel considering that Henriques seems to aim at the reconciliation of two traditionally conflicting outlooks (2011: 253), namely monism and dualism, by means of a stance that is explicitly close to the position proposed by the British emergentists.[8] The emergentist position claims that the world is made up of different levels (as in the ToK system) hierarchically organized from the simplest to the most complex. Each level emerges from the one that is hierarchically beneath it and is characterized by the feature of novelty: the new level is something qualitatively different from the one from which it emerges. In other words, the elements of the level below add together and originate something new that is not the simple sum of those elements: it is more than that. This is the non-additivity principle (Morgan, 1923). As in the purpose of emergentism, Henriques aims at gaining an authentic autonomy for the explanation of human events, without abandoning the solid grounds of the monistic perspective, and thus maintains a traditional account which honors the requirements described in Chapter 1.

In more detail, the unified theory seems to support, as Morgan does (1923: 282), a deterministic view of the world that also affects human events: every event has its causes and it is integrated in a causal chain. However, this perspective turns out not to be compatible with the statement that each emergent level is more than the sum of the elements of the level beneath. In fact, this assumption would infringe on the deducibility requirement,[9] which is logically connected to determinism. In other words, if the level above cannot be determined by the one beneath, determinism turns out to be false as the level above is not deducible from the level beneath. Hence, the adoption of a deterministic stance rules out the non-deducibility principle and vice versa. This problem, shared by the supporters of a certain kind of emergentism, would lead to an epistemic, not ontological, interpretation of the ToK system, although Henriques claims the opposite elsewhere, explicitly postulating the autonomy of different dimensions of complexity (Henriques, 2011: 15). From this perspective, the philosophical position of Henriques can be reasonably compared to Morgan's, which can be defined as property dualism (Corradini, Gaj, and Lo Dico, 2005: 272–7). Such a position claims the existence of a unique primary substance (in the ToK system vocabulary, energy) without refusing the attribution of autonomous causal powers to the other levels of the hierarchy (matter, life, mind, culture), whose features are the results of evolutionary processes. Thus, the proposal outlined constitutes a sort of discontinuity in the monism–dualism debate, placing Henriques' unified theory in an unusual position compared with other proposals of unification.

Such a position, which takes shape from Morgan's emergentism, weaves methodological aspects tightly with ontological aspects. Henriques' system explicitly rejects reductionism and "grants genuine ontological status to mental behaviors" (2011: 173). But what is mental behavior? The author claims that everything can be defined as behavior, so psychology cannot be the science of behavior; the problem of defining which kind of particular behavior falls into the psychological domain. Psychology deals with mental behaviors, which are "behaviors of the animal as-a-whole mediated by the nervous system that produces a functional effect on the animal–environment relationship" (Henriques, 2011: 72). The adjective "mental" refers to the information instantiated in and processed by the nervous system; thus, the term "mind" refers to something that can be "conceptually separated from the biophysical material that makes up the brain in the same way a story can be separated from a physical book" (Henriques, 2011: 186). According to this definition, the author seems to describe the mind in a rather functionalistic fashion: mental events are caused by other mental or environmental events and they can cause, in turn, other mental or behavioral events. In other words, mental events are described as events to which typical causes belong and which produce typical effects. These processes, which are generically called information, can be instantiated (or realized) via different means: the brain is just one candidate, as is the computer. In fact, the functionalistic tradition is accustomed to describing mental processes as a software, while remaining silent about the hardware, that is, the material that permits the software to operate (Crane, 2001; Blackburn, 2005). Henriques supports a functionalistic position about mental events, but, as we saw above, he doesn't declare himself a reductionist, so he cannot support an identity theory, a position which claims that mental events are identical to physical events. In fact, the ToK system entails a certain degree of autonomy for mental events. If mental events are not identical to physical events, then mental properties are different from physical ones (Crane, 2001: 57). Therefore, there are two kinds of things or, in the case of the ToK system, four kinds of things (matter, life, mind, culture) whose origin is one, energy. In fact, this position is compatible with emergentism and with property dualism, the claim that there is a unique primary substance which turns out to have different kinds of autonomous properties.

Emergentism and property dualism are also compatible with a position called non-reductive physicalism, which can shed light on the relationship between the primary substance (energy) and its properties (in the unified theory: matter, life, culture, and, particularly, mind). Non-reductive physicalism is non reductive because it refuses the identity theory and the ontological reduction of the properties (levels). As already illustrated, the properties are autonomous at the ontological level, that is, each level is independent, even if is connected to the others. Now, it is clear why this position is non reductive, but why it is called physicalism? Non-reductive physicalism supports the idea that mental (or biological, etc.) properties depend on physical properties, in the sense that every change in A (e.g., a physical event) also entails a change in B (e.g., a mental event): this relationship is called supervenience. However, beyond that, for those who support a non-reductive physicalistic stance, the connection between the levels must be further specified by means of two requirements, which Henriques seems to espouse. First, non-reductive physicalism claims the causal efficacy of the mental (Crane, 2001: 58): the unified theory argues that the ToK levels have causal powers on the levels below (Henriques, 2011: 173), and hence argues that mental events are not epiphenomena, i.e., incidental products caused by lower processes. Second, non-reductive physicalism entails a stronger relationship than the dependence relationship between the levels. This relationship can be called constitution, and it is illustrated by the relationship existing between a statue and the material it is made of (say, marble). This relationship is not symmetrical, as the identity relationship is, and respects the requirement above illustrated: there cannot be a change in A (e.g., the statue) without a change in B (e.g., the marble it is made of). The relationship between the statue and the marble is not only a correlation between two distinct existences, it is tighter: if you take away the marble, you would take away the statue (Crane, 2001: 58), and vice versa. Such a stance perfectly fits with the unified theory's view of the relationship between mind and brain, which is clearly described as the relationship existing between a story and the material of which the book is constructed (Henriques, 2011: 186).

In this general theoretical frame, is there room for intentionality? The relative autonomy of the psychological domain would suggest a positive answer, even if Henriques doesn't explicitly deal with this issue and his position doesn't appear to be in line with the general framework so far described. With respect to purposiveness, humans are described as individuals provided with "a decision-making system that calculates the value of the resources obtained and the losses avoided, relative to the costs of spending the actions in the first place, the risk involved, and the value of other avenues of investment" (Henriques, 2011: 46). In other words, according to the BIT, the consequences of human actions have progressively shaped the direction for future allocations of mental resources. Besides those primary needs that humans share with animals, humans fundamentally strive for the achievement of social influence in order to influence others' actions, according to the individual's interests and aims; this is consistent with the IM.

That being specified, human beings are considered as processing systems whose operations are described in a third-person perspective and whose goals are established by evolutionary processes (Henriques, 2011: 51, 85). From this perspective, humans are described similarly to machines which, on the basis of the features of their environment, produce actions directed towards aims in line with hard-wired, evolution-based goals. The statement that individuals produce actions which help them aim for goals is compatible with the assertion that human behavior is oriented toward intentional targets and that there is an irreducible diversity of human beings (see Chapter 1).

However, the unified theory does not appear to support the notion of intentionality, which is understood as the directedness of conscious mental states or, in other words, as the existence of states of mind directed toward bringing about a given state of affairs (Crane, 2001; Blackburn, 2005). Indeed, individuals process information in order to produce outputs which are consistent with their goals, but they may or may not have intentions. The narratives they produce do not necessarily refer to the reasons that moved the individual's actions toward a specific goal. According to the JH, these narratives only have the aim of building socially acceptable justifications that legitimize the individual's actions and claims (Henriques, 2011: 115). In other words, the content of those narratives do not refer to existent reasons, understood as mental triggers of behaviors, but can be considered as a collection of *post hoc* justifications of one's behavior. From such a perspective, behavior is first emitted, then justifications about which reasons produced that behavior are created.

In my opinion, this position implicitly claims that what is real are the evolutionary motivations and goals illustrated by BIT and IM, while the reasons provided by individuals in order to explain their behaviors are just means to obtain, or to increase, social influence and legitimation. If this interpretation of the unified theory is sound, then this theory refuses the traditional notion of intentionality, bringing the issue back to naturalistic stances connected to evolutionary processes.

To summarize, as a whole, the general philosophical structure underlying Henriques' theory seems to be rather mutually coherent, other than a few incoherent and obscure aspects. Lloyd Morgan's emergent evolutionism provides the structure for the ToK system and sketches the relationships between the levels. Accordingly, the details about the relationship between the levels are provided by the adoption of a non-reductive physicalistic stance, which seems to fit neatly with the unified theory's perspective on reality. Then, the notions of mind and mental events are described in a functionalistic frame, as is the relationship between the mind and the material from which it rises, i.e., the brain.

Having these premises as a background, it is worth noting that the unified theory considers the human world as continuous with the animal world, in line with the other proposals so far reviewed. In fact, as above illustrated, the first piece of the proposal is the BIT, whose six principles can be applied to humans as well to animals. Indeed, as Henriques explains, those principles constitute a sort of brief but exhaustive summary of animal behavioral literature (2011: 48). Posing BIT as the first piece of the unified theory, Henriques definitely suggests a continuity between the two worlds, which are connected. However, in line with the above-mentioned philosophical positions, the two worlds also exhibit a certain degree of discontinuity, as Henriques attributes to the human world particular features (illustrated by the IM and the JH) that are not reducible to the animal principles pointed to in the BIT:

> Whereas Behavioral Investment Theory provides a framework that allows for the understanding of how human behavior is continuous with other animals, the Justification Hypothesis provides the framework for understanding what makes people such unique animals.
>
> *(2011: 113)*

This two-faced position, oscillating between continuity and discontinuity with the animal world, is reflected in the organizational division of psychology that the author proposes at the end of his book. It is precisely the assumptions that human facts are in one way continuous with animal facts but in another way are discontinuous, that pushed Henriques to separate what he called psychological formalism (or basic psychology) from human psychology. Psychological formalism is defined as the basic science of psychology and deals with phenomena relating to the mind level. It is worth noting that psychological formalism, even if it has mental behavior as a subject matter, doesn't focus on human behavior only, but on those principles which are shared by humans and animals. Ironically, this would lead to the assumption that what humans and animals share is mind, as mental behaviors are "behaviors of the animal as-a-whole mediated by the nervous system that produces a functional effect on the animal–environment relationship" (Henriques, 2011: 72). Actually, in Henriques' opinion, what makes us human is not our mind, which is something that can be studied by a "purely natural science discipline"; what makes us properly human is an additional dimension of complexity that is called culture (2011: 192, 184), in the ToK system. Indeed, human psychology, the second part of psychology, is part of the social sciences and cannot be a purely natural discipline, as it deals with values and cultural relativism (Henriques, 2011: 194). From this perspective, human psychology, having the human individual as object, deals with the smallest unit of analysis in the social sciences. The details about this position are clearly illustrated by this quotation:

> Human psychology should be thought of as existing at the base of the social sciences and should be thought of as a hybrid between psychological formalism and the social sciences. Moreover, it is human psychology that is a subset of psychology more generally. Humans are, after all, a subset of animals, rather than the reverse.
>
> *(2011: 196)*

In other words, human psychology has its feet in the natural sciences and its head at the very beginning of the social sciences.

According to Henriques, psychological formalism and human psychology would constitute the whole body of psychological knowledge, on which is based another separate component: professional psychology. The task of professional psychology is not to increase psychological knowledge, but to generally improve the human condition (Henriques, 2011: 198). The connection with the needs of those who benefit from psychological interventions makes professional psychology something different from the other two branches. In line with the psychologist Donald Peterson (1991), Henriques claims that the goals of the scientist are completely different from those of the practitioner. The latter has the task of using the available psychological knowledge in order to better meet the needs and the conditions of the client, while the former has virtually no limits to the development of knowledge. In this perspective, professional practice is an applied social science, grounded on scientific psychological knowledge. This knowledge is a means to the end – improving human condition – not the end itself, as it is for the scientist.

Accordingly to their contents, the three parts composing psychology are supposed to cooperate in order to increase psychological knowledge (particularly, psychological formalism and human psychology) and to better contribute to human development (professional practice). Thus, in the aim of unifying psychology, the discipline appears rather composed of different parts that reciprocally interact.

In conclusion, it is arguable that Henriques' proposal is a kind of grand theory, which has the main aim to provide psychology (and, ambitiously, science in general) with a broad theoretical framework. This framework constitutes a sort of meta-perspective – encompassing animal as well as human events – that is able to attribute univocal meanings to terms like mind, brain, behavior, cognition, and so on, specifying their reciprocal definitions and the mutual relationships (2011: 13). In this sense, the unified theory has the ambitious goal of providing a general syntax where traditional psychological concepts may acquire univocal meanings and may lay the foundations for a unified approach that contains both theoretical and professional aspects.

However, this syntax is evidently not theoretically neutral; as has been illustrated above, it rests on definite philosophical grounds, whose acceptance is required in order to espouse the whole theory. This rather explicit reference to the philosophical stances that constitute Henriques' proposal is no doubt praiseworthy, in particular considering that the other proposals described here are not so philosophically explicit. However, these references are not always coherently presented and this makes the thorough reconstruction of the whole philosophical outlook a difficult task.

Notes

1 Perception is defined as the process that integrates sensory inputs which result in a meaningful representation of an object or event (Henriques, 2011: 74).
2 Motivation is defined as a valued goal state that the organism is working toward (Henriques, 2011: 75).
3 According to this hypothesis, individuals build narratives following common rules and biases. For example, people tend to explain bad outcomes in terms of external, temporal, and local causes and good outcomes in terms of internal, stable and general causes. Consequently, individuals tend to think and feel about themselves positively, try to provide thorough, consistent, and accurate reasons founding their narratives (Henriques, 2011: 135–8).
4 Henriques puts the so called Freudian filter between sentience, which is also called the experiential self, and the private self. It provides protection against unjustifiable or painful images and impulses – coming from the sentience – which are reinterpreted to be consistent with the individual's social justification system. Instead, between the private and the public self stands the Rogerian filter, which deals with the building of a proper image that proves to be socially satisfactory (Henriques, 2011: 127–30).
5 More about this issue will be said in the next section.
6 This is justified by the assumption that the human mind is deeply embedded in the cultural dimension (according to the JH) and thus human psychology can be considered as a hybrid between psychological formalism and the social sciences.
7 This view is consistent with Peterson (1991) who advocates different kinds of training for professional psychologists, on the one hand, and psychologists who will deal with academic research on the other.
8 In fact, Henriques explicitly refers to C. Lloyd Morgan's emergent evolutionism.
9 The assumption that one level can be naturally explained by the effects of the level below.

References

Blackburn, S. (2005). *Dictionary of Philosophy, 2nd Edition*. Oxford: Oxford University Press.
Corradini, A., Gaj, N., and Lo Dico, G. (2005). Emergenza: Le origini di un concetto. *Rivista di Filosofia Neo-Scolastica*, 2: 263–279.
Crane, T. (2001). *Elements of Mind: An Introduction to the Philosophy of Mind*. New York: Oxford University Press.
Hacking, I. (1996). The disunities of sciences. In P. Galison and D. J. Stump (eds.), *The Disunity of Science. Boundaries, Contexts and Power* (pp. 37–74). Stanford, CA: Stanford University Press.
Henriques, G. R. (2011). *A New Unified Theory of Psychology*. New York: Springer.
Morgan, C. Lloyd (1923). *Emergent evolution*. London: Williams & Norgate.
Peterson, D. R. (1991). Connection and disconnection of research and practice in the education of professional psychologists. *American Psychologist*, 46(4): 422–429.
Staats, A. W. (1996). *Behavior and Personality. Psychological Behaviorism*. New York: Springer.

9

NORMAN ANDERSON'S INFORMATION INTEGRATION THEORY (IIT)

The author's intention behind the book *Unified Social Cognition* (2008) is to condense years of work on the Information Integration Theory (IIT), which in his view provides "a simple, effective framework for unifying human psychology" (Anderson, 2008: ix). The book presents a collection of research works elaborated over time and spanning different areas of psychology and more particularly learning and memory, judgment and decision, perception and psychophysics, and language. From this perspective, IIT can be defined as an experimental-based unifying proposal. Here, I will only illustrate the main aspects of IIT, without going into the details of the rich store of research presented in the book. I will try to extrapolate the theoretical principles which guided the experimental works illustrated therein.

IIT is a cognitive theory based on the idea that information and its modes of processing are the unifying principles of psychology. Within a traditional cognitivistic view, stimuli are considered as informers, which are elaborated in order to reach specific goals[1] (Anderson, 2008: 11). This notion is central since for Anderson all psychological inquiry can be viewed as an attempt to come to grips with the issue of intentionality and the achievement of goals, as will become clearer later in this chapter.

Psychological science from the IIT perspective rests on two axioms: the *axiom of purposiveness* and the *axiom of integration*. These are axioms in the sense that their existence is "biologically based" (Anderson, 2008: 1) and that they can be found in every domain dealing with cognitive phenomena. On one hand, the axiom of purposiveness deals with affect and motivation, which are the forces that guide behavior to goals related to the individual's survival. Purposiveness refers to goal-directed actions in terms of approach/avoidance behavior. Parenthetically, every human action has a purpose in every different circumstance: the interaction between the individual and the environment causes his or her purpose to change continuously. The axiom of purposiveness accounts for the organization of the great amount of available information toward a simplification that permits goal-directed behavior to be produced in every circumstance (Anderson, 2008: 29). On the other hand, we have the axiom of integration, which accounts for the "general integrational propensity to take account of multiple elements in a stimulus field" (Anderson, 2008: 1). The function of integration refers to how multiple informers (stimuli) are integrated and influence behavior and thought. This axiom claims that every human behavior is the product of multiple determinants which are integrated by the individual (Anderson, 2008: 30). Together, the two axioms describe human action as it is understood within the IIT framework. The upshot of complex integration processes of multiple inputs, coming from the internal or the external environment, is behavior whose specific characteristic is that it is goal-directed. This is the general conceptual frame of IIT in Anderson's view.

The integration diagram (and Figure 9.1), Anderson's main theoretical device, shows how the two axioms are implemented in human information processing and represents a schematic description of how information is processed in order to give rise to goal-directed behavior. Looking at Figure 9.1, on the left side we find multiple inputs (A, B),[2] e.g., physical stimuli coming from the environment. They are transmuted into psychological representations (a, b) by means of the valuation operator (V). Then, the integrator operator (I) integrates those psychological representations to produce an internal response (r) which is transformed by the action operator (A) into an observable behavior (R) at the right side of the diagram.

The valuation process (V) is an organizing process that involves the interaction between the informers, the individual's knowledge system and the goal that the individual wants to achieve. Here, informers are transmuted into goal-relevant representations (Anderson, 2008: 20), through a "largely nonconscious" operation

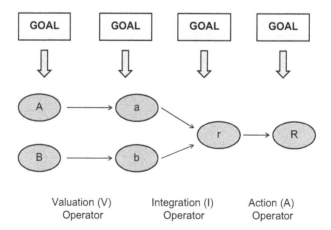

FIGURE 9.1 Information integration diagram. Chain of three operators, V, I, A, leading from observable stimuli, A and B, to observable response, R

Source: adapted from Anderson (2008)

(p. 276). In other words, inputs are unconsciously elaborated on the basis of the goal that the individual consciously wants to achieve. The second operation is Integration (I), which involves the integration of the functional[3] (that is, relative to the selected goal) values of multiple stimuli into a unitary internal response which will produce an observable, conscious, goal-directed action by means of the A operator. The overall process is adjusted and directed toward the achievement of a specific goal (G).

Beside the axioms that form the conceptual basis of IIT, Anderson proposes the existence of three psychological laws – averaging, adding, and multiplying (2008: 4) – which represent the natural applications of the two axioms. These laws show that the integration of informers exhibits simple algebraic forms and this is applicable to almost every area of human psychology and thus can provide a solid basis for psychological unification (Anderson, 2008: 402). Every kind of law has two conditions of application, one of which is shared by all of them. This condition is response linearity, which states that the observable response (R) is a linear function of the implicit response (r). For Anderson, this condition entails that "the observed response R is a true measure of the unobservable response r" (2008: 36). The other peculiar condition deals with the specific mode of integration of the psychological representations (in Figure 9.1: a, b): psychological representations can be integrated through adding, averaging or multiplying. In other words, once the subject has attributed values to constructs of different kinds (such as in the many experiments reported in the text), the interaction between these constructs can be described through the use of those laws.[4] To take an example using hypothetical data reported by the author, two people have to cast blame in a children's story where a child threw a rock that harmed another child. Each person has to attribute subjective values to Intent (degree of intentionality) and Harm (seriousness of the harm), according to their personal views. The data shows that both people follow the addition schema: Blame = Intent + Harm (Anderson, 2008: 6–8), according to the addition law, even if the values subjectively attributed by the two people are different. Hence, what still remains the same is the formal character of the law, while subjective values evidently vary.

Psychological laws, like the addition law illustrated in the example above, embody the structure of the internal world (Anderson, 2008: 269) and thus can be considered as the key elements underlying human psychology.

From a general point of view, Anderson defines his model as constructionistic and contextualistic. The constructionistic aspect resides in the fact that valuation involves construction. In fact, the same stimulus may take different values depending on operative goals, and thus values have to be constructed on the basis of operative goals (2008: 8). Also, integration involves construction because the unified response (r) is constructed on the basis of the integration of multiple stimuli. In general, the conscious experience is constructed because it is considered as an integration of multiple unconscious determinants (2008: 15, 275). Moreover, IIT is considered to be grounded in contextualism, because "perception, thought, and action always occur within some particular context or situation, which may be considered a complex field of information, internal as well as external" (2008: 9). The fact that valuation and integration processes are strongly influenced by operative goals shows the importance of environmental contexts in IIT.

To summarize, Anderson's proposal of unified psychology rests on the specification of two axioms, which account for the general features of human cognition, and of three laws, which describe different ways to integrate psychological representations within a traditional input–elaboration–output frame of reference.

What kind of psychology is suited to Anderson's IIT?

From the methodological point of view, one of IIT's main purposes is to unify two traditionally opposing ways to scientifically address phenomena: the nomothetic approach, which seeks universal laws that go beyond individuality, and the idio-graphic approach, which conversely emphasizes the uniqueness of each individual. These two opposing approaches turn out to be unified by means of the three psychological laws (averaging, adding, and multiplying). On one side, the fact that all experimental data gathering follows the laws of information integration accounts for a nomothetic explanation of psychological data. On the other hand, the fact that each individual attributes his/her own personal values to the considered con-struct accounts for an idiographic explanation of the same data. So, this approach "Allows, or rather, insists on individual differences in value while seeking general integration laws" (Anderson, 2008: 15).

This unifying perspective, in Anderson's opinion, comes from an inductive mode of theory development in the sense that absolute priority is given to the features of the phenomena at stake (2008: 12, 14). It can be said that theory has the unique function of "ratifying" the behavior of the data, without further theoretical elaboration; the weight of theorization is minimum, because the "adherence to a theory often constricts attention to favorable conditions, short-changing the phenomena" and "the neatness and pleasure of assumptions and deductions can so readily slight empirical substance" (2008: 406). This very tight connection to empirical phenomena has a price, of which the author is aware of: IIT cannot predict values of stimulus informers nor when a particular law will apply. This entails that IIT is a descriptive theory which "seeks to reveal psychological process directly in the data" (2008: 72). In more detail, individual values in addition to the specific kind of law that is applied to a particular psychological phenomenon are not predictable aspects and can be assessed only after the observation of the phenomenon itself. Once the data are observed those theoretical aspects can be ascertained or applied.

This open refusal of deductive procedures seems to be based on the failure to distinguish between the descriptive perspective and the evaluative perspective. When Anderson claims that everyday life is a primary concern and hypothesis testing is secondary, and that deductive philosophy sees scientific inquiry as hypothesis testing, "especially tests of competing hypotheses" (2008: 406), the above-mentioned distinction is missing. It is well known that the testing of

competing hypotheses is usually something that occurs during the process of discovery, when different ways to view a phenomenon are mutually competing; here,
the aim is to describe the phenomenon in question. On the other hand, the
deductive use of the (resulting) better hypothesis is routine in the ordinary process
of evaluation which is normative in character, i.e., it follows procedures in order to
determine whether a hypothesis can be accepted based on specific rules of method
(what the philosopher Thomas Kuhn would call "normal science"). Anderson
doesn't consider the different use of deductive methods in science and this makes
his refusal of the deductive methods not solidly justified, especially considering that
the absence of predictive power is a high price to pay for IIT. Another related
point is worthy of attention. Anderson also seems to be aware of the fact that each
inductive operation is guided by our conceptual framework which "embodies our
view about what phenomena are important as well as their interpretation in our
symbolic world" (2008: 15). This leads to the finding that every empirical investigation is deductive in character, even if that conceptual framework "should evolve
in an inductive mode that respects the phenomena" (2008: 15). In other words, the
deductive dimension is ineludible.

Although these stances might occupy a methodologically equidistant position
between the monistic and the dualistic approaches, Anderson's proposal seems to
be closer to a monistic account which sees psychology as methodologically continuous with other scientific disciplines whose main method should be empirical
investigation and whose priority is the study of some observable behavior of the
phenomenon of interest.

However, the emphasis on the empirical observation of behavior and its relevance
to the exploration of the psychological world raises an interesting issue regarding
the relationship between stimuli, responses, and their measurement. One of the
characteristics of the integration diagram (see Figure 9.1), the linearity of the
response measure (Anderson, 2008: 31, 36), claims that responses R, those referring
to observable behaviors, are *true measures* of the unobservable, internal response r.
In other words, the observable behavioral events are considered nothing less than
faithful images of what occurs in the internal, unobservable world. The analysis of
what is observable makes the unobservable directly accessible. These assumptions
make it clear that for IIT whatever is observable and measurable is interesting and
worth studying: there is not an impenetrable border between internal and external
worlds, since the latter perfectly mirrors (i.e., is) the former. From such assumptions
follow that measurement theory is not considered as a prerequisite of scientific
investigation as usually is the case, but it becomes an organic part of the investigation, closely interwoven with the latter (Anderson, 2008: 36). The measurement of
psychological constructs *is* those constructs and hence it is defined as true measurement (Anderson, 2008: 257, 401). This stance derives from the assumption that
metric measurements of individual responses – often refused by other psychological
approaches to measurement – are useful and legitimate, since they permit a linear
connection to be established between the values of the stimulus and the values of
the response and provide crucial information about the individual psychological

functioning: "A theoretically adequate scale of the dependent variable opens up the possibility of scaling the underlying (stimulus) variables" (Anderson, 2008: 257).

Now, measurement can be rather unanimously defined as follows:

> [It] is the assignment of numbers to events or object according to rules that permit important properties of the objects or events to be represented by properties of the number system. The key to this definition is that properties of the events are represented by properties of the number system.
>
> *(McBurney and White, 2009: 124)*

This definition supposes that measurement is a way to increase our knowledge about something using numbers and their properties. The quality (appropriateness, soundness, relevance) of this knowledge depends on which properties of the objects are considered and on the rules by which numbers and their properties are attributed to the properties of the object or the event in question. In other words, measurement procedures involve and require important methodological choices to be made. *Per se*, measurement cannot provide comprehensive truth about an event and *it is not* the event it describes. From this perspective, Anderson's position seems to run the risk of reifying the process of measurement and those properties of the event that are under scrutiny: the targets of the measurement procedures seem to be real objects or events of the real world (attitudes, thoughts, memories), while those targets should be considered as constructs, i.e., abstract and theoretically informed concepts used to indicate aspects of the real object (see Chapter 5). In other words, psychological constructs are not considered as theoretical entities, but become real objects whose features emerge from measurement. As illustrated above, what a measurement theory can do is to provide some theoretically biased, though useful, information about the object, while in IIT the measurement theory *is* the functioning of the object at stake, since the three psychological laws are "true foundation for the theory of psychological measurement" (Anderson, 2008: 259). This problem has obvious reverberations for the ontological issue, as will be clear below.

Turning back to the previous issue, though Anderson supports a monistic vision of science, the concept of intentionality – which is usually refused by those who defend such a stance – seems to play a strategic role. Here, I refer to the axiom of purposiveness, whose universality and centrality is often evoked during the book (Anderson, 2008: 1, 2, 399). Is it possible to approximate Anderson's notion of purposiveness to the notion of intentionality? As we saw above, the axiom of purposiveness briefly claims that all human psychological activity is motivated toward goals. In general terms, intentionality can be defined as the fact that states of mind have, or are directed to, an object. Each object is present to the mind in a certain way and is considered from a certain perspective under which it is given to the mind (Crane, 2001: 7, 18–19). From these definitions, it seems clear that IIT's position about purposiveness may be properly called intentional: the subject tends to a state or object (the mind is directed on an object) whose achievement is considered desirable (goal). IIT can be defined as intentionalistic in character, since the pervasiveness of purposiveness, in the integration diagram (and Figure 9.1) is easily noticeable by the fact that the G (Goal) factor is present in all the operations pointed to in the diagram.

Nevertheless, intentionality is not defined in terms of teleological explanations, nor in terms of reason giving (see Chapter 1), but in a kind of "behavioral" mode: intentions are understood in terms of "goal approach/avoidance" (Anderson, 2008: 2). In particular, two measurable indexes seem to account for the notion of intention and to define it. On one hand, intentions can be defined as approach or avoidance behaviors and, on the other hand, intentions can also be defined by the variability of values attribution to stimuli.[5] Therefore, in general terms the notion of intention accounts for the fact that individuals tend to approach objects or events and to avoid other objects or events; moreover, individuals tend to attribute different subjective values to these objects or events, according to their behavioral tendencies.

Another related problem refers to the fact that the operations described in the integration diagram (and Figure 9.1) are carried out at an unconscious level, while only the outputs are experienced consciously. If those operations, as it now appears clear, are goal-directed and are also "largely nonconscious" (Anderson, 2008: 276), the question is: how can the individual's intentional conscious experience affect those unconscious processes that permit the elaboration of information in order to achieve that goal? What is the connection between the intentional experience of, e.g., wanting A, and the unconscious processes which are organized to reach that specific goal A? In IIT, such questions remains unanswered. Thus, the assumption that every human action is oriented toward goals doesn't seem to entail that these goals are consciously available: the theory is not explicit about which kind of relationship the conscious experiences hold with the goals (G) in the integration diagram (and Figure 9.1)

Hence, Anderson's notion of intention is "behavioralized," that is, defined in terms of observable and measurable behavior, and thus doesn't refer to the literature which considers intentionality as the factor that makes human beings unique (see Chapter 1). In fact, the individual is described as a sort of automaton whose behavior is directed toward goals and aims of which he/she is not aware, in the sense that they are not consciously available. In this sense, IIT keeps a monistic vision – considering human beings in the same way as natural events – despite the reference to the notion of purposiveness.

In IIT, another methodological issue is detectable that seems to be quite problematic; the issue concerns the level of abstraction of the theory or, in other words, the weight attributed by the theory to the specific features of the entities at stake. As we saw in Chapter 1, the more a theory is distant from its object, the more it can ignore some of its (alleged peculiar) features; the more it is close to it, the more it will deal with them. The former approach can be defined as syntactic, the latter as semantic. From this perspective, Anderson's proposal – attempting to fill the gap between the nomothetic and the idiographic outlooks – seems to take a middle position in the traditional debate. However, a deeper analysis of the theory seems to uncover a view that is closer to a syntactic position. In fact, Anderson's contextualism entails that every psychological event can be considered as a complex field of information where elements (stimuli) are elaborated relative to the operative goal. Despite the fact that "the same physical stimulus may take on different values, depending on operative goals" (Anderson, 2008: 8, 9), IIT methodological structure is syntactic in character because it is focused on the logical and systematic aspects of psychology (see Hempel, 1979: 357) and on a concept of evidence which is not relative to, and variable with, individuals (Hempel, 1961–2: 82). In other words, what is peculiar to IIT is a view on the object that permits those general aspects of human cognition to be grasped which are independent of elements pertaining to the individuality of the subject. These latter individual elements are included in the larger, syntactic frame as values attributed by the individuals in that specific situation.

Such a perspective also reflects in the language of IIT. Following Carnap's proposal (1928), stimuli are considered in their relational aspects, that is, they are described in terms of the relations they hold with each other within the same informational field (see Chapter 3). The consideration of those relational aspects is functional to avoid the inaccuracies of the common language, which doesn't befit science. Indeed, IIT has the goal to "purify concepts from common language and develop them into true scientific concepts" (Anderson, 2008: 8). Such an outlook provides an account of phenomena from a high level of formalization, which fosters a unified approach to psychology and consequently provides a complete account of the internal world (Anderson, 2008: 269).

Hence, it is plausible that Anderson's IIT holds a syntactic view of the scientific enterprise, thus keeping in line with the monistic perspective of the whole theoretical framework.

When it comes to issues connected to the object of psychological inquiry, it can be said that what Anderson proposes is a reductivistic theory, in the general sense illustrated by Nagel (see Chapter 4). To elaborate, Anderson's aim is to explain a theory or a set of laws established in other areas of inquiry by means of his own theory, initially formulated in another domain[6] (Nagel, 1961: 338). What Anderson proposes is not the explanation of qualitatively different objects – compared with those for which the theory has been initially developed – by means of his own theory; rather, IIT seem to be a case of homogeneous reduction, that is, the broadening of the scope of a theory, once formulated for a certain kind of phenomena and now extended to cover additional, similar, phenomena.

However, it must be argued that such a similarity can be ascertained only on the basis of a very high level of abstraction, such as the one provided by IIT. This means that the similarity of the phenomena explained by IIT can be assessed only on the basis of the high level of their syntactic aspects. These aspects, in turn, assure that the generality of the psychological laws, originally formulated in some areas of social psychology, can be applied to all psychological phenomena which are thus considered similar. In doing so, the adoption of IIT and the psychological laws can provide a new way of thinking for all of psychology and a base upon which to unify the psychological field (Anderson, 2008: 25). In other words, according to

Anderson's intentions the generality of such an approach regarding the objects of psychology makes IIT applicable to virtually every aspect of psychology, at the expense of ignoring many peculiar features of the objects which, inevitably, may fall out of the scope of the theory. Thus, psychological laws seems to apply only to very general aspects of the objects, at a high level of abstraction where the peculiarities of objects are likely to fade away into similarities.

Delving into more detail about the nature of the object of psychology, Anderson assumes that psychology deals with the processing of information in order to produce actions directed toward goals. Although he is not explicit about this, it is arguable that from this perspective psychology is an attempt to scientifically account for how humans behave in their environment. In IIT, many concepts that constitute the core of the psychological discipline are described in common-sense terms, according to the assumptions that the theory "puts phenomena before theory" (Anderson, 2008: 72) and that "everyday life is a primary concern" (p. 406). To give some examples, a person's cognition is defined as the "cognition of any person – parent, spouse, ex-spouse, friend, self" (p. 51). Group dynamics are generically defined as "interpersonal interaction" (Anderson, 2008: 222–3). Moral phenomena such as deserving and obligation are defined, respectively, as fitting entitlement to some outcome (reward or punishment), and as the degree of motivation to perform some action, which may be felt or attributed as fitting the circumstances (Anderson, 2008: 199). From this it follows that Anderson is not interested in taking a definite onto-logical position about the existence of psychological entities: psychology as a discipline must deal with the way people normally refer to mental phenomena, but it doesn't say anything about their real existence. In IIT, mental phenomena, as they are described in common-sense terms, are not interesting *per se* for science and do not seem to provide relevant information about the real world. On the contrary, what seems to constitute the ontological core of the psychological reality are the three psychological laws which represent the internal structure of the psychological world (Anderson, 2008: ix, 18, 269). In other words, what really exists are the mechanisms underlying the functioning of common sense entities; those mechanisms, the psychological laws, constitute the ontological horizon of IIT.

Such an ontological claim appears to be strongly connected to the issue of reifi-cation illustrated above. In fact, the laws discovered through experimental designs acquire the status of ontological entities, while they only represent empirical regularities. More specifically, it seems that the interpretation of the experimental results entails a terminological equivalence between the experimental design language and the theoretical language, so that the theory is not conceived as a possible interpretation of the data (Katzko, 2002: 264–5; see Chapter 5), rather, the data regularities *become* the theory. Thus, the data *are* the theory, which is reality, as this quotation shows very effectively: "Success of the algebraic law supports the hypothesis that the stimulus and response terms represent cognitive entities; otherwise they would be unlikely to obey an exact law" (Anderson, 2008: 36).

As a concluding remark, it is worth noting that although IIT is presented as effective in nearly every field of human psychology, its possible professional applications are not even mentioned. Indeed, the fact that IIT has no predictive power (Anderson, 2008: 72) makes it ill-suited for professional application. Moreover, in contrast to other proposals previously illustrated, IIT is not even interested in the relationships between human and animal cognition, since the aim of psychology is assumed to be human cognition.

Finally, IIT is a cognitive theory of human cognition with strong unifying aims based on an ontological stance that assumes the existence of psychological laws which underlie the majority of human phenomena. Its main problem seems to reside in the relationship between the experimental data and the theory, whose interplay is highly questionable and results in a controversial philosophical position.

Notes

1 This process can be integrated with prior information relevant to the issue at stake. Here, prior information is considered as a knowledge system (Anderson, 2008: 44). Affect, as well as motivation, are considered to be information too (2008: 9–10) in the broad sense that they play a role in the process of input elaboration.
2 For simplicity's sake, only two inputs are shown, but more are allowed.
3 Anderson calls functional measurement the method that measures the values attributed in the integration operation.
4 The specific shape of the data graph will reveal the law that best describes the data. Regarding this point, Anderson reports a lot of research where he and his colleagues illustrate in detail the methodology they used in many areas of psychological inquiry. Readers interested in these issues should consult Anderson (2008) for more detail.
5 Here Anderson refers to those experimental works by which IIT developed, where subjects are supposed to attribute subjective values to stimuli.
6 Person cognition, as stated by Anderson (2008: 51).

References

Anderson, H. N. (2008). *Unified Social Cognition*. New York: Psychology Press.
Carnap, R. (1928). *Der Logische Aufbau der Welt*. Leipzig: Felix Meiner. [Italian translation *La costruzione logica del mondo*, Milan: Fabbri]
Crane, T. (2001). *Elements of Mind: An Introduction to the Philosophy of Mind*. New York: Oxford University Press.
Hempel, C. G. (1961–62). Explanation and prediction by covering laws. In J. H. Fetzer (ed.) (2001), *The Philosophy of Carl G. Hempel* (pp. 69–86). Oxford: Oxford University Press. [reprinted from *Philosophy of Science: the Delaware Seminar*, vol. 1, by B. Baumrin (ed.), New York: Interscience]
Hempel, C. G. (1979). Scientific rationality: Normative vs. descriptive construals. In J. H. Fetzer (ed.) (2001), *The Philosophy of Carl G. Hempel* (pp. 358–371). Oxford: Oxford University Press. [reprinted from *Wittgenstein, the Vienna Circle, and Critical Rationalism. Proceedings of the third International Wittgenstein Symposium*, August 1978, by H. Berghel, A. Huebner, and E. Koehler (eds.), Vienna: Hoelder-Pichler-Tempsky]
Katzko, M. W. (2002). The rhetoric of psychological research and the problem of unification in psychology. *American Psychologist*, 57(4): 262–270.
McBurney, D. H. and White, M. L. (2009). *Research Methods*. Belmont, CA: Wadsworth.
Nagel, E. (1961). *The Structure of Science. Problems in the Logic of Scientific Explanation*. Cambridge, MA: Hackett.

10

THE UNIFIED PSYCHOLOGY OF ROBERT STERNBERG AND COLLEAGUES

It is worth noting that the unified psychology proposed by Robert Sternberg and colleagues is grounded in a rather deep analysis of the sources and the modes of fragmentation in psychology (for details, see Chapter 5). The authors detected many areas of psychology relating to professional practice as well as to research, education, and academic organization which display various aspects of fragmentation and which turn out to pose a threat to both scientific credibility and institutional organization. Thus, this perspective can be considered a way to resolve "psychology's potential loss of identity as a field" (Sternberg, 2005: 3), via a methodological and theoretical analysis which aims to better organize the institutional aspects of psychology as a scientific and academic discipline. In contrast to the other proposals discussed so far, Sternberg and colleagues' proposal does not deal with the content of psychological inquiry, but rather with the strategies aimed at integrating psychological knowledge.

This chapter will focus on two works which may be considered to cover Sternberg and colleagues' view on unified psychology: "Unified psychology," Sternberg's 2003[1] work with Elena Grigorenko, and "The role of theory in unified psychology," his article published in 2001 with Elena Grigorenko and David Kalmar.

In the first paper, the authors consider their proposal as a sort of interlevel theory, that is, a theory for which the aim is to bridge different levels of analysis about phenomena. Regarding the issue of unification, such interlevel theories can be compared to traditional grand theories. Grand theories, such as psychoanalysis, cognitivism, or behaviorism, aim is to extend principles and concepts which are formulated on the basis of research in one area of psychology in order to provide a general explanation of human behavior. In this way, grand theories entail a two-level strategy of theory construction, which involves the formulation of a theory in a restricted area of the discipline and then the generalization of that theory to other fields of psychology, or even to the whole discipline (Staats, 1996: 9). In contrast, an interlevel theory attempts to bridge different and distant approaches of analysis of the same phenomenon, based on the idea that psychology's disciplinary target is to have different scholars studying the same problem with different methods and from different perspectives (Sternberg and Grigorenko, 2003: 25). This is exactly the central claim of the converging operations principle. This principle refers to the use of multiple methodologies for studying a single psychological phenomenon or problem (Sternberg and Grigorenko, 2003: 27). The basic idea is that any one methodology, or operation, in the authors' language, is, in all likelihood, inadequate for the appropriate and comprehensive study of any psychological phenomenon. The main reason is that each methodology has its own biases and involves the adoption of a peculiar perspective on the object of interest. In other words, it may be said that the use of a single methodology supports the assumption that what has been found is the object of analysis, whereas it is only an aspect of it, the aspect that that particular methodology is able to detect and analyze. The use of a single methodology is misleading, as this parable of the blind men and the elephant illustrates:

> Consider the well-worn parable of the blind men each touching a different part of the elephant and each being convinced that he is touching a different animal. In psychology, the situation is like always studying the same part of the phenomenon and thinking that this part tells you all you need to know to understand the whole phenomenon.
>
> *(Sternberg and Grigorenko, 2003: 34)*

The use of converging operations permits psychology's grip to be strengthened on the features of the phenomena which interest psychologists, expanding their view through the integration of different aspects of the same object, but detected with different methodologies.

So far some crucial methodological issues of the proposal of Sternberg and colleagues have been presented. But every discipline must also deal with the issue of theory development, one of the core issues of the scientific enterprise. How is the process of theory development addressed by the authors? This topic is illustrated in the 2001 work by Sternberg, Grigorenko, and Kalmar. In this paper, the authors claim that theory development as currently practiced in psychology involves the juxtaposition of different theories which compete in terms of predictive power (p. 106). This turns out to be a so-called "segregative" approach which has some crucial disadvantages. First, such an approach can make psychologists focus on *different aspects* of the same phenomenon, while they believe they are studying the same phenomenon. In fact, theories are developed and refined on independent tracks, these being compared based on empirical control: theories are accepted or rejected based on the strength of their empirical predictions vis à vis their competitors (Sternberg, Grigorenko, and Kalmar, 2001: 107). Moreover, this approach fosters the adoption of a single perspective regarding the phenomenon, ignoring other ways to study it. In other words, the use of this segregative approach, emphasizing the predictive power of theories, tends to isolate different theories, rather than to integrate their strengths, and narrows the view on the problem at stake, rather than increasing the knowledge of its different aspects.

In contrast to this approach, the authors' proposal of theory development is integrative and called "theory knitting." This view gives priority to explanation, rather than prediction, and argues that science – psychology more specifically – most profitably progresses in the direction of increasing explanation as opposed to increasing prediction, as psychology especially needs the contribution of conceptual, rather than empirical insights. Furthermore, the integrative approach insists that psychology needs to develop conceptually more comprehensive theories, rather than to refine many different theories which are unlikely to be wholly correct in and of themselves (Sternberg et al., 2001: 107). This approach aims to formulate broad theoretical frameworks, rather than to separately develop and refine narrow, independent theories. In sum, theory knitting involves integrating the best aspects of existing theories with one's own view about the phenomenon under investigation (Sternberg et al., 2001: 108). This leads to the integration of previous theories into a higher-order theory, which functions as a general theoretical framework.

But how can the strength of these theories be assessed? The authors pragmatically claim that this integration entails the introduction of new elements that knit the theories together and "that account for aspects of the phenomenon for which neither of the previous theories accounted" (Sternberg et al., 2001: 109). In other words:

> Typically, one may find that both theory A and theory B are correct in some respects and incorrect in others. One thus seeks a higher order theory that integrates those aspects of the two theories that are empirically supportable, and that discards those aspects of the two theories that are not supportable. In essence, one unifies the theories.
>
> *(Sternberg et al., 2001: 109)*

According to the authors' methodological position, theory knitting permits scientific inquiry to better stay on course. They contend that approach is less likely to mislead the course of research on a certain phenomenon since the emphasis is on conceptual integration rather than on predictive power. In fact, the definition of the construct at stake becomes a crucial point (Sternberg et al., 2001: 110).

Beyond the already mentioned advantages in using theory knitting, the authors warn that it is not advisable to use this approach in the initial stages of research, when "there is not enough 'yarn' with which to knit" (p. 110). Indeed, theory knitting is more appropriate when a certain number of theories exists for approximately the same phenomenon.

To summarize, as now is clear, the methodological and the theoretical aspects so far discussed turn out to be mutually compatible: in fact, converging operations provide methodological integration while theory knitting provides theoretical integration (Sternberg et al., 2001: 111). The common ground of these two aspects of Sternberg and colleagues' unified psychology is the concern for important institutional issues related to the organization of psychology as an academic discipline, as will be discussed. In this sense, converging operations and theory knitting are intended as tools which suggest prolific directions for the scientific development and the disciplinary organization of psychology.

Regarding the issue of psychology's organization as a scientific and academic endeavor, the authors believe that the discipline of psychology could be better organized on the basis of psychological phenomena, rather than on the basis of current traditional fields of psychology. The reason is that these fields and their contents (i.e., the objects or phenomena with which they deal) are largely arbitrary and, in the authors' opinion, do not fit well with the methodological requisites psychology should achieve. In other words, this proposal fosters a *phenomenon-based approach*, where problems, rather than sub-disciplines, become the key basis for the study of psychology (Sternberg et al., 2001: 104; Sternberg and Grigorenko, 2003: 35–6). According to the authors, such a view is supported by the fact that the current academic organization has many problems, the principal ones of which are the following:

1. The current organization hinders the study of the same phenomenon under different theoretical or methodological perspectives, whose scientific benefits have already been mentioned.
2. The current organization creates conflict between researchers who are studying the same phenomenon from different perspectives, thereby hindering the integration of different methodological perspectives regarding the same phenomenon.
3. The current organization does not give value and scientific credibility to those researchers dealing with phenomena at the interface of different fields which, arguably, may be the most interesting and worthy of study.

Such an organization perpetuates a state of fragmentation within psychology and provides inappropriate grounds to establish and develop a sound and reliable psychology, both from the scientific and academic viewpoints. In conclusion, converging operations and theory knitting embody methodological and theoretical directions for researchers who aim to create general, higher-order disciplinary frameworks, and may thus be considered a means for promoting the scientific advancement of psychology. In addition, this approach aims to allow a better academic organization for the discipline, according to its scientific requirements and goals.

What kind of psychology is suited to Sternberg and colleagues' unified psychology?

As illustrated in Chapter 5, one of the three bad habits of the psychological community according to Sternberg and Grigorenko (2003) is the exclusive or almost exclusive reliance on a single methodology. The use of converging operations would help to remove this hindrance to a proper development of psychology. From this perspective, their proposal of unified psychology seems to be pluralistic in character. Since the knowledge about psychological phenomena is hard both to accrue and to apply (Henriques and Sternberg, 2004: 1058), it requires the use of different kinds of methods in order to grasp meaningful aspects of such phenomena. The background of such an approach is evidently methodologically dualistic, because it supports the view that the various phenomena of reality can only be investigated through the use of different methods which respect their differences. The authors' point is that the complexity of the object of psychology requires the utilization of multiple methodologies, since "any one operation is, in all likelihood, inadequate for the comprehensive study of any psychological phenomenon" (Sternberg and Grigorenko, 2003: 27). We may compare this view with the positions of the authors discussed in Chapter 1. Interestingly, Sternberg and colleagues do not explicitly refer to those issues that originally justified the appeal to the use of methods other than those used in the natural sciences, namely the alleged uniqueness of human facts, the notions of intention and purposiveness, and the importance of goals in the explanation of human behaviors. For Sternberg and colleagues, the need for plurality is oriented toward the achievement of a comprehensive, detailed and sound knowledge of the phenomena at stake: "multiple [methodological] paradigms can contribute to our understanding of a single psychological phenomenon, locking oneself into any single paradigm reduces one's ability fully to grasp the phenomenon of interest" (Sternberg et al., 2001: 106).

The use of multiple methodologies, besides the above illustrated advantages, can also help to face the problem of reification, whose impact on psychological fragmentation is evident (see Chapter 5). In fact, the use of multiple methodologies removes the common belief that one is studying the whole phenomenon when, in fact, one is studying just a small part of it. For example, let us assume that a psychologist studies intelligence on the basis of school performances. The analysis of the students' marks, their frequencies, the mean and the observation of whatever regards school performances will lead our non-philosophically oriented psychologist to the belief that intelligence *is* school performances and that it is appropriately and solely measurable through this methodology. Using converging operations provides a methodologically more correct and reliable way to address psychological problems, because it helps to keep in mind that what one is touching is nothing more than a part of the elephant, not the elephant itself.

So far in this discussion, the authors support the analysis of psychological phenomena understood as complex wholes, whose features and their relationships are the epistemic aim of psychology. From this perspective, this position seems to tend toward a semantic view of psychological inquiry, which turns out to be committed to the properties of the objects at stake, that is, to those particular features which make them interesting and worth studying among others. In other words, the combined approach of methodological pluralism − provided by the use of converging operations − and theory knitting tends to uncover those aspects of the phenomena whose understanding requires an approach that favors and is oriented to their particularities. In other words, the relationship between the phenomenon and the respective theories seems to be strongly connected, and this may eventually entail a one-to-one isomorphism (see Chapter 1) between the data and the higher-order framework theory at stake.

The prescription of using different kinds of methods and integrating theories opens up the issue of language, mainly in the case of theory knitting procedures. The particular issue at stake is that of the connection among the theories and between the theories and the higher-order theoretical framework. The authors (Sternberg, Grigorenko and Kalmar, 2001) do not discuss the ways that this connection can be achieved, claiming nothing more than that, after evaluating the empirical validity of two or more theories to be knitted, "one thus seeks a higher-order theory that integrates those aspects of the two [or more] theories that are empirically supportable, and that discards those aspects of the two theories that are not supportable" (p. 109). Hence, the problem of the connection – or translatability (see Chapter 3) in terms of the new higher-order framework theory – remains open and needs further attention.

The issue of the linguistic relationship between theories leads straight to the issue of the reduction of theories. Sternberg and colleagues' proposal seems to offer an integrative vision of psychology, rather than a proper reductionistic outlook, which would entail the reduction of minor, more specific theories, to one grand theory. Indeed, in theory knitting "one attempts to integrate previous theories into a single higher order theory, rather than to segregate a new theory from previous ones" (Sternberg et al., 2001: 108). This kind of relationship between the theories seems to entail the fulfillment of Nagel's condition of connectability (1961: 353–4; see Chapter 4), which prescribes the introduction or the specification of terms which establish connections between the entities outlined by the theories at stake. In fact, in the process of theory knitting, those selected theories' aspects must find common ground by which to establish a certain kind of connection, "identifying the mutual overlapping and non-overlapping scope of the theories with regard to the phenomenon of interest" (Sternberg et al., 2001: 109). In contrast, it seems that theory knitting does not require the fulfillment of the other condition illustrated by Nagel, that of derivability (1961: 354). This condition prescribes the derivability of the laws of the reduced theories to the laws of the reducing theory. Theory knitting may dispense with this condition because the higher-order theory provides for a new theoretical structure where previous theories' laws or principles seems to somehow change their original configuration and nature by virtue of the new framework itself. From such a perspective, the relationship between the theories involved in the knitting is symmetrical – rather than asymmetrical, as in the case of reduction – and this is due to the fact that the higher-order theory constitutes a framework whose aim is the coordination of those aspects of the theories-to-be-knitted by means of "the introduction of new elements that knit the theories together" (Sternberg et al., 2001: 109). This puts the theories-to-be-knitted somehow on the same level.

From what has been discussed so far, it is clear that this proposal of unified psychology is grounded on the need to better understand psychological phenomena, which can be seen as the starting point of the psychological inquiry and as a means by which to reorganize the academic discipline of psychology.[2] The extreme importance of the object of psychology is evident: converging operations and theory knitting are aimed at the exploration of the different aspects of psychological phenomena. But how are those phenomena defined? It may be said that the methodological and theoretical positions held here have the explicit aim of uncovering different aspects – through different methods and theories – which all turn out to belong to the same phenomenon, just as the single parts of the elephant (objects of the theories-to-be-knitted) touched by each blind man (the theories-to-be-knitted) end up belonging to the same elephant (the phenomenon at stake). The consequence of such an approach is that phenomena are better understood through the adoption of different perspectives, each of which sheds some light on the object at stake (Sternberg et al., 2001: 110). Each perspective – both methodological or theoretical – offers the possibility to recognize those aspects of the phenomenon to which each perspective refers (Sternberg et al., 2001). For the authors, "There is no one correct perspective. Each perspective presents a different way of understanding the problem" (Sternberg and Grigorenko, 2003: 37; see also Sternberg et al., 2001: 106). This approach, on one hand, fosters a pluralistic and integrated knowledge of the phenomenon, and, on the other hand, helps the scientist to make explicit statements about the construct at stake.[3]

Such a view is defined as constructionistic by the authors, since it "holds that each person has idiosyncratic ways of looking at the world" (Sternberg et al., 2001: 107). However, in my opinion, the features so far illustrated do not necessarily justify such a philosophical stance. Conversely, Sternberg and colleagues' proposal seems to be consonant with the position of the philosopher John Dupré (see Chapter 4). Indeed, Dupré claims that each theoretical (and hence methodological) perspective about reality is justified by the purposes of the investigation and the peculiarities of the object at stake (Dupré, 1993: 57). In other words, there are many possible points of view for looking at the world and each one sheds some light on the world itself. The position of the philosopher is based on the consideration that common sense – as well as science – tends to classify things by the individuation of fragmentary and diverse categories, which turn out to have the aim of comprehending particular aspects of the object, according to the purposes of the observer and the features of what is observed. This approach seems to be in line with Sternberg and colleagues' proposal: in theory knitting, indeed, one of the major targets is to uncover those implicit assumptions that guide scientific research, "by forcing the theorist to grapple with the problem of recognizing the aspects of the phenomenon to which each theory refers" (2001: 110). The authors recognize, as does Dupré, the availability of different, legitimate ways to investigate psychological phenomena, and in contrast to the philosopher, maintain that this is solely justified by the fact that people have different, idiosyncratic perspectives of the world. In fact, the already mentioned reference to constructionism leads to a weak ontological position: the objects of scientific inquiry do not exist independently from the observers, but are mind-dependent. In contrast, Dupré claims that what is highlighted by each theoretical perspective is not in any sense illusory or unreal: the unearthed aspects really exist on the grounds of the adoption of that specific theoretical position which unearthed them. Thus, one doesn't need to be a constructionist to account for a pluralistic vision of the scientific enterprise. Conversely, the proposal of Sternberg and colleagues arguably better fits a realistic position about the world, such as that of Dupré, since it aims at progressively identifying more and more aspects of the construct at stake, striving for an account of it which is as exhaustive as possible. In other words, the higher-order theoretical framework held by theory knitting seems to postulate the possibility of progressively approaching what really exists (the phenomenon) by means of the integration of different theoretical points of view. Accordingly, the phenomena investigated by psychology can be understood as real phenomena, thus preserving a pluralistic outlook on reality.

Coming to the issue of the relationship between theory and practice, it must be noted that Robert Sternberg and Gregg Henriques wrote a paper in 2004 which was specifically dedicated to the professional aspects of their proposals and to the relationship between theory and practice. Hence, what follows reasonably refers to the position of Sternberg and colleagues and serves as an integration of Henriques' proposal which was discussed in Chapter 8.

The perspective endorsed in the 2004 paper basically considers the professional practice as intrinsically different from, although connected to, scientific psychology according to the position of the distinguished psychologist Donald Peterson (1991), one of the most prominent leaders of the movement that advocated a specific training for professional psychologists. From such a perspective, the crucial difference between science and practice deals with the fact that scientific psychology is descriptive in character, i.e., its aim is to describe and explain psychological phenomena, while professional practice is prescriptive in character, i.e., it is oriented toward the goal of change in order to increase psychological health and thus "begins and ends in the condition of the client" (Peterson, 1991: 426). This would seem to justify the independence of psychological professional practice from scientific psychology in terms of targets and procedures. However, science and practice are clearly connected and intertwined. Indeed, psychological knowledge, which is the aim of scientific psychology, is but a means to the aim for those who practice. Hence, the authors' position is that science and practice have different but complementary roles and "are seen as both necessary and good" (Henriques and Sternberg, 2004: 1059).

On this basis, unified professional psychology (UPP, as it is called) claims the need for a new professional model that is capable of addressing the problems which plague the applied dimension of psychology (see Chapter 5), and whose competencies "cut across the practice areas[4] and thus provide a clear foundational training base for an integrative and generalist practitioner model" (Henriques and Sternberg, 2004: 1057).[5] In general, the UPP model highlights the critical aspects of the science–practice connection, in order to better define the features of professional practice as an autonomous field. Going into more detail, the UPP practitioner supports evidence-based practice that is ecologically valid and relevant to the problems to be addressed. Science, in this regard, provides for scientific tools which have to meet some additional criteria, other than those of empirical and conceptual validity: these are the criteria which account for the professional relevance of those tools in the real world (Henriques and Sternberg, 2004: 1059; Sternberg, 2005: 6, 7). According to this position, the aim of science is to increase psychological knowledge that is empirically sound and conceptually reliable, while the aim of professional practice is to assess this knowledge, evaluating its practical relevance and the conditions of its application in the real world.

Within such a framework, professional practice is defined as the applied part of scientific psychology (or human psychology, in Henriques' vocabulary), even if the two – professional practice and scientific psychology – are both commonly connoted as "psychology." In fact, the use of different names may help, as in the case of biology and physics whose applications are connoted by the different names, respectively, medicine and engineering. Following such a parallelism, according to the UPP perspective, "professional psychology is to medicine and engineering what the basic science of psychology is to biology and physics" (Henriques and Sternberg, 2004: 1060). In the same manner as physicians and engineers, professional psychologists can be properly considered as scientific practitioners: on one hand, they are "scientific" because their practice is scientifically informed and grounded in empirical knowledge; on the other hand, they are "practitioners" because their actions are oriented to practical goals and must respect ecological criteria.

Finally, it is worth noting that Sternberg and colleagues' unified psychology does not explicitly refer to the continuity between the human world and the animal world, as do other proposals so far discussed. In a sense, this is because this proposal does not directly deal with the content of psychology, but provides a general outline for the integration of the discipline. However, by virtue of the pluralistic approach so far outlined, such a continuity cannot be ruled out in principle.

In conclusion, Sternberg and colleagues' perspective shows the merit of illustrating general methodological and theoretical strategies, of which the aim is to better organize existent and future psychological knowledge. Such an outlook is not another "psychology," but can be understood as a framework thanks to which the development of psychology and the connections between theories can be managed in such a way as to enhance the effectiveness of both scientific and professional psychology, while respecting their intrinsic differences.

Notes

1 Reprinted from the original paper published in 2001 in *American Psychologist, 56*: 1069–79.
2 "We believe that a more sensible and psychologically justifiable way of organizing psychology as a discipline and in departments and graduate study is in terms of psychological

phenomena … rather than so-called fields of psychology" (Sternberg and Grigorenko, 2003: 35).
3 As already noted above, this aspect is very important with regard to the issue of reification.
4 The recognized practice areas in the USA are clinical, counseling, and school psychology.
5 It is worth noting that this is consistent with Henriques' tripartite model, where professional psychology is understood as different both from psychological formalism and human psychology.

References

Dupré, J. (1993). *The Disorder of Things. Metaphysical Foundations of the Disunity of Science.* Cambridge, MA: Harvard University Press.

Henriques, G. R. and Sternberg, R. J. (2004). Unified professional psychology: Implications for the combined-integrated model of doctoral training. *Journal of Clinical Psychology*, 60(12): 1051–1063.

Nagel, E. (1961). *The Structure of Science. Problems in the Logic of Scientific Explanation.* Cambridge, MA: Hackett.

Peterson, D. R. (1991). Connection and disconnection of research and practice in the education of professional psychologists. *American Psychologist*, 46(4): 422–429.

Staats, A. W. (1996). *Behavior and Personality. Psychological Behaviorism.* New York: Springer.

Sternberg, R. J. (2005). Unifying the field of psychology. In R. J. Sternberg (ed.), *Unity in Psychology. Possibility or Pipedream?* (pp. 3–14). Washington, DC: American Psychological Association.

Sternberg, R. J. and Grigorenko, E. L. (2003). Unified psychology. In A. E. Kazdin (ed.), *Methodological Issues and Strategies in Clinical Research*(3rd edn) (pp. 23–47). Washington, DC: American Psychological Association.

Sternberg, R. J., Grigorenko, E. L., and Kalmar, D. A. (2001). The role of theory in unified psychology. *Journal of Theoretical and Philosophical Psychology*, 21(2): 99–117.

PART 4

11

A FRAGMENTED CLINICAL PSYCHOLOGY

It is customary to say that clinical psychology, as a peculiar ambit of psychology was born in 1896, when Lightner Witmer, a pupil of Wilhelm Wundt in Leipzig, founded the first Psychological Clinic at the University of Pennsylvania. It was Witmer's intention that clinical psychology, borrowing a typically medical term, should be an autonomous psychological rather than medical discipline. The term clinical applies to all methods whose object is the study of the mental states of individuals by means of observation and experimental research. Witmer's clinical psychology dealt not only with maladjusted children but also included in its scope normal subjects, the aims being the same, namely to foster the individual's development and well-being. The birth of a new kind of psychology was based on the need to exceed the limits, on one hand, of psychologies that obtained psychological principles from philosophical and pedagogical speculations and, on the other hand, of psychologies that directly implemented experimental outcomes to real-life contexts (Witmer, 1907). Indeed, its founder deemed inadequate both alternatives.

Clinical psychology is at present the largest sub-discipline of psychology and perhaps one of the most prominent field of applied psychology. It is worth noting that, despite its influential weight on psychology as a whole and its social appeal, its birth, development, and professionalization underwent many hardships, both on methodological and theoretical levels, thus complicating the stabilization of its institutional organization and scientific legitimacy. Clinical psychology developed as a profession at a time within societies where the need for flexible mental health providers, aware of the new social needs, became frankly urgent.[1] This social demand for clinical psychology was combined with the fact that the training in psychology (including clinical psychology) had always been – and continued for many years to be – conducted within research-based programs in academic contexts. Therefore, on one hand, the new challenges of society, more and more inclined to accept psychologists as credible professionals, required new and creative ways to address ever growing problems pertaining to psychology. On the other hand, the people and the institutions responsible for the education of young psychologists were new to the application of psychology, and often skeptical in this respect.[2] These two coexisting spheres – the connection with the world "out there" and its research-based grounds – make clinical psychology an interesting crossroads between different traditions and methodological approaches.

Even though Witmer's early proposal had a fairly influential scientific legacy, clinical psychology underwent huge growth only after World War II (Reisman, 1991), when it became a profession in every respect (Bootzin, 2007: 11). It can be argued that clinical psychology was considered by many to be one of the most promising candidates for a "second psychology," a discipline which would address aspects of human mind and behavior within the real world, in ecological contexts, in response to and as a complement to the historically and methodologically earlier laboratory-based tradition of academic psychology (Cahan and White, 1992: 224), the "first psychology." As Chapter 5 revealed, when a new branch of psychology came into existence, it did not have the proper methodological toolbox with which to adequately respond to issues related to those needs: this was specifically true for clinical psychology. The success and the social visibility of clinical psychology, in addition to the urgency to efficiently and rapidly respond to growing social needs and thereby strengthen its credibility as a new branch of the profession, left little room for careful scientific reflection concerning the discipline and its methods. Many psychologists began to worry about the growing number of theories, methods, and practices that characterized the development of clinical psychology after World War II, and thus sensed signs of disciplinary weakness (Reisman, 1991). Even today, the field of psychology appears simply "too large and diverse to be unified" (Leahey, 1992: 479). The same can easily be said about clinical psychology.

In the United States such a fragmentation can be recognized well before the period when clinical psychology developed as a profession (i.e., after World War II). Indeed, psychology's successful role during World War I provided a stimulus for a stronger focus on applied psychology, but the American Psychological Association (APA) displeased many of its members in the first attempt to develop standards for clinical practice in 1917 (Reisman, 1991; Bootzin, 2007: 9). From this moment on, clinical psychologists made numerous efforts to organize themselves and their growing discipline in a consensual way for political as well as for methodological reasons, often in a reciprocally conflicting attitude with the APA: many associations have been formed, disbanded, or rejoined the APA, such as the American Association of Clinical Psychologists (AACP) (1917–19), the American Association of Applied Psychology (AAAP) (1937–45 rejoined the APA), the American Psychological Society (1988–2006, now renamed Association for Psychological Science), the American Association of Applied and Preventive Psychology (AAAPP, 1991–2004), and the Society for a Science of Clinical Psychology (1966, still existing) (Bootzin, 2007: 9–20). Such divisions evidently reflect strong disagreements among those who practice clinical psychology in its variety of expressions, not only concerning organizational issues, but also concerning more substantial issues about the scientific outlook of the discipline (see Benjamin, 2005: 23).

Perhaps one of the most controversial points remains the connection between science and practice in the training of clinical psychologists. Two different models and philosophies concerning education in clinical psychology have historically competed in the United States, based on two different ways of understanding the professional and scientific role of the clinical psychologist. The first is the so-called Boulder Model[3] which endorses a scientist-practitioner model: clinical practice must be performed and developed on a scientific basis. In this model, academic departments are in charge of education in clinical psychology, whose roots are indeed in scientific research. Clinical psychologists' practice is considered to be directly grounded in psychological science: the professionals have to be trained both in research and practice. The second is the Vail Model[4] which endorses a scholar-practitioner model, whereby the practitioner is taught to understand and apply research, but not to be a researcher. The rationale of this model concerns the recognition that professional practice, while needing to be grounded in research, has different problems and aims, thus practitioners must be "local scientists" (Trierweiler and Stricker, 1998), oriented to the specific features and constraints of contexts, clients, and organizations, that are the environment where the psychological work takes place (Peterson, 1991). In general terms, the core of the controversy deals with the role of psychological knowledge obtained through research-based procedures in the design and development of clinical psychological interventions: is scientific research as it is carried out today in academic settings crucial for clinical practice or is it non influential? In fact, the coin of science-based professions has two faces, since "practice can be restricted to fit the science, or the science can be developed to fit the practice" (Peterson, 1991: 429).

Beyond the existence of these two rather structured kinds of training models, clinical psychology education and practice still has enormous variability in the extent to which both professional psychologists and educational programs emphasize science or practice (Bootzin, 2007: 17). Therefore, the issue of the connection between science and practice which is relevant for psychology in general (as discussed in Chapter 5) is especially relevant for clinical psychology. This is a topic which characterizes not only American clinical psychology, but also European and, in particular, Italian clinical psychology. As already mentioned, when (clinical) psychology met the "real world out there" – after World War II – all its inadequacies as a credible profession showed up, also in Europe and especially Italy, where psychologists began to be included in the National Health System and were asked to design and coordinate interventions of social interest. In particular, in Italy the only specificity clinical psychology could boast about was the practice of psychotherapy, even though this was not exactly a real specificity, because it was (and it still is) shared with physicians. In this context, clinical psychologists addressed the real world with the implicit idea that psychology – as it was practiced and taught in academic settings – was not useful or adequate to answer socially relevant requests for psychological intervention.[5] Psychotherapy had been long considered as the only transformative (i.e., applied) area clinical psychologists could count on. Only psychotherapy, not psychology, could provide tools aimed at addressing the problems and issues presented for psychologists' consideration (Carli and Grasso, 1991: 177). However, psychotherapeutic techniques were originally designed mostly for individual interventions in private settings: the multiplicity of needs which clinical psychologists found in the wide range of settings where they were asked to work brought out all the limitations of the traditional psychotherapeutic approaches. But those psychotherapeutic traditions – despite their many differences – provided a strong base from which to define clinical psychologists' own practice and identity as credible professionals (Berdini et al., 1992). Given this situation, it may be argued that the development of clinical psychology as a profession in Italy has been characterized by two relevant sources of fragmentation.

On one hand, the fact that psychology was considered incapable of providing sound tools for psychological interventions – and psychological education struggled to train future psychologists as clinical psychologists – laid the foundations for the identification of many clinical psychologists with other kinds of professions that were deemed more socially credible. In other words, many psychologists ceased to consider themselves as psychologists and began to generically define themselves as (health) *operators*. This is now considered to be as an ideological attempt to remove the professional differences and specificities among people working together, in order to legitimate and justify the presence of clinical psychologists in the health settings where physicians, nurses, and social workers served. In this way, many clinical psychologists gave up their own professional specificity, camouflaging themselves within the comforting boundaries of more socially acknowledged professions (Carli, 1989). This evidently hindered the development of clinical psychology as an autonomous discipline and brought about a sort of fragmentation of the profession, whereby clinical psychologists renounced not only their theoretical and methodological specificity but also their social role as psychologists.

On the other hand, the reference to psychotherapy as the only viable practice for clinical psychologists has been another crucial source of fragmentation. Indeed, in Italy, as elsewhere, the psychotherapy traditions have been diverse and self-referential for a long time. As Robyn Dawes (2005: 1245–6) asserted about a common attitude in clinical psychology, everyone tended to fish on his own side of the lake and no one was really interested in fishing in the middle. The connections between practitioners of different approaches received a suspicious or, at best, cautious attitude and contact was rare or occasional. Isolation has been the rule for a long time. Moreover, the strong professional identity provided by the reference to the different orientations of psychotherapy brought about the reinforcement of this kind of reciprocal isolation: often, if not always, the only scientific, methodo-logical, and social references for many Italian clinical psychologists were provided by the affiliation to a psychotherapeutic tradition (Berdini et al., 1992; Malato et al., 1993). This evidently fed fragmentation and hindered the development of a clinical psychology that would be capable of transcending the hodgepodge of psychotherapeutic traditions.

In the course of time, the idea of psychotherapy as the main and most legitimate professional practice for clinical psychologists has begun to slowly collapse, as clinical psychology has progressively found its place as a profession in Western societies and has been asked to respond to new social challenges and to prove its scientific validity. Since the early 1990s, it can be argued that clinical psychologists began to be dissatisfied with single-school approaches and the traditionally prudent isolation between different traditions started to break down, at least in the United States (Norcross, 2005: 3–4). The progressive opening of the borders has been the result of many factors related both to the professional practice and to the scientific research in the psychotherapy field. Again, the relevance of psychotherapy for clinical psychology can be well ascertained.

From the point of view of professional practice, psychologists found that some problems could be better addressed by other methodological or theoretical tools which might complement their own primary orientation's weaknesses. The awareness was growing that "no one approach is clinically adequate for all patients and situations" (Norcross, 2005: 5). Differences began to be deemed as resources, not only as insurmountable barriers. Experimentation and heterodoxy in psychotherapy flowered, fostered by the intellectual and sociopolitical climate (Norcross, 2005: 6). Moreover, the increased availability of manuals and videotapes facilitated the appreciation of differences and commonalities of various treatment approaches, effectively spreading knowledge about psychotherapies.

From the point of view of scientific research, a plethora of theories and techniques are now proliferating, making the traditional psychotherapeutic scenario more and more complex and rich: new approaches integrate, substitute, or modify traditional approaches, or simply support them. Several factors contribute to a progressive departure from the exclusive reliance on a single psychotherapeutic technique. Among these is the recognition that different treatments help specific psychological problems in different ways, in addition to the rise of evidence-based and manualized treatments, together with the recognition that the so-called common factors – properties of the patient–therapist relationship – heavily contribute to the therapy effectiveness.

Such a situation has two main consequences for the issue at stake. On one hand, this cultural turmoil is disbanding the traditional boundaries among the various approaches. In this way, psychotherapeutic traditions may no longer be considered strong methodological and professional references for clinical psychologists: somehow, clinical psychologists are compelled to give up their psychotherapeutic "clothing" with a view to putting on new clothes. For example, it is worth noting that a recent study shows that in the United States fully 90 percent of psychologists embraced several orientations (Norcross, Karpiak, and Lister, 2005), that is, declared themselves not be rigidly bound to a single therapeutic approach. On the other side, such an integrative or eclectic attitude is idiosyncratic and deemed rather "instinctive" in character, within the clinical psychology community. A psychotherapy integration movement arose and developed in the last three, four decades as an autonomous area of interest (Goldfried, Pachankis, and Bell, 2005: 24), including

its related literature, and proposing various models of integration which favor theoretical, actuarial, or technical dimensions in the quest for unification (Arkowitz,
1992). Nevertheless, in clinical practice the managing of different clinical psychological tools, their integration, the examination of their theoretical basis, and similar
processes have so far been left often to the initiative of individual professionals
within their everyday practices, since research on the unification of psychotherapy
has not acquired much popularity among practitioners.[6] In other words, in the face
of this exciting professional and scientific challenge, clinical psychologists seem to
try to orient themselves through the jungle of techniques and theories without a
proper compass, endowed only with their intuition and expertise. A bottom-up
approach, where individual psychologists' initiatives inform theoretical and methodological issues, take the place of a top-down approach whereby theoretical and
methodological bases inform psychologists' initiatives. Sure enough, this state of
affairs – which emphasizes the role of expertise and "instinct" of individual practitioners rather than the role of scientific and philosophic knowledge – does nothing
so much as feed the fragmentation of clinical psychology.

Before examining in more detail how clinical psychology is generally defined via
the review of the American and the Italian definitions of its peculiar disciplinary
content, it is worth considering some data about the clinical psychologists' community
that highlights its state of affairs and the specificities of the current fragmented scenario
so far described. In a relevant paper, Norcross, Karpiak, and Santoro (2005)
reviewed the data provided by significant researches about crucial features of the
professional community of clinical psychologists, namely Kelly (1961), Garfield and
Kurtz (1974), Norcross and Prochaska (1982a, 1982b, 1982c), Norcross, Prochaska,
and Gallagher (1989a, 1989b), Norcross, Karg, and Prochaska (1997a, 1997b), and
compared the outcomes with those of their 2003 study,[7] which is the core of the
2005 paper. Here I will report some interesting data gathered by Norcross, Karpiak,
and Santoro that reveals the state of fragmentation of the clinical psychology
community today, together with the data gathered in Italy by the psychologist
A. Claudio Bosio in a 2011 study[8] about the professional and scientific features of
the Italian psychological community.

Norcross and colleagues show that in every data gathering, from 1960 to 2003,
the modal orientation[9] as concerns the theoretical orientation of the community
was eclecticism or an integrational approach (29 percent in 2003; see Norcross,
Karpiak, and Santoro, 2005: 1471). Since 1960, more or less one-third of the
sample declared endorsed an eclectic theoretical attitude as the primary orientation.
Behavioral orientations remain constant during this time, while the cognitive
approaches continuously increase in popularity, almost reaching eclecticism in 2003
(28 percent). On the other hand, the influence of psychodynamic orientations
progressively decreases, to 15 percent of the sample in 2003. The data show a
rather fragmented scenario; the fact that the modal orientation has always been
eclecticism provides evidence for an even more serious situation. In fact, while
those who endorsed a traditional approach (behavioral, cognitive, constructivist,
humanistic, psychodynamic orientations, etc.) may be associated with well-known

professional and scientific traditions, those who endorsed eclecticism were not associated with any known or scientifically qualified theoretical approach. In other words, whereas the traditional orientations can be easily, *albeit* approximately, traced back to a limited numbers of core principles and primary methods, eclecticism may be considered as a vast terrain where different kinds of approaches coexist. The problem is that these eclectic approaches are not explicitly defined and cannot be intersubjectively reviewed; rather, their blend seems to be idiosyncratic in character. Thus, it can be argued that the relevance of eclecticism actually increases the state of fragmentation beyond the boundaries of traditional psychotherapeutic approaches, rather than representing a common ground among orientations. For example, Norcross (2005: 12) reports the outcomes of an impressive study where 90 percent of psychologists reported to embrace several orientations. Here, the crucial question is: do all these psychologists combine those different orientations in the same way? And if so, how? It is evident that fragmentation does not only stem from the existence of different codified approaches, but also to a greater extent from eclecticism.

The Italian situation has both similar and different aspects. When psychologists were asked to indicate their theoretical orientation, different schools and approaches were mentioned. Most of them (25 percent) declared to be devoted to approaches that can be somehow traced back to the psychodynamic area (Freud, Klein, Adler, Lacan, Jung, transactional analysis). This datum seems to diverge from the American trend, where the psychodynamic approaches are progressively losing ground. In addition, 11 percent of psychologists endorse a systemic approach, while cognitive-behavioral orientation is endorsed by only 9 percent (Bosio, 2011: 51). It is quite clear that the psychodynamic tradition is still very relevant among Italian practitioners, while the behavioral and cognitive approaches are far less prevalent than for American practitioners. It is worth noting that eclecticism, in the Italian study, is mentioned by only 1 percent of psychologists, a very different outcome from the American study (23 percent). Evidently, eclecticism plays a marginal role among Italian clinical psychologists, at least on the basis of what they verbally report. Indeed, eclecticism may be just an unpopular label in Italy, although it may actually be practiced. In general terms, the Italian and American situations show the same coexistence of different orientations among clinical psychologists, though these orientations show different degrees of relevance in the two professional communities. At first sight, it may be reasonably argued that, on one hand, American clinical psychology, dominated by eclectism, seems to be more concerned with the pragmatic aspects of the discipline, whose components (theories, techniques, methodologies) are deemed to be tools which may be creatively combined, based on the individual practitioner's targets. On the other hand, Italian clinical psychology, dominated by the strong reference to psychotherapeutic schools, seems to be more concerned with the social image of the community, whose identity and professional legitimation seems to be uniquely or mainly achievable through the reference to strong psychotherapeutic traditions.

A relatively similar scenario stems from the activities of clinical psychologists. In the US in 2003, psychotherapy was still the predominant activity, with 80 percent of the sample spending 34 percent of their professional time in its practice. Although psychotherapy was prevalent, almost half of psychologists were routinely involved in six activities other than psychotherapy such as diagnosis/assessment, teaching, clinical supervision, research/writing, consultation, and administration (Norcross et al., 2005: 1474). Even though the Italian sample comprises psychologists and not specifically clinical psychologists (as in the American study), when they are asked to report about the activities in which they are engaged, 55 percent of them turn out to be devoted to activities that can be easily defined as clinical (psychological support, counseling, psychotherapy and clinical interview), while 25 percent are devoted to interventions performed in schools settings (school interventions, education) (Bosio, 2011: 49–50). In general terms, from these data psychologists seems to be rather focused on interventions oriented to help people and promote health in a traditional fashion. However, it is worth noting that the prevalence of psychotherapeutic or para-psychotherapeutic activities does not provide *per se* a proper anchorage for the profession. Indeed, the reference to psychotherapy provides a general frame which includes tremendously different practices, theories, and methodologies. In other words, the reference to psychotherapy, though representing a useful social label that legitimates psychologists' professional practice, enhances the state of fragmentation, rather than representing a common ground for the discipline. In addition, it can be argued that this strong reference to psychotherapy as a recognized source of professional legitimation and social credibility may be somewhat risky, as it can be considered a hindrance to a serious inquiry into the targets, methodologies, and social usefulness of psychological interventions, beyond the cliché of the psychotherapy umbrella.

To better evaluate such a fragmented situation, it is worthwhile to briefly review the issue of training in clinical psychology. In the United States, clinical psychologists are trained through graduate studies (PhDs, mainly awarded from universities, or PsyDs, mainly awarded from freestanding professional schools). As already illustrated, the main controversy about this education is focused on the role played by science and research in the education of professional clinical psychologists. In general terms, those who maintain that clinical practice must be research-based and that clinical psychologists must be trained both to provide services and to conduct research (i.e., the Boulder, or scientist-practitioner, Model) are opposed to those who maintain that clinical psychology is a local enterprise whereby research-based principles provide a basis for clinical practice whose main aim is to face real, unique problems which require a proper application of these principles. The latter type of practitioner is trained to be a skilled consumer of research, and not a producer of research (i.e., the Vail, or practitioner-scholar, Model). In other words, two different conceptions of clinical psychology are at stake, where the connection or disconnection between opposite components of the discipline, such as science vs. practice and generality vs. individuality, is a crucial issue. Such a debate has longstanding origins, since it directly reflects the different positions supported by those who contributed to the birth and development of scientific psychology (see Chapter 5) and it indirectly reflects the controversy between the supporters of monistic and dualistic approaches (see Chapter 1).

As in the United States, in Italy clinical psychologists are trained through graduate studies, but this is mostly delegated to freestanding psychotherapy schools, which are therefore in charge of the education of clinical psychologists. It is clear that this situation is problematic: to become a clinical psychologist one must be trained by a psychotherapy school, as if clinical psychology *is* psychotherapy, nothing more, nothing less. Even from this simple fact, outwardly just an organizational issue, the relevance of psychotherapy in Italy as the main reference for clinical education and practice turns out to be evident. Therefore, the training in clinical psychology is inherently fragmented: psychotherapy, as already illustrated, is but a holder where diverse kinds of treatment and intervention coexist. Thus, the great importance of psychotherapy in the education of clinical psychologists makes their education clearly diversified and fragmented, since psychotherapy as a whole is diversified and fragmented.

Let us now consider two features of this situation. First, psychotherapy schools embody strong therapeutic traditions, such as psychoanalysis, behaviorism, cognitivism, etc. Second, these schools also embody idiosyncratic and minute variations of those traditions which may often be considered as mere sub-schools. Those facts clearly jeopardize the integrity and autonomy of Italian clinical psychology. Some recent data on psychotherapy schools will confirm this scenario. In a study about the quality of training organized by the Italian Department of Education (Ministero dell'Istruzione, dell'Università e della Ricerca), 212 Italian freestanding psychotherapy schools participated (Maffei et al., 2015). In this study, 64 percent of schools shared an orientation with at least another school, while 36 percent of them didn't have any shared orientation, that is, they had a unique orientation.[10] These data are impressive and they confirm what was mentioned before: the world of psychotherapy training and practice is fragmented and this fragmentation stems both from the existence of well-known, self-referential, great traditions, and from the existence of a large number of "new" schools whose theoretical and methodological references cannot be neatly traced back to well-known traditions. It is worth noting that the schools, when asked to specify their own scientific orientation, declared to endorse 102 different orientations. This means that for each orientation there are barely more than two schools!

The qualifications of those who provide education for clinical psychologists is also important for the issue at stake. In the study of Maffei et al. (2015), 66 percent of the teaching staff in the sample of 212 schools are formed by "skilled psychotherapists," while only 34 percent comes from academic settings. Now, it is arguable that those skilled psychotherapists gain expertise mainly from their practice and from their professional experience, under the guidance of their school's orientation. This situation contains the implicit assumption that the practice of psychotherapy, based on that specific orientation, is capable of developing an expertise that legitimates the possibility of teaching that technique. If this hypothesis is sound, what is taught by those skilled professionals in many freestanding schools has little or, in the worst case, no reference to research-based practice or general psychological principles, since most of the teaching staff members establish their competence on expertise and professional experience. The relevance of clinical psychologists employed in private practice (i.e., not connected to academic settings) in the training area is evidently growing (Bosio, 2011: 59–66; see also Norcross et al., 2005: 1474), and this may be viewed as a further source of fragmentation for clinical psychology. The risk is that clinical psychology may be progressively more disconnected from procedures based on science and psychological principles and become more connected to procedures based on expertise and "clinical sense."

Two definitions of clinical psychology

But what precisely is clinical psychology? A comparison between two influential definitions seems to be a useful way to approach the issue of how to set the boundaries of clinical psychology. For this purpose, I will deal with the definition provided by Division 12 (Society of Clinical Psychology) of the APA,[11] representative of the American outlook on clinical psychology, and the definition provided by the Collegio dei Professori Universitari e dei Ricercatori di Psicologia Clinica (Board of University Professors and Researchers in Clinical Psychology), the Italian Association which promotes and develops clinical psychology, both on scientific and applied levels (Molinari and Labella, 2007: 315–16). Let us first discuss the common aspects of the two definitions. Both describe clinical psychology as a psychological discipline which addresses problems relating to psychological uneasiness and suffering, such as maladjustment, disability, discomfort, dysfunctional mental processes. The target is at the individual, interpersonal, or group level. The interventions are designed in order to work on single individuals or on relationships in general, including groups or families. While soothing psychological discomfort seems to be its primary aim in both definitions, clinical psychology is also devoted to the promotion of psychological health, according to a model which considers the integration and the interdependence of the biological, social and psychological aspects. In other words, psychological health is considered to be strongly intertwined with biological and social conditions, so clinical psychology cannot ignore those aspects in its mandate. Given those boundaries, clinical psychology generally aims to understand (APA; Molinari and Labella, 2007), explain, interpret, reorganize (Molinari and Labella), predict, and alleviate (APA) psychological distress. While generally committed to unraveling interpersonal problems relating to psychological discomfort and to promote health, clinical psychology as defined by the Italian board seems to emphasize those aspects pertaining the intellectual understanding and explanation of phenomena (understanding, explaining, interpreting), rather than the pragmatic dimension of the prediction and the alleviation of distress, as emphasized by the APA.

This last remark points to some slight differences in the two visions of clinical psychology, beyond the commonalities already discussed. In the Italian definition, where the intellectual aspects of the inquiry seems to be slightly prevalent, the pluralistic character of clinical psychology is repeatedly mentioned as both an intrinsic feature and as a virtue of the discipline: clinical psychology operates through "natural science standards as well as human science standards" (Molinari and Labella, 2007: 316, my translation), psychotherapy has "different strategies and methods" (Molinari and Labella, 2007: 315, my translation), the research and applied dimensions are "profitably fed by a plurality of models" and their methods are "legitimated by different traditions of study" (Molinari and Labella, 2007: 315, my translation). Every expression of clinical psychology seems to be under the auspices of plurality and inner diversity. The American definition, on the other hand, seems to identify the diversity within clinical psychology focusing on the gap between science and practice (see Chapter 5). According to those who wrote the definition, this gap seems not to be a virtue, but something that needs to be filled through the integration of the two aspects, no matter what "integration" means: "the field of Clinical Psychology integrates science, theory, and practice" (APA), "the Clinical Psychologist is educated and trained to generate and integrate scientific and professional knowledge and skills" (APA), "researchers study the theory and practice of Clinical Psychology" (APA). Therefore, both definitions recognize some sort of fragmentation within clinical psychology: while the American definition seems to strive for filling that gap, the Italian definition describes a discipline where different aspects (traditions) coexist with little or no room for comparison and exchange. Such a scenario may be similar to the one described by the psychologist Robyn Dawes, who suggested that when he entered the field, the state of clinical psychology could be finely described by the complex and unintelligible name "Chargoggaggoggmanchargagoggcharbunagungamaug"[12] (the ancient name of Lake Webster, in Connecticut; Dawes, 2005: 1245–6). Different approaches were legitimated by their own traditions and their research, methods and professional applications operated quite independently from those of other traditions. Indifferent independence was (and perhaps still is?) the prevailing attitude. It may be suggested that the American definition, emphasizing the pragmatic side of clinical psychology, is more inclined to strive for the integration of the scientific and professional aspects; it describes a field that strives for connecting the basis (science) to the applied dimension (practice), which is depicted as very relevant. Though, the expressed intention of connecting theory and practice doesn't specify the modes of that connection. On the other hand, the Italian definition, emphasizing the intellectual, speculative side of the discipline, simply recognizes a state of pluralism which seems to be rather unproblematic. This definition describes a field that is more oriented to the preservation of an existent, legitimate, unproblematic pluralism: sentences like "the research tradition ... is profitably fed by a plurality of models," "such models are guided by different epistemological and theoretical–methodological assumptions" and "[they] are characterized by indefeasible differences" (Molinari and Labella, 2007: 316, my translation) are meaningful expressions. The origins of such a plurality are argued to be rooted in the variety of traditions that developed in the course of time within the scientific community.

One last point to be noted concerns the issue of subjectivity. In the Italian definition, subjectivity has a pivotal role in clinical psychology, specifically as a tool for designing and performing clinical interventions. The "subjective system of the clinical psychologist" is argued to be one of the most relevant tools for the practice of clinical psychology. The professional, properly trained through a "specific training and clinical practice," makes his/her own "emotional, cognitive and relational system" (Molinari and Labella, 2007: 316, my translation) a methodological device in the service of his/her professional practice. This reference to subjectivity is completely missing in the American definition where the education of clinical psychologists is centered on scientific and professional knowledge which seems to constitute a sort of double core of the discipline. This odd position of subjectivity – completely ignored by the American definition, though deemed as crucial in the Italian definition – may somehow be connected to the different views that the two definitions hold about the intrinsic plurality of clinical psychology. As a matter of fact, the emphasis on subjectivity fits fairly well with a legitimate state of methodological and theoretical plurality: the professional use of subjectivity, after receiving proper training, is supposed to give rise to a variety of procedures which are, in turn, legitimated by the fact that one of the most relevant tools of clinical psychology is argued to be subjectivity itself. In other words, it may be reasonably assumed as a hypothesis for the time being that the legitimization of subjectivity as a sound device for clinical practice is connected to the unproblematic, pluralistic nature of clinical psychology, as defined by the Italian board.

Notes

1 This is approximately true in the United States as well as in Europe, and in particular in Italy, although with substantial differences. However, it is not my intention to historically reconstruct the development of clinical psychology as a profession, but to highlight some crucial aspects of it in order to address the issue from a theoretical and methodological point of view.
2 This can be argued for Italy (Bagnara et al., 1975) as well as for the United States (Cahan and White, 1992).
3 In August 1949 a conference on graduate education in clinical psychology was held at the University of Colorado at Boulder, sponsored by the National Institute of Mental Health.
4 Another conference was held in Vail, Colorado, in 1973, where the award of PsyDs was set forth, which is commonly awarded by freestanding professional schools of psychology, rather than by university-based programs.
5 This was somehow endorsed and confirmed by those who dealt with psychological education within the academic departments. On one hand, psychology was considered by many as a scientifically immature discipline, thus not capable of constituting the basis for a proper profession. On the other hand, academic psychologists mainly disagreed about the possibility of the development of a professional scientific psychology (Lombardo, 1993: 125–7).
6 This is due to and fostered by the gap existing between practice and research discussed in Chapter 5.
7 The authors mailed a self-administered questionnaire to 1,500 randomly selected members and fellows of the APA Division 12 (clinical psychology) living in the United States, concerning their professional practice. The final sample consisted of 654 clinical psychologists; 649 questionnaires were returned, but 40 of them were not usable for various reasons, primarily due to retirement (n=36).
8 The author administered a structured interview, by telephone, to 1,947 Italian psychologists selected among the members of the Regional Psychological Associations in Italy

(Ordini Regionali); 79 percent of them (n=1,541) accepted to be interviewed and constitute the final sample.

9 The most frequently occurring score in a batch of data.

10 It is interesting to note that these data are basically coherent with those gathered by Lombardo and colleagues more than twenty years ago. Indeed, in their study, 31 percent of freestanding psychotherapy schools declared to be devoted to a "specific and original vision of psychotherapy" (Lombardo et al., 1991: 301, my translation) elaborated by their own founders.

11 http://www.apa.org/divisions/div125/AboutClinicalPsychology.html

12 Native American for "I fish on my side, you fish on your side, and no one fishes in the middle."

References

Arkowitz, H. (1992). Integrative theories of therapy. In D. K. Freedheim, H. J. Freudenberger, J. W. Kessler, S. B. Messer, D. R., Peterson, H. H. Strupp, and P. L. Wachtel (eds.), *History of Psychotherapy: A Century of Change* (pp. 261–303). Washington, DC: American Psychological Association.

Bagnara, S., Castelfranchi, C., Legrenzi, P., Minguzzi, G., Misiti, R., and Parisi, D. (1975). Per una discussione sulla situazione della psicologia in Italia. *Giornale Italiano di Psicologia*, 3: 285–305.

Benjamin, L. T. (2005). A history of clinical psychology as a profession in America (And a glimpse at its future). *Annual Review of Clinical Psychology*, 1: 1–30.

Berdini, G., De Berardinis, D., Masina, E., Mazzotta, M., Orgiana, C., Rubino, A., and Tavazza, G. (1992). Immagine del lavoro dello psicologo clinico. *Rivista di Psicologia Clinica*, 2: 212–237.

Bootzin, R. R. (2007). Psychological clinical science: why and how we got to where we are. In T. A. Treat, R. R. Bootzin, and T. B. Baker (eds.), *Psychological Clinical Science* (pp. 3–28). New York: Psychology Press.

Bosio, A. C. (2011). *Fare lo psicologo. Percorsi e prospettive di una professione*. Milan: Cortina.

Cahan, E. D. and White, S. H. (1992). Proposals for a second psychology. *American Psychologist*, 47(2): 224–235.

Carli, R. (1989). Tema del numero: Lo psicologo clinico nei servizi socio-sanitari. *Rivista di Psicologia Clinica*, 1: 6–14.

Carli, R. and Grasso, M. (1991). Psicologia clinica e psicoterapia. *Rivista di Psicologia Clinica*, 2: 172–188.

Dawes, R. M. (2005). The ethical implications of Paul Meehl's work on comparing clinical versus actuarial prediction methods. *Journal of Clinical Psychology*, 61(10): 1245–1255.

Garfield, S. L. and Kurtz, R. (1974). A survey of clinical psychologists: Characteristics, activities, and orientations. *Clinical Psychologist*, 28(1): 7–10.

Goldfried, M. R., Pachankis, J. E., and Bell, A. C. (2005). A history of psychotherapy integration. In J. C. Norcross, and M. R. Goldfried (eds.), *Handbook of Psychotherapy Integration* (pp. 24–60). New York: Oxford University Press.

Kelly, E. L. (1961). Clinical psychology – 1960. Report of survey findings. *Newsletter: Division of Clinical Psychology of the American Psychological Association*, 14(1): 1–11.

Leahey, T. H. (1992). *A History of Psychology*. Englewood Cliffs, NJ: Prentice Hall.

Lombardo, G. P. (1993). Teorie sul ruolo dello psicologo. Storia e modelli dell'intervento clinico. *Rivista di Psicologia Clinica*, 2–3: 123–149.

Lombardo, G. P., Stampa, P., Cavalieri, P., Ciuffo, E., Farnese, M. L. (1991). Struttura e risorse degli Enti privati di formazione alla psicoterapia: una ricognizione. In G. P. Lombardo (ed.), *Storia e modelli della formazione dello psicologo. Le teorie dell'intervento* (pp. 292–315). Milan: Franco Angeli. [reprinted from *Rivista di Psicologia Clinica*, 5(1)]

Maffei, C., Del Corno, F., Dazzi, N., Cioffi, A., and Strepparava, M. (2015). Private psychotherapy training in Italy: A systematic analysis. *European Journal of Psychotherapy and Counselling*, 17(1).

Malato, D., Masiello, S., Niccolucci, C., Nuovo, M., Raffaele, A., and Verrienti, D. (1993). Psicologi in formazione: alla ricerca di una competenza. *Rivista di Psicologia Clinica*, 1: 98–109.

Molinari, E. and Labella, A. (2007). *Psicologia clinica. Dialoghi e confronti*. Milan: Springer.

Norcross, J. C. (2005). A primer on psychotherapy integration. In J. C. Norcross and M. R. Goldfried (eds.), *Handbook of Psychotherapy Integration* (pp. 3–23). New York: Oxford University Press.

Norcross, J. C., Karg, R. S., and Prochaska, J. O. (1997a). Clinical psychologists in the 1990s: I. *Clinical Psychologists*, 50(2): 4–9.

Norcross, J. C., Karg, R. S., and Prochaska, J. O. (1997b). Clinical psychologists in the 1990s: II. *Clinical Psychologists*, 50(3): 4–11.

Norcross, J. C., Karpiak, C. P., and Lister, K. M. (2005). What's an integrationist? A study of self-identified integrative and (occasionally) eclectic psychologists. *Journal of Clinical Psychology*, 61(12): 1587–1594.

Norcross, J. C., Karpiak, C. P., and Santoro, S. O. (2005). Clinical psychologists across the years: The division of clinical psychology from 1960 to 2003. *Journal of Clinical Psychology*, 61(12): 1467–1483.

Norcross, J. C. and Prochaska, J. O. (1982a). A national survey of clinical psychologists: Characteristics and activities. *Clinical Psychologists*, 35(2): 1–8.

Norcross, J. C. and Prochaska, J. O. (1982b). A national survey of clinical psychologists: Affiliations and orientations. *Clinical Psychologists*, 35(3): 1–6.

Norcross, J. C. and Prochaska, J. O. (1982c). A national survey of clinical psychologists: Views on training, career choice, and APA. *Clinical Psychologist*, 35(4): 1–6.

Norcross, J. C., Prochaska, J. O., and Gallagher, K. (1989a). Clinical psychologists in the 1980s: I. Demographics, affiliations, and satisfactions. *Clinical Psychologist*, 42, 29–39.

Norcross, J. C., Prochaska, J. O., and Gallagher, K. (1989b). Clinical psychologists in the 1980s: II. Theory, research and practice. *Clinical Psychologist*, 42, 45–53.

Peterson, D. R. (1991). Connection and disconnection of research and practice in the education of professional psychologists. *American Psychologist*, 46(4): 422–429.

Reisman, J. M. (1991). *A History of Clinical Psychology*. Philadelphia, PA: Hemisphere Publishing Corporation.

Trierweiler, S. J. and Stricker, G. (1998). *The Scientific Practice of Professional Psychology*. New York: Kluwer Academic.

Witmer, L. (1907). *Clinical psychology. Psychological Clinic*, 1: 1–9, http://psychclassics.yorku.ca

PART 5

12

A THEORETICAL AND EMPIRICAL DISCIPLINE

Psychology as a science and as a profession

What has thus far been illustrated in this work are some – I hope interesting – theoretical and methodological issues connected to the main topic of this work, namely the unity or disunity of psychology. In Part 1, some general, philosophical issues were discussed, in order to provide a sort of framework in which to ascertain the state of psychology and, subsequently, of clinical psychology. A primary dialectical tension emerged between authors who supported a monistic, method-oriented science and those who supported a dualistic, object-oriented science.[1] As is now clear, similar oppositions unsettled the development of psychology; instead of a cohesive discipline, different levels of fragmentation have been uncovered, showing psychology's vulnerability from a theoretical point of view and also from that of practice (Part 2). Various proposals of unification were discussed in Part 3, with various aims and different degrees of complexity.

Despite such attempts to unify psychology, the traditional tensions and vulnerabilities of the discipline are apparent; sometimes authors hold a clear position, sometimes they are not explicit about their assumptions. Following the brief exposition of clinical psychology's roots and the analysis of the Italian and American definitions of the scope of the discipline, this work showed the emergence of different, mutually incoherent, seemingly uncritical conceptions of clinical psychology which display their deficiencies. Indeed, this situation highlights the problematic inclination of psychologists to minimize and not render explicit their fundamental philosophical and theoretical assumptions.

The present chapter presents an empirical study concerning the manner in which psychologists see their discipline as a science and as a profession. This topic has not yet been treated substantially in the psychological literature. As was illustrated in detail in Chapter 5, in 1984 Kimble found that psychologists implicitly endorse two conflicting epistemological cultures and thus two different ways of conceiving psychology as a scientific discipline. Norcross, Karpiak, and Santoro (2005; see

Chapter 11), summarizing the outcomes of six significant research studies conducted from 1960 to 2003, present a similarly fragmented scenario about the theoretical references psychologists use in their professional practice. In the latter study, the modal orientation reported by psychologists is eclecticism, which is idiosyncratic in character and thus feeds an inclination toward fragmentation.

The limits of these studies is that their outcomes are based on self-reports and closed question-based measures, which do not allow for the exploration of hidden, underlying dimensions of psychological practice beyond the quantitative analysis of self-reported data coming from the subjects. In other words, those studies focused on denotative aspects only, that is, on the objects to which terms refer. The connotative aspects, those connected to the abstract, idiosyncratic meaning of terms, turned out to be ignored, precisely because of the authors' methodology. These outcomes are surely useful, but fail to grasp deep dimensions of how psychologists represent their own practice.

Professional practice is a strategic area where both the theoretical and the applied dimensions of the discipline strive to find a reciprocal and efficient balance. Indeed, the relevance of professional practice lies in its double concern about theoretical issues, whose purpose is to direct professional behavior toward specifiable and desirable ends, and practical issues relating to the specificities of what the user requires from the practitioner in ecological contexts. From this standpoint, it is useful to explore connotative aspects of the link between theory and practice among practitioners. This issue is examined in the empirical study which will be discussed presently.

The aim of the study presented in this chapter is to explore the practitioners' different perspectives on psychology and to uncover the kind of features that they attribute to their work as practitioners in a scientifically based field. The focus lies in those emerging aspects that may be compared with the theoretical issues illustrated in the previous chapters. Indeed, the approach underlying the theoretical remarks presented here is substantially top-down, in the sense that theory precedes and should inform professional practice. This kind of approach strongly reflects the academic way of creating and managing knowledge: the privileged perspective is the theoretical one. In contrast, the present empirical study is based on a bottom-up approach, in the sense that professional practice provides data that are potentially useful for theory construction. This kind of approach is strongly related to the practitioner's way of creating and managing knowledge. According to this perspective, research should integrate the traditional top-down approach and the bottom-up approach by giving voice to issues coming from professional practice in the field. This, in turn, must be strongly connected with the work of those who deal with theory construction, as it was noted in Part 2, so as to give applied psychology a solid, scientific basis and to render academic research significant and useful for practitioners.

Premise

In order to explore and understand practitioners' different perspectives on psychology it is fundamental to ask practitioners what they believe psychology is and how they operate as psychologists in their everyday practice. As already noted, this can be revealed through a bottom-up approach, i.e., an approach devoted to exploring how psychology is done starting from the practice itself, namely the ways practitioners operate while addressing real-life problems. Practice thus understood presumes implicit beliefs and assumptions about the discipline, which in turn shape and influence practice. These beliefs and assumptions are emotionally characterized, in the sense that they deal with emotional aspects related to how psychology is understood and performed by individual practitioners. In this regard, the following considerations about group-functioning can help to provide theoretical and practical foundations for the exploration of this subject.

Theoretical background: emotions and their social display

The study which will presently be discussed stems from the assumption that emotions are the primary source which determines human behavior. Emotions are usually defined as complex reaction patterns by which the individual attempts to deal with a personally significant matter or event (VandenBos, 2007). The quality of the emotion is determined by the significance and the meaning of the stimulus, so as to readily react to cogent aspects of the environment. Emotions are predominantly associated with individual processes, which are hard-wired, fixed ways of moderating the connection between the individual and the environment. Primary emotions, those that are biologically determined, trigger automatic behavioral responses which have an evolutionary relevance, protecting the individual from potential dangers to self or valued others. Emotions are aimed at reacting to relevant environmental aspects in an economic way, i.e., involving primitive, direct ways to connect relevant stimuli to (supposedly) best reactions. In other words, emotions aim at bypassing complex cognitive operations, which are very demanding in terms of cognitive resources and useless in potentially dangerous situations, where prompt reactions are required. However, emotions are not just important determiners of individual behavior, but also play a primary role in group and organizational processes.

The Italian psychologist Renzo Carli and his colleagues developed over time an analysis of the role of the emotions in organizational settings in order to understand the dynamics of the behavior of social groups. In line with the literature on group dynamics, the authors noticed that the behaviors of organized social groups such as groups carrying out teamwork, sports teams, professional groups or simply groups that share common objectives are not only guided by rational considerations which would permit them to achieve their explicit (i.e., productive) goals in the most direct and effective way. It is perhaps assumed that behaviors of groups and organizations are usually determined in such a way, but they are not. Rather, their behaviors are influenced by factors that are completely unrelated to those goals, although such groups or organizations are naturally expected to be focused on those goals for which they were formed or established. In fact it is observed that groups or organizations appear to show two different dimensions (for more detail, see Carli and Paniccia, 1981). On the one hand, there is a "productive" dimension which concerns the rational planning oriented to the achievement of explicit goals, through processes such as the specifications of roles, the division of tasks, the adoption of goal-oriented strategies, and so on. It is the most evident, explicit dimension of an organized social group. On the other hand, the second dimension concerns the emotional aspects that influence the explicit functioning of that group and the way the members emotionally experience the context they share. Here, emotion refers to the way the members of a group sharing a context define an aspect of reality, experiencing it in its emotional dimension or the way an individual (or members of a group) idiosyncratically relates to specific aspects of his or her reality. Although the two dimensions, the explicit (pragmatic) and the implicit (emotional), may be mutually coherent, they also may not be. In other words, the emotional aspects that substantiate a specific social group can either serve or hinder the achievement of its explicit goals.

As was previously remarked, emotions are triggered by the attribution of a certain meaning to selected stimuli of the environment. In operational terms, meaning may be defined as the mediator between a stimulus and a response. In other words, meaning is the process or state which is assumed to be a necessary consequence of the reception of a stimulus and a necessary antecedent for the production of a specific response (Osgood, Suci, and Tannenbaum, 1957). In this perspective, meaning is the theoretical term that accounts for the connection between an environmental event and the specific response of a subject. In general terms, meaning is the way in which a stimulus is perceived, or interpreted; the way it is perceived evidently influences the response to that stimulus.

Carli's two-dimensional proposal – dealing with explicit and implicit groups' functioning – requires a clarification of the underlying processes of meaning attribution to environmental stimuli. Indeed, the implicit, emotional dimension reflects the idiosyncratic attribution model shared by those who are members of that group, in addition to the explicit, rational dimension. In this attempt at clarification, it may be useful to refer to Charles Osgood and colleagues' proposal concerning meaning (1957). The authors maintain that the concept of meaning deals with stimuli that reliably elicit predictable patterns of behavior. For example, the presence of a wild, dangerous animal elicits a predictable pattern of escape and avoidance. However, this example refers to the biological hard-wired mechanisms connected to self-preservation. In our complex world, it is understandable that subjects attribute meaning to initially meaningless stimuli because they learn associations between them (conditioning), between stimuli with an already conditioned meaning and stimuli which "borrow" some properties of that meaning. In more detail, when a stimulus appears somehow repeatedly contiguous with the original meaning stimulus, it will acquire some properties of the original stimulus, i.e., it will be increasingly associated with some portion of the behavior elicited by the original stimulus. For example, the buzzer signaling food distribution becomes a stimulus of salivation for the animal. The contiguous unconditioned stimulus – or sign of the original stimulus – then becomes associated with some parts of the total behavior elicited by the original stimulus itself: for example, the sound of the buzzer will elicit saliva-tion. Such a process is defined as *representational* because it is part of the same behavior elicited by the original stimulus, evoking internal responses comparable to those elicited by the original stimulus. Moreover, the process is defined as *media-tional* because this sort of internal stimulation may now mediate the production of a variety of behaviors (in our example, escaping, leaping, hiding, etc.). In reference to Figure 12.1, the first stage – namely, the association of signs with representational mediators – may be called *decoding* or interpretation. The second stage – namely, the association of mediated self-stimulation with overt behaviors – is called *encoding* and is connected to the expression of opinions and ideas.[2]

In this perspective, "words represent things because they produce in human organisms some replica of the actual behavior toward these things, as a mediation process" (Osgood et al., 1957: 7). What makes this approach interesting is that it permits one to grasp the connection between real objects and events and their attributed meanings, which are influenced by the repeated associations between the original stimuli and the series of contiguous reactions that the individual has had to it. Such a theoretical framework for meaning and interpretation is able to oper-ationally account for the production of individual, idiosyncratic meanings, since the meanings attributed to signs by different individuals will vary to the extent that their behaviors toward the things signified have varied. In this sense, the meanings attributed to signs belonging to a specific context will reflect the specificity of subjects' experiences within that context, in agreement with Carli and colleagues' work. In this sense, emotions as a reaction triggered by a process of meaning attribution are considered to be equated with meaning, one being the necessary antecedent of the other.

How are such processes displayed in organizations or groups sharing some cogent environmental stimuli? Renzo Carli tried to detail this phenomenon through the notion of *collusion*.[3] Such a word comes from Latin *cum-ludere*, to play

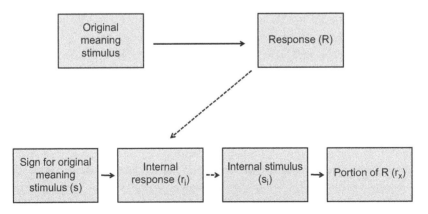

FIGURE 12.1 Meaning as a representational mediational process: the development of a sign and associated meaning
Source: adapted from Osgood, Suci, and Tannebaum (1957)

with, together, and *colludere*, conspire, and thus it suggests the idea of sharing something within a group of people. In fact, collusion, as a psychological term, refers to the common way the members of a social group emotionally experience, or attribute meaning to, the context to which they belong (Carli, 1993: 14). In other words, there are common, shared, emotional components among those who belong to the same context. For example, the members of a school class share a common emotional representation of their context (their belonging to that class, to that school with that faculty) beyond the explicit goals (i.e., learning). By context, we specifically mean those elements of the real world which turn out to be cogent environmental stimuli for those who share the belonging to the context itself. From such a perspective, collusive processes keep social cohesiveness within those who belong to that group, serving as a sort of common, shared view with reference to that specific context.

The local culture

Returning to the central subject of this chapter, we can consider the case of being a psychologist in a specific cultural and social context and how this can influence the way psychologists understand their profession. Being a psychologist entails the experience of a specific context and learned responses to a number of cogent environmental (i.e., political, professional, theoretical, etc.) stimuli toward which the group (the psychologists belonging to that professional community, association, country, etc.) develops a sort of "common attitude." Collusive processes – being social displays of emotions – specify the way the members react to cogent aspects of the environment. This is the reason why emotions *de facto* always refer to a relational system or context, that is to a relation of some kind between the subject and some selected cogent portion of the environment. The analysis of collusive processes allows for the investigation into the emotional, meaning–attribution processes shared by the members of a group in a particular context. Such an analysis may reveal important aspects of the relational patterns of a group as a whole by means of the disclosure of their shared emotional models of reality, beyond the explicit and rational goals for which the group was originally formed or established.

   The collusive processes characterizing a specific social group within a specific context form a *local culture*[4] (Carli and Paniccia, 2002: 15–17). In behavioral terms, a local culture may be defined as the usual meaning attribution pattern of the members of a group sharing common experiences within a specific context. These collusive processes are mainly conveyed by language, both spoken and written. It is plausible that such processes may also be displayed by non-linguistic cues such as nonverbal behaviors, as Osgood and colleagues suggest, but these cues are cumbersome to record and probably insensitive to subtle meanings. Thus, the crucial point here is that the analysis of language allows for the best possible investigation of the important aspects of a local culture, disclosing its deeper features. In other terms, the key hypothesis is that language is the main door to exploring the emotional world of a social group. However language and its formal structure also, and we may even say mainly, convey aspects relating to the explicit achievement of organizational goals: the literal meaning of language. Thus, in what sense does language convey emotions, or meaning–attribution processes?

Language and local culture

The main assumption of the study presented in this chapter is that the analysis of the recurrence of, so-called, "dense" words – by means of proper software – reveals important features of the local culture of the social group whose members produced language (both spoken or written). From this perspective it may be said that there is a sort of isomorphism between the local culture and the emotional structure of language (Carli and Paniccia, 2002: 57). The assumption behind the above hypothesis is that every word has an emotional value, namely a history of associations with other, contiguous, repeated experiences. Some words have a low value (such as articles, adverbs, pronouns, conjunctions) while others have a high value. Those words which have high emotional value are called dense words (Carli and Paniccia, 2002: 23). For example, "bomb" is a dense word, because it conveys polysemic emotional meanings and evokes many emotional hints. In contrast, a word such as "and" is not a dense word, as it needs to be inserted within a sequence of words in order to organize emotional dimension. Alone, it contains ambiguity and does not convey emotional meaning. Dense words can be defined as symbolic expressions whose emotional meaning precedes the intentional meaning as it is organized by the syntactic and rhetorical structure of language (Carli and Paniccia, 2002).

From this perspective, what is relevant in order to uncover the collusive processes is not the intentional network of connections among words, which conveys the intentional meaning of a text as we read it. Rather, it is the assumption that, beyond this connecting structure of the text, the analysis of selected recurring words (i.e., dense words) can show a new and different meaning among those words. Thus in order to understand the emotional dimension of the texts under analysis it is not necessary to analyze the syntactic connections between words conveying intentional meanings. The goal is not language *per se*, but the sequences of single (dense) words, parceled out from the linguistic structure of the original text. These words, making up new sequences not present in the original text (ordinary language), may suggest new emotional meanings that have to be interpreted in inferential ways.

Emotional analysis of texts

The analysis of the recurrence of dense words may be undertaken by using a specific method called emotional analysis of texts (AET, for *analisi emozionale del testo*), developed over time by the Italian psychologist Renzo Carli and his colleagues. AET uses both quantitative and qualitative methods in order to catch those hidden dimensions emerging from the language of clusters of subjects sharing a common view of the issue at stake. AET has given rise to a theory about the analysis of the emotional relations among the dense words of a text. Sequences of dense words are highly polysemic, that is they can convey many different meanings; AET works on sequences of words extracted from a text in order to reduce their polysemy, unraveling the emotional meaning of the text.

AET has been used in very different contexts and with different aims, depending on which kind of data are collected and the way they are collected. As mentioned above AET is used to interpret the emotional meaning conveyed by sequences of those dense words which result from computer analysis. The researcher attempts to connect the sequences of dense words with the features of the social group at stake and its context, in order to better reconstruct the emerging local culture. The choice of the dense words depends on the consideration of two aspects: the stimulus – in response to which the text has been produced – and the context – which represents the common salient aspects of reality shared by those who produced the text.[5] Indeed, these are crucial aspects of the local culture to be analyzed.

The methodology is fully presented in Carli and Paniccia (2002) and good examples of its potential applications are Battisti (2006), Carli and Paniccia (2006) and Dolcetti, Giovagnoli, Paniccia, and Carli (2006). The first is a study of the representations of students of the psychology faculty about their future profession, compared with the representations of psychology of the potential users of psychological services. Battisti (2006) investigates the representations of students of the psychology faculty about their internship experience before the degree examination, exploring different kinds of professional representations. Carli and Paniccia (2006) employ this method to explore the hidden dimensions emerging from the transcript text obtained from psychotherapy that lasted four years. Dolcetti et al. (2006) explore the hidden dimensions emerging from texts produced by clients and psychotherapists about the nature of problems addressed during psychotherapy.

We may consider the following example of a sequence of dense words of a text produced by a client receiving a psychotherapeutic treatment. The sequence may be: to be afraid of – late – session. The reconstruction of the emotional meaning can be accomplished in many different ways: for example, "I am afraid to come to session, then I come late"; "I am afraid to come late, then I come to session"; "The session comes late in my life, alas! I fear for myself," and so on. The dense words must be organized in reference to the context of the subject who has produced the text from which the sequence of dense words have been drawn out. The "correct" meaning can only refer to the specificity of the circumstances at stake, reconstructing the emotional meaning (i.e., the meaning–attribution processes) by means of associative inferences, starting from the sequence of the dense words at stake (Carli and Paniccia, 2002: 53). This is the reason why the researcher must have at least a preliminary knowledge of the context to explore so that the meaning of words may be reconstructed by means of temporary working hypotheses, which are tested through the process of polysemy reduction among the words extracted by the software.[6] In this sense, the same sequence of dense words may convey different meanings in different contexts, so knowledge of the features of the context is essential. Then, once the intentional, linguistic meaning has been deconstructed, the interpretation of the sequences of dense words permits another kind of (emotional) meaning to be reconstructed, often very different from the literal meaning of the text.

In the present study, the material for analysis was collected from reports produced by psychologists. The key assumption is that a report is a sort of description of an event based on idiosyncratic interpretative models of meaning attribution; in other words, the description of the object of the report (the stimulus) is strongly influenced by those models which emerge within the report itself. Indeed, proposing to someone to produce a report about a specific object/event induces him/her to clarify his/her theoretical preconceptions about the object/event itself (Battisti, 2006: 122). To produce a report fosters a reflection on what has been experienced within the relation with the object/event about which the report is written. Thus, the creation of a report brings to light the meaning attribution processes about the object/event at stake, since it promotes the passage from the episodic dimension (i.e., each episode with which the relation with the object/event is made) to the procedural dimension (i.e., the meaning the producer attributes to the flow of such episodes) (Carli, 2007: 188). In other words, by means of the creation of a report, the producer has the opportunity to think about the meaning of the relation with the object/event as a whole, revealing his/her own subjective way to emotionally experience that relation. These assumptions support the use of the report as the main object of study in the present study, with the further aim of uncovering/discovering those meanings attribution models that make up collusive processes.

Introduction to the present research

The study presented here is intended as a preliminary exploratory endeavor of a general area of concern in order to try to identify research issues which can be further investigated in the future, in accordance with the exploratory methods of inquiry (Tukey, 1980). The perspective adopted is factual, in the sense that the goal is to accurately describe the collected data through proper procedures (Hoyningen-Huene, 1987: 511). For this reason, the research is based on multivariate text procedures which are intended to formulate hypotheses rather than to test hypotheses. The aim is to discover preliminary hypotheses to test, which are made provisionally in order to organize the available data. Generating provisional hypotheses allows knowledge about the context at stake to be constructed. The outcomes of the hypotheses here formulated can then be tested empirically at a later stage, with a larger degree of generality, by means of confirmatory analyses.

The present research deals with the way practitioners view their discipline, considering psychology's double soul: theory and practice. We hypothesize that the texts produced by a sizeable number of psychologists can convey important aspects about the way psychologists emotionally represent their profession, beyond the formal, often trite aspects that emerged from the reading of such texts. Those emotional aspects are relevant for the present work because they necessarily inform the practice of psychology which, like any other human activity, is heavily influenced by the theoretical preconceptions of those who practice it. Our hypothesis is that the emotional dimensions revealed by the present analysis can shed some light on the way theory and practice are really articulated in everyday professional practice, showing those hidden conceptions that most characterize psychology as a professional endeavor. This would also show possible symmetries and asymmetries between those two spheres of psychology – practice and academy, practice and theory – which have been shown to be too often divergent or of insignificant mutual impact.

Subjects and procedures

During a period of one year, the author emailed a self-administered questionnaire to 716 Italian psychologists working in different disciplinary areas and living in two regions of Italy, Lombardia and Lazio. The email addresses were collected through the website of the professional psychologists association in Lombardia[7] and through personal relationships with colleagues. Two weeks after the first email, those who didn't answer were requested again via email to answer the attached form. After two attempts, the contact was considered not included in the research. Of 716 contacted psychologists, 94 answered and returned the reports (response rate: 13.1 percent). The creation of the reports was encouraged through a target question: "We ask you to think about your professional experience regarding psychology as a science and as a profession and to write your considerations down."[8]

The subjects who answered were 62 females and 32 males between the ages of 25 and 69 (M = 40.8, SD = 11); 20 of them lived in Lazio, the rest in Lombardia; 62 of them declared themselves to be licensed psychotherapists. As shown in Table 12.1, psychodynamic orientation was predominant (54 subjects, 50.8 percent), followed by other orientations (19 subjects, 17.9 percent), cognitive-behavioral orientation (9 subjects, 8.5 percent) and systemic orientation (7 subjects, 6.6 percent); 5 subjects didn't answer (4.7 percent).

With regard to their professional activity (Table 12.2), 28 subjects declared that they worked in the health field (26.3 percent), 20 in other fields (18.8 percent), 13 in

TABLE 12.1 Primary theoretical orientations as a percentage of the sample

Primary theoretical orientation	n	%
Psychodynamic	54	50.8
Cognitive-behavioral	9	8.5
Systemic	7	6.6
Other	19	17.9
No answer	5	4.7

TABLE 12.2 Primary professional areas as a percentage of the sample

Professional areas	n	%
Health	28	26.3
Child/adolescence	13	12.2
Psychiatry	11	10.3
Rehabilitation	9	8.5
Forensic	3	2.8
Drug abuse	2	1.9
Other fields	20	18.8
More than one area	8	7.6

child and adolescence psychology (12.2 percent), 11 in psychiatry (10.3 percent), 9 in the rehabilitation area (8.5 percent), 8 in more than one of these areas (7.6 percent), 3 in forensic psychology (2.8 percent), 2 in the drug abuse area (1.9 percent). Regarding the employment conditions, most of our sample were freelance professionals (80 subjects, 85.1 percent), 9 subjects declared that they were employees (9.5 percent), 3 subjects declared that they both worked freelance and were be employed (3.2 percent), 2 answers were missing (2 percent).

The form presented the study as "a multidisciplinary research aimed at describing the way psychologists consider their own discipline." Participants were asked to consider the target question as a stimulus for better illustrating their opinion about the issue at stake. The form also suggested writing down one's opinion at two different times. The subjects were advised to write their first opinion, then to wait until the following day to complete their thoughts about the issue, in order to foster a deeper and broader analysis of it. Furthermore, the form asked some information about the education and the professional practice of the compiler. The explanatory variables considered were: sex (two levels, male/female), age (two levels, younger/older than 35), residence (two levels, Lombardia/Lazio), type of degree (two levels, psychology/other),[9] year of graduation (three levels, up to 1987/1988–99/from 2000 on),[10] psychotherapy license (two levels, yes/no), theoretical orientation (four levels, psychodynamics/cognitive-behavioral/systemic/other), area of practice (eight levels, psychiatry/drug abuse/child psychology/forensic psychology/health psychology/rehabilitation/more areas/other).

The reports collected have been analyzed by the software Alceste (Analyse Lexicale par Contexte d'un Ensemble de Segments de Texte), by Max Reinert (1993). This program is able to operate on the text and to perform factor and cluster analysis, which can show how dense words organize and create clusters, according to their statistical relations. This kind of relation displays those collusive processes that differentiate each cluster (also called *cultural repertoire*).

The procedure followed envisaged the following steps. A corpus was created, that is, a complete text (a Word document) upon which the analysis was carried out, and which was composed of the 94 reports collected. Next, the corpus was prepared for the analysis. Homographic words with different linguistic meanings were differentiated: the words underwent a process of disambiguation, for example differentiating between words with different meanings, but written in the same way (for example, in Italian "legge" can be either "law" or "he/she reads"). Graphic signs (commas, periods, etc.) were removed, because they were irrelevant for the software analysis. Furthermore, in the preparation of the corpus explanatory variables were selected which were considered interesting for consideration (those specified above). This allowed the matching of each cluster found by the software with the most distinctive variables. Then, the software produced a list of words (or, better, lexemes)[11] to be analyzed. This step involved the choice of the dense words to be included in the analysis. Afterward, the software executed the analyses on those lexemes in order to identify the clusters, which were themselves differentiated by the presence of the same recurring, specific dense words. Then, factors were found with regard to the number of clusters (factors = number of clusters −1). Every sequence of dense words is composed of words recurring within a specific text unit, namely a unit selected by the software on the basis of specific words recurring within portions of the corpus. Every sequence of dense words significantly differs from other sequences recurring in other text units (Carli and Paniccia, 2002: 55), thus determining the reciprocal diversity of each cluster. The assumption is that the recurring words of a text unit illustrate the specific features of a local culture, the one identified by each cluster thanks to the process of cluster formation. Within each cluster, dense words (lexemes) are hierarchically organized, from the more statistically significant to the less statistically significant. Such an arrangement allows for the reconstruction of the emotional meaning conveyed by each cluster by means of a procedure whose goal is to decrease the polysemy that characterize each lexeme (if considered individually). Indeed, for each cluster, words (lexemes) are arranged in a list where their chi2 values progressively decrease: the meaning of each word has a limiting function on the polysemy of those words that precede it in the statistical importance (Carli and Paniccia, 2006). In this way, AET unveils the relations between the dense words within each cluster that determine the meaning of the cluster (cultural repertoire) at stake.

Results

The complete corpus is rather large: 55 pages, type Times New Roman, point size 12. The total number of words is 35,244; the actual number of lexemes considered (reduced forms) is 1,612. Within those lexemes, 447 lexemes were analyzed. The clusters (cultural repertoires) emerged on the basis of 528 ECUs (elementary context units), that is 55.17 percent of the total ECUs (957); this is considered to be a valid value, showing the reliability of the analysis (Reinert, 1993). The average number of dense words (lexemes) analyzed for each ECU was 5.42. Table 12.3 shows the variance referring to the factors in the factorial space.

TABLE 12.3 Factor loadings for exploratory factor analysis

Factors	Variance (%)	Cumulative variance (%)
1	31.20	31.20
2	27.02	58.22
3	22.89	81.11
4	18.88	100

TABLE 12.4 Chi2 values for cluster analysis

Cluster	1	2	3	4	5
1	**303**	0	−16	-37	−23
2	−24	**284**	−5	-30	−54
3	−25	−13	**200**	21	−45
4	−12	0	−3	**98**	−31
5	−19	−117	−21	0	**375**

Note: Values indicating clusters' specificity in boldface

Table 12.4 shows the statistical specificity of each cluster (chi2 values) found by means of the cluster analysis. The data are rather cohesive, indeed almost all chi2 values are negative or zero, so the clusters are significantly different from each other (an exception is the relationship between cluster 4 and 3, which is slightly positive).

In Table 12.5, the statistical relation between factors and clusters is shown. Factors are latent variables that make up the factorial space (or cultural space, in AET terms) where clusters form. These are the values that show the relation between the clusters and the factors in the factorial space: the values which identify the strongest relations between clusters and factors (in their negative and positive sides) are in boldface.

Table 12.6 (see the Appendix for the Italian version) shows the dense words (lexemes) that make up each cluster, arranged in a decreasing manner according to

TABLE 12.5 Chi2 values indicating the relations between clusters and factors

	Factor 1	Factor 2	Factor 3	Factor 4
Cluster 1	0.231	**−1.156**	−0.475	0.100
Cluster 2	**−0.711**	−0.170	0.678	−0.403
Cluster 3	−0.357	**0.703**	**−1.118**	−0.179
Cluster 4	−0.322	0.282	0.348	**1.410**
Cluster 5	**0.782**	0.401	0.095	−0.157

TABLE 12.6 Chi2 values of main lexemes involved in clusters formation

Cluster 1		Cluster 2		Cluster 3		Cluster 4		Cluster 5	
Chi2	*lexemes*	*Chi2*	*lexemes*	*Chi2*	*lexemes*	*Chi2*	*lexemes*	*Chi2*	*lexemes*
67.89	project<	85.55	client<	72.94	objective<	35.86	human<	44.46	work
52.92	institution<	42.23	theor<	47.49	subjective<	33.34	job	34.02	medic<
43.35	organization<	21.94	intervention<	44.09	assum<	33.34	stimul<	24.35	patient
38.37	citizen<	20.15	thought<	44.09	skill	26.01	therap<	15.99	educat<
38.37	territor<	19.50	relational	36.60	limit<	24.09	grow	15.57	hospital<
29.64	cultur<	19.49	useful	32.06	epistemolog<	22.79	method<	14.05	pay<
29.17	group<	16.55	complexity	32.06	philosoph<	18.17	outcome	13.60	accept<
26.19	social	14.84	ortopedic	21.83	intuit<	16.54	read<	12.12	apprenticeship
23.66	commissioner<	13.64	explore	19.35	nature	16.54	protocol<	11.63	contract<
21.38	famil<	13.53	techni<	16.95	variable<	15.93	life	11.63	money
19.62	adult<	13.27	lose	15.84	scientific	15.10	duty	10.66	psychotherap<
18.86	coexist<	12.01	share<	14.96	rigour<	11.50	verif<	10.22	university

their chi2 values, which points out the statistical importance of each lexeme in the process of cluster formation. In the analysis, only those lexemes with significant (higher) values were considered. The analysis ended when the meaning of the cluster at stake seemed to fully emerged through the consideration of its dense words (lexemes).

Table 12.7 shows the chi2 values of the explanatory variables that turned out to be significantly associated to the clusters. It shows the statistical relations between clusters and explanatory variables. In other words, those are the explanatory variables that statistically associate with each emergent cluster and define some features which are strongly associated with those who contributed to the formation of that specific cluster. In the table are reported only three variables with the highest chi2 values, those that are the most representative of each cluster.

Figure 12.2 shows the factorial space (or cultural space) where five clusters (or cultural repertoires) emerged. The space is organized by two axes, the vertical (first axis) and the horizontal (second axis). Two clusters are in the upper-left quarter (clusters 3 and 4), one in the upper-right quarter (cluster 5), one in the lower-left (cluster 2), and one in the lower-right (cluster 1).

The clusters and their meanings

Here we begin the analysis of the co-occurrence of dense words within each cluster, discussing their reciprocal relations and their positions in the factorial space.

TABLE 12.7 Highest chi2 values associated with professional characteristics for each cluster of subjects

	Cluster 1	Cluster 2	Cluster 3	Cluster 4	Cluster 5
Psychotherapy license – no	50.92	119.90			
Area of practice – other	54.49	107.58			
Residence – Lazio	49.84	168.84			
Year of graduation – up to 1987			47.90		
Theoretical orientation – systemic			39.94		
Sex – m			25.30		
Area of practice – health				44.69	
Age > 35				27.97	
Psychotherapy license – yes				23.67	83.54
Residence – Lombardia					126.64
Theoretical orientation – other					89.27

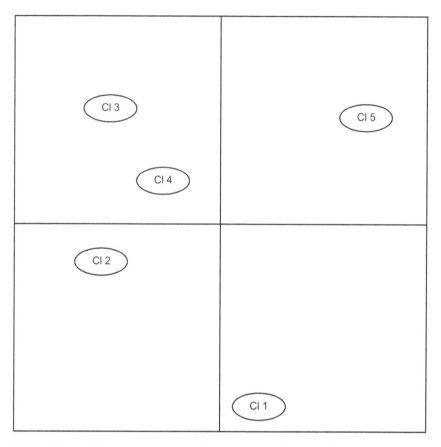

FIGURE 12.2 Graphical representation of the clusters (Cl; cultural repertoires) in the factorial (cultural) space

It is worth remembering that each cluster is thought to be representative of a local culture, where typical, idiosyncratic models of meaning attribution to cogent stimuli of the environment emerge. In other words, each cluster is somehow representative of different ways to interpret the stimulus question and, thus, to organize meanings connected to the content of the question itself. Each cluster represents different ways of perceiving psychology, uncovering different points of view toward the same issue, namely psychology as a profession and as a science. That being said, we shall consider the meanings emerging from each cluster in detail (see Table 12.6). The analysis will report the lexemes in hierarchical order, starting from the most relevant in statistical terms. For each cluster, all the lexemes analyzed will be reported, in order to make understandable the process of polysemic reduction.

For clarity, the analysis will start with cluster 5, with the aim of better organizing the outcomes. Cluster 5 is on the right side of the first axis. This cluster is characterized by dense words that are associated with illustrative variables such as: psychotherapy license = yes, theoretical orientation = other, residence = Lombardia. This means that psychologists expressing those features significantly contributed to the formation of cluster 5. Here we present the inferential process that led to progressively decreasing the polysemy of the dense words characterizing cluster 5. Table 12.6 provides the list of lexemes (see also the Appendix for the Italian version).

Lavora< (to work, job, practice)

The lexeme with the highest chi2 value is lavora<, from *labor*, effort, strenuous physical or mental work. To devote physical or mental energy to a productive activity. To have a turnover, to have many clients. This first lexeme is very polysemic and it points to an activity with highly emotional value, especially, for the psychological community in Italy where the employment opportunities are scarce (Bosio, 2011). The lexeme is connected to issues relating to employment, but also to underemployment and unemployment, which are basic concerns of the current psychological profession in the current social and economic context. The primary organizing factor of this cluster is the issue of working and employment; it may be deemed to be an extremely desired dimension, even though it may evoke concerns about the future.

Lavora< (to work, job, practice)
Medic< (medical, physician)
Pazient< (patient)

Employment, the possibility to work and earn money, may be anchored to the medical profession, which is socially strong and highly esteemed. This may lead an individual to give up a specific professional psychological identity, fostering the identification with the medical profession. In other words, psychology as a profession may be considered legitimate only if it merges with the medical profession, thus acquiring its particular features, among the others, the existence of a disease which connotes that the client is in fact an ill individual. Such considerations may lead to a model of psychology that is highly medicalized: in the relation with the psychologist the client acquires a passive role, the role of patient. In this view, the psychologist would possess the means to heal the disease. The merging of these two professions would permit one to work, to practice, to have a job. It may be said that for those who contributed to the formation of this cluster, the psychological profession may be conceived in this way, provided that the clients' pain is deemed a (medical) pathology.

Lavora< (to work, job)
Medic< (medical, physician)
Pazient< (patient)
Educa< (to teach, to train)

Educa< derives from *e*, outside, and *ducare (ducere)*, to lead, to draw, to raise. To train one's character and personality, especially young people; to drill. This word may refer to the kind of psychological intervention provided by the professional model so far illustrated: the psychologist brings an ill body to health. In a sense, the educational intervention is an orthopedic intervention, that is it fosters the elimination of the deviations from the norm, consonant with the medical model. In other words, the asymmetrical relation between the client and the psychologist (borrowed from the physician–patient relationship) is considered as the means of bringing back the illness to normality (*restitutio ad integrum*). Here, the psychologist is considered to be a skilled professional, who autonomously determines what is healthy and what is not and whose expertise doesn't require the active client–patient participation. The psychologist is an external observer of the client's system, about which he is an expert. Another important aspect evoked by Educa< in this model of psychology is the evident psychologist's need to be trained in order to be allowed to practice, as if the psychologist should be required to be accepted by those who already practice the profession and occupy a privileged position. The need to be trained seems to be required in order to become part of the establishment, with the aim of acquiring those skills that constitute the psychological expertise.

> *Lavora< (to work, job)*
> *Medic< (medical, physician)*
> *Pazient< (patient)*
> *Educa< (to teach, to train)*
> *Ospedal< (hospital)*

The hospital is the place *par excellence* where the medical profession is practiced. It is the place that legitimizes the value and the social recognition of the profession. It is the place where the professional training is accomplished, within the lines thus far illustrated. The hospital is the place where the processes connected to training and practice acquire social visibility and legitimacy.

> *Lavora< (to work, job)*
> *Medic< (medical, physician)*
> *Pazient< (patient)*
> *Educa< (to teach, to train)*
> *Ospedal< (hospital)*
> *Paga< (to pay, wage)*
> *Accett< (to accept, desk, reception)*
> *Tirocin< (apprenticeship, internship)*

Proceeding with the analysis, it is clear that the strong merging between the psychological profession and the medical profession opens up the possibility to earn money (Paga< to pay, wage), to be paid for one's work. However, the inclusion of the psychological profession in the medical profession seems to be uncertain, because it is dependent on the acceptance (Accett< to accept, desk, reception) of other people (future colleagues), by means of a specific training – the internship (Tirocin< apprenticeship, internship) – which is the entrance to the professional world. In order to work with, and in the same manner as physicians, psychologists must be accepted and included in that system. Thus, this model seems to abdicate a specific psychological identity, in favor of a different professional identity that is not specifically psychological, but which offers many benefits. It is a different identity, considered to be socially more legitimate and able to guarantee a good income (later in the analysis there are lexemes with lower chi2 values but meaningful in this sense: soldi [money], guadagn< [gain], stipendi< [salary]).

The analysis of key words in cluster 5 will end here, since the meaning of the other following lexemes did not add much to the meaning of those already specified.[12]

It is worth noting that the first reference to a psychological service, namely psychotherapy (however it is shared with the medical profession), shows up rather late in the analysis, with a low chi2 value (10.66; not reported in the table). This is coherent with the hypothesis that in this model the prevalent emotional meaning system is about the merging with the medical world, which guarantees a strong social identity and prospects of income. However, the inclusion in this élite is problematic because it is not immediate; indeed, it is connected to a specific training, to the uncertainty of being accepted by the group. Such a possible inclusion in the élite is not based on expertise. This is made clear by the fact that no words about specific psychological (or medical) services or methods are mentioned in the corpus. Precisely, psychotherapy seems to be the only shared area with the medical profession, representing a sort of "anchorage" to it. Here, the professional identity of psychology is accomplished through the merging with the medical profession, which guarantees employment, prospects of income, social legitimacy and credibility.

Let us now deal with cluster 2. Cluster 2 is on the left side of the first axis, but it is in an opposite position (compared with cluster 5) in respect to the second axis (see Figure 12.2). This cluster is characterized by dense words that associate with the illustrative variables: psychotherapy license = no, area of practice = other, residence = Lazio. This means that psychologists with those features significantly contributed to the formation of cluster 2. The words included in the cluster are the following (see Table 12.6 for the list).

Client< (client)

The lexeme with the highest chi2 value, Client< (client), comes from Latin *colere*, to farm, or from *klyo* (Ancient Greek), to listen to, to lend an ear, so to give attention, to follow. This word reveals the recipient of the psychological intervention. The client is the one who actively asks for a qualified service on the basis of specific needs. The professional collaborates with clients with the aim to design and deliver psychological services, as in all other kinds of services production (see Normann, 1984).

Client< (client)
Teori< (theory)

The lexeme comes from the Ancient Greek *theoros*, to behold, to regard, to contemplate, to observe, to look at. The two words together seem to suggest the need to establish a connection with the client, whose needs' analysis will reveal core features of his/her requirement for a psychological intervention. In other words, the client needs to be considered through the lens of a specific theoretical outlook, in order to better understand his/her needs. Here, there seem to be two emotional meanings connected to the notion of theory: on one hand, theory can be understood as a valuable outlook that fosters knowledge about the client, which is the basis for the design of a tailor-made psychological intervention. On the other hand, the notion of theory may be emotionally understood as a model that is imposed and is irrespective of the client's needs, which are considered in an unproblematic way. Such a polysemy may be decreased by the analysis of the following words.

Client< (client)
Teori< (theory)
Interven< (intervention)

The lexeme Interven< comes from *inter*, between, among, and *venire*, to come; it means to "come among," to participate, to contribute. The word seems to suggest a sort of mediation between the psychological expertise (held by the professional) and the needs of those who may be the users of psychological services (the potential clients). Thus, the word refers to a relational dimension, where people interact and collaborate. This word sheds light on the seemingly more adequate interpretation of the previous lexeme, Teori< (theory). Since each psychological intervention implies the connection between the professional and the client, the necessary theory seems to be understood in a constructive way, as a means to foster the gathering of data about the potential client and the identification of different ways to better meet the client's needs. In other words, interven< seems to clarify the meaning of teori<, which may be positive and constructive in the present cluster.

Client< (client)
Teori< (theory)
Interven< (intervention)
Pensier< (thought)
Relazional< (relational)

Pensier< (thought) comes from *pensum*, the amount of wool (which had been weighed)[13] that spinners had to handle. It means to weigh, and also refers to issues to be treated, to be pondered, to be examined. In the sequence of dense words, this lexeme seems to reveal that the connection between professionals and clients has to be pondered, to be carefully examined. The professionals perform competent actions, which have to be thoughtful.

Relazion< (relation) comes from *relatus*, past participle of *referre*, to lead back, to relate. It refers to the way of being of a thing in respect to another thing. Here seems to emerge a specific psychological expertise which is developed by means of the thoughtful connection with someone else, the client, within a relational frame.

The connection between professionals and clients turns out to be somehow symmetrical. Once again, the connection with the client is understood as a primary element in psychological interventions; it is not an unspecific connection, but it seems to be a thoughtful relation led by a theory about the relation itself. Here we have the core of the psychological expertise, as it seems to be described by those who contributed to this cluster.

What has been said so far seems to reveal an outlook where science and practice are integrated elements, focused on the applied aspects of psychology. Indeed, among the lexemes with higher chi2 values, there are lexemes referring both to the applied side (clien<, chi2 = 85.55; interven<, chi2 = 21.94; relazional<, chi2 = 19.50) and to the theoretical side (teori<, chi2 = 42.23; pensier<, chi2 = 20.15) of the discipline. Those who contributed to the formation of cluster 2 propose a model of psychological expertise based on the relation between professionals and clients.

Let us now turn to cluster 1. It is at the low end of the first axis and slightly on the right side of the second one. This cluster is characterized by dense words that associate with the same illustrative variables as cluster 2: psychotherapy license = no, area of practice = other, residence = Lazio. That means that psychologists with those features significantly contributed to the formation of cluster 1. Here follows the analysis of the dense words characterizing this cluster. See Table 12.6 for the list of lexemes.

Progett< (project)

From *pro*, ahead, and *jacere*, to throw, is the action to throw something ahead, to make something move forward, what one has the intention to do in the future. Here, the issue is the construction of future things on the basis of what is known in the present. Here, proactiveness and openness are hypothesized to be key dimensions.

Progett< (project)
Istituzion< (institution)
Organizzazion< (organization)

Istituzion< comes from *in statuere*, to put in a certain place, to establish, to give rise, to ratify. Organizzazion< comes from *organum* (Latin) or *organon* (Ancient Greek), tool, and *ergo*, to work. The constitution and the arrangement of the organs in an animal body. To lay out, to arrange. Here, the issue may be the need to standardize, to organize, to institutionalize the psychological work, so as to make applied psychology a set of codified procedures within the social context. Indeed, the social context may be identified as the means by which psychology's usefulness and validity is ascertained. Psychology is included in the broader context of society and its structures, where individuality seems to be somehow outdated. Projects and planning, for psychologists, seems to be valid and rightful within the framework of social institutions.

Progett< (project)
Istituzion< (institution)

Organizzazion< (organization)
Cittadin< (citizen)
Territor< (district)
Cultur< (culture)

A citizen (cittadin<) is a member of a community, while a district (territor<) is an area which is a judicial and administrative unit (the lexemes cittadin< and territory< have the same chi2 value = 38.37; see Table 12.6). The citizens may be represented as those who benefit from the psychological work; here, they are described as members of a whole (the district), which is defined by a specific culture. Individuality is overcome through the consideration of the social dimension which defines its members, the citizens. Psychological work is characterized by a specific cultural frame (cultur<) within a social organization whose members are those who benefit from it. The design of the psychological work occurs within the society, which is constituted by members who are defined by such a membership. Thus, psychology deals with issues regarding the coexistence of individuals, giving rise to a discipline whose focus is the relationships between the individuals and the social context where they live.

Concluding the analysis of cluster 1, it is worth noting that there are lexemes which seems to point out − even though with low chi2 values − the various forms the social dimension can take as targets of the psychological work: we find grupp< (group, chi2 = 29.17), famili< (family, 21.38), adult< (adult, 19.62), uten< (user, 15.94), disagi< (distress, 14.84), coppi< (couple, 14.68), adolescen< (adolescent, 14.15), popolazione (population, 5.25), scolastic< (scholastic, 3.10) (from uten< to scolastic< not reported in Table 12.6). Patients (persons defined by their own diseases, see cluster 5) and clients (persons defined by the act of asking for a service, see cluster 2) are no longer depicted as the recipients of the psychological work; the recipients are described as citizens, people who take part in a social organization, within a district. This is reasonably the context within which psychological work arises and acquires legitimacy for those who contributed to the formation of cluster 1.

Cluster 3 is at the left side of the first axis and on the upper side of the second one. This cluster is characterized by dense words associated with illustrative variables such as year of graduation = up to 1987, theoretical orientation = systemic, sex = m. This means that psychologists with those features significantly contributed to the formation of cluster 3. Here is the analysis of the dense words characterizing cluster 3 (see Table 12.6 for the list of lexemes).

Oggettiv< (objective)
Soggettiv< (subjective)

Oggettiv< (objective) comes from *obiectum*, object, which comes from *obicere*, to put in front, what can be seen or thought. On the other hand, soggettiv< (subjective) comes from *sub*, under, and *jacere*, to throw, to place, to put. What is beneath one's thought or sight, something that escapes from one's thought or sight.

Somehow, these two words refer to the object of psychology *par excellence*: the pair objectivity–subjectivity. This is a key juxtaposition for psychology, which is a discipline that strives to find a balance between those two critical dimensions. It is worth noting that the highest chi2 value benefits objectivity (chi2 = 72.94).

> *Oggettiv< (objective)*
> *Soggettiv< (subjective)*
> *Assu< (acquire, assume)*
> *Capacità (ability, skill)*

Capacità (ability, skill) comes from *capax*, which derives from *capio*, to take, to understand, to comprehend. It refers to what can be contained, or metaphorically, what can be understood. It seems that the *proprium* of psychology is the action of revealing what is concealed from view and from thought. Psychology is depicted as being able to contain, to unveil both objective and subjective dimensions, through the acquisition (assu<) of specific skills which may be hypothesized to form the core of the discipline itself.

> *Oggettiv< (objective)*
> *Soggettiv< (subjective)*
> *Assu< (acquire, assume)*
> *Capacita (skill)*
> *Limite< (border)*

Limite< (border) comes from *limes*, transverse road, a path which serves as a border. The friction between the objective and subjective dimensions may set limits on psychological knowledge as the product of a scientific discipline. The inclination toward the objective dimension finds a limit in the subjective dimension. Psychology, as depicted in this cluster, seems to be focused on the following issues: a scientific discipline which deals with its own intrinsic contradictions, the conflict between objectivity and subjectivity, the impulse to investigate their relations and the awareness of the limits of psychology's capacity to produce reliable knowledge. Psychology, although able to uncover important aspects of reality, seems to be aware of its limits.

> *Oggettiv< (objective)*
> *Soggettiv< (subjective)*
> *Assu< (acquire, assume)*
> *Capacita (skill)*
> *Limite< (border)*
> *Epistemolog< (epistemology)*
> *Filosofi< (philosophy, philosophers)*

Here, psychology seems to be sketched as a "fringe science," on the border of philosophical and epistemological enterprises, a scientific discipline which is aware of its foundational issues and its limits. The limits are those regarding objectivity and subjectivity, knowledge and its borders, but also those between psychology and "close" disciplines such as philosophy and epistemology. Here, the limits seem to be epistemological, foundational, not limits regarding the pragmatic application of psychology. The issues at stake are theoretical in character, rather than pragmatic.

Within cluster 3 there are other lexemes with lower chi2 values which cover the same issues as above, namely lexemes recalling some theoretical or methodological tensions in psychology (see Table 12.6): Intuit< (intuition, chi2 = 21.83), Natura (nature, 19.35), Variabil< (variable, 16.95), Scientific< (scientific, 15.84), Rigor< (rigour), Dubbi< (doubt), Setting (setting, 14.96), Sperimentar< (experiment, 10.86), Contraddiz< (contradiction, 8.43) (from Dubbi< to Contraddiz< not reported in Table 12.6).

It is worth noting that the practical, applied side of psychology doesn't appear in this cluster: the first lexeme which refers to this dimension, cura (care, treatment), has a very low chi2 value (7.87). In line with that, those who benefit from the psychological work also do not appear, in contrast with the other clusters (namely, clusters 5, 2, 1) where they were pointed out respectively as patients, clients and citizens. Concluding the analysis of cluster 3, the outlook emerging displays a critical consideration of psychology as a problematic scientific discipline, which seems to minimize or to exclude its practical and applied dimensions. The theoretical aspect has the upper hand over the practical aspect.

Let's now turn to the last cluster considered, cluster 4. It is positioned at the left side of the first axis and slightly on the upper side of the second. This cluster is characterized by dense words that are associated with illustrative variables such as area of practice = health, age > 35, psychotherapy license = yes. This means that psychologists with those features significantly contributed to cluster 4 formation. Here follows the analysis of the dense words (see Table 12.6 for the list of lexemes).

   Uman< (human)

This is a dense word that deals with the issue of being human. "To be human" is a common saying. To be human is tantamount to being good or generous, and it refers to one's belonging to the human race. It is a generic lexeme, whose meaning is unspecific. It may refer to both those who benefit from the psychological work and those who practice psychology, in an indistinct way.

   Uman< (human)
   Mestier< (profession, expertise)
   Stimol< (stimulus, incitement)

Mestier< means profession, but also expertise, to have skills. "Agire con mestiere" (to act skillfully) means to perform a task with ability due to experience. In this line, "mestiere," as a kind of ability obtained through experience, may even be considered opposed to the former above specified meaning (i.e., profession). Indeed, to have skills (as included in the Italian meaning of "mestiere") means to learn something through direct experience, while the term "profession" refers to a formal educational training. Psychology deals with humans, and it is also practiced by humans. In this sense, psychological skills seems to refer to a sort of natural competence, not specifically a learned, professionally acquired competence. The human dimension is both the stimulus and the target of psychology, but may also be the tool through which psychology is practiced. In the same way as above, the lexeme stimol< (stimulus, incitement) has a double meaning: on one hand, the human is a stimulus for psychologists to develop and apply their knowledge; on the other hand, psychologists, through their interventions, are a sort of stimulus for those who benefit from their work. In this way, a practical knowledge without a specific, formal competence seems to take shape for psychology. Psychological knowledge may be hypothesized to be constituted by personal, human features based on experience, rather than on a specific, learned professional proficiency. Thus, psychological work seems to be based on an unspecific kind of knowledge, made of personal features, rather than of professional proficiencies.

Uman< (human)
Mestier< (profession, expertise)
Stimol< (stimulus, incitement)
Terap< (therapy)
Cresc< (to grow, growth)

The lexeme terap< (therapy) points out that psychology deals with care, but those who benefit from psychology do not explicitly appear. Indeed, uman< (human) is a very general lexeme and it identifies both those who practice psychology and those who benefit from psychology. This suggests that the psychological work entails a sort of mutual (involving both psychologists and users) path of personal growth (cresc< refers to growing, growth) produced and stimulated by a generic human contact. Psychology seems to be defined by the mutual encounter between human beings, whose contact is hypothesized to be therapeutic *per se*. The sharing of the human condition seems to be the guarantee that both the psychologist and the user serves as stimulus for each other; moreover, such an encounter is able to trigger a reciprocal personal growth. Therefore, psychology is intended to be a discipline made by humans for humans, a discipline whose expertise is based on the sharing of the common human condition between the psychologist and the user.

Cluster 4 depicts the image of a psychology that seems only to foreshadow a science-based profession. Such a profession is generic, not oriented toward the users, and based on personal, rather than professional, skills. In the analysis, lexemes may be found that recall the dialectical tension between objectivity and subjectivity which emerged in cluster 3, being in the same quarter of the factorial space. Such lexemes as metodo< (method, chi2 = 22.79), risultat< (outcome, 18.17), proto-coll< (protocol, procedure, 16.54), verific< (test, 11.50) semantically contrast with lexemes such as artistic< (artistic, 9.36) and creativ< (creative, 9.22) (not reported in Table 12.6). Thus, within psychology some dialectical tensions are outlined:

being human may be understood as a blanket that serves as the foundation of psychology, in order to solve those tensions. Indeed, it may be hypothesized that the tensions are somehow solved adopting a framework based on common sense, on human closeness and on the sharing of the common experience of being human. This may strongly involve giving up the possibility of establishing a psychology founded on specific professional and scientific knowledge.

Discussion: some remarks on the clusters and the factors

After the cluster analysis is completed, the software automatically assigns a number of factors equal to the number of clusters − 1. The spatial arrangement of the clusters in the factorial space may highlight the relevance of some factors over others. Indeed, it is the spatial contiguity of the clusters to the factors assigned by the software which attributes a particular relevance to some factors over others with regards to the dimensions of meanings which they convey. Table 12.5 shows the relations between the clusters and the factors. In other terms, these factors may reflect important dimensions organizing the meanings conveyed by the reports produced by our sample. In fact, they are the main dimensions of meaning through which our sample emotionally organizes the relation with the independent variables, namely the stimulus question and the shared belonging to the psychological professional community. In our case, four of the five clusters may be considered as poles of two relevant factors within the factorial space (or cultural space). They locate important dimensions which may be considered as the supporting structure of meaning extracted from the texts produced by our sample. Let us now consider the contents of those two factors, through the analysis of the clusters which represent the two opposite, polar dimensions of the meanings conveyed by the factors themselves.

Factor 1 is defined by clusters 5 (on the positive side) and 2 (on the negative side; see Table 12.5). It seems to express, on one hand, the issue of creating and defining psychology's clients and, on the other hand, the issue of the uncritical adoption of a producer/consumer model borrowed from a socially strong discipline, namely medicine. On one hand, one pole of this factor sees the user of psychology as an active individual, directly involved in the process of designing and supplying psychological activities, starting from the features of the issues brought by the user himself/herself. On the other hand, the other pole of the factor sees the user as a passive individual, identified *ab origine* by his/her own disease. Here, the user is represented as an individual whose problems and personal features are already known, are understood as "starting points" (for example, as illnesses), rather than as objects to progressively uncover via the psychological work. From this perspective, psychological work is considered as a sort of branch of medical work. Thus, in factor 1 the conception of psychology is organized on two opposing poles: on one hand, psychology involves the collaboration between psychologists and users while, on the other hand, psychology renounces a specific competence and adopts a successful professional model (a sort of medical model) where the user has a substantially passive role (i.e., defined by his/her own disease). In other words, the relation between clusters 2 and 5 deals with these two opposing poles: first, the image of psychologist as a practitioner who gives up his/her specific competence, which is the origin of professional identity in order to embrace a vicarious identity, based upon the acceptance and the endorsement of those who take part to the medical establishment. From this view, their approval will ensure the credibility and the earning capacity of physicians. Second, there is the image of a psychologist who seeks a proper professional identity, based on the skills underlying a specific competence. Here, psychology deals with the possibility of working with the client on the basis of a theoretical account which is able to orient the psychological intervention toward a specific direction (i.e., a goal). To summarize, cluster 5 seems to aggregate around the issue of the substitution of a proper professional and scientific identity with a "stolen" identity from medicine. However, cluster 2 seems to aggregate around the issue of psychology as a discipline grounded on its own theoretical tools, which are to be applied and to make knowledge a practical endeavor, and where clients are active parts of the endeavor.

Let us now turn to factor 2. It is defined by cluster 1 (on the negative side) and cluster 3 (on the positive side). On one hand, factor 2 presents some (meta) scientific reflections on the theoretical foundations of psychology, which turn out to be deprived of its applied dimension (cluster 3). On the other hand, the individual conception of psychological work is overtaken on behalf of an opening to the social dimension, where the institutional contexts and the users orient and shape psychology as a profession. In other words, this factor may be considered to be organized by the juxtaposition of the theoretical reflections on psychology as a science and the social dimension as psychology's cornerstone. However, those aspects seem to mutually exclude each other, being at opposite positions in the factorial space. In our sample, it may be hypothesized that the scientific reflections on psychology exclude from their scope the applied and professional dimensions of the discipline (cluster 3), while the emphasis on a professional psychology based on the collaboration with social actors seems to take up space for theoretical observations (cluster 1). Factor 2 seems to dialectically represent psychology's dilemma concerning the connection between theory and practice: psychology may be represented as a creature with theoretical feet which lacks an applied head. Or psychology has an applied head but lacks theoretical feet. Factor 2 seems to highlight a dimension where theoretical reflection did not concern practice, and practice did not concern theoretical reflection. Theory is self-sufficient, and so is practice.

Apart from factors 1 and 2, the other two factors, 3 and 4, may be considered as independent, since they do not convey a dialectical meaning as those conveyed by the first two factors and do not add any further information (see Table 12.5).

Let us now make a brief comment about the quarters, which are the four spatial dimensions through which the factorial space is organized (see Figure 12.2). In general, the clusters are rather scattered, since they are located in the whole factorial space, filling all the quarters. Only in the first quarter are located two clusters, namely 3 and 4. It is worth noting that this reflects an important problem characterizing psychology as represented by our sample, which has already been considered while illustrating the meaning associated with factor 2. In this quarter the image of psychology as lacking in its applied and professional dimension (cluster 3) juxtaposes the image of psychology as a discipline which turns out not to be established on specific professional competence: no theoretical models are provided (cluster 4). In other terms, the quarter deals with a tension between two relevant aspects of psychology, namely theory and practice. These two important dimensions seem to be ironically considered as mutually exclusive, as if theory did not need practice or practice did not need theory. As is now clear, this tension is paradigmatically expressed by factor 2, as well as by the whole quarter.

To summarize, on the basis of the analysis of the clusters, two main dimensions emerge from the data collected (see Figure 12.3). One dimension, represented by factor 1, fundamentally deals with different conceptions of the users of psychological services, understood as those who benefit from psychological work. The user is understood as someone who actively cooperates in the design and in the implementation of the psychological work. The reason for such a collaborative role may lie in the need – emerging from this view of psychology – to devote the application of psychology to the fulfillment of the client's needs. Psychological work is designed to be established from the nature and the features of the clients' problems. As an alternative view of factor 1, the user is understood to be someone whose role is passive, relegated to the status of patient. The role of the psychological user is not

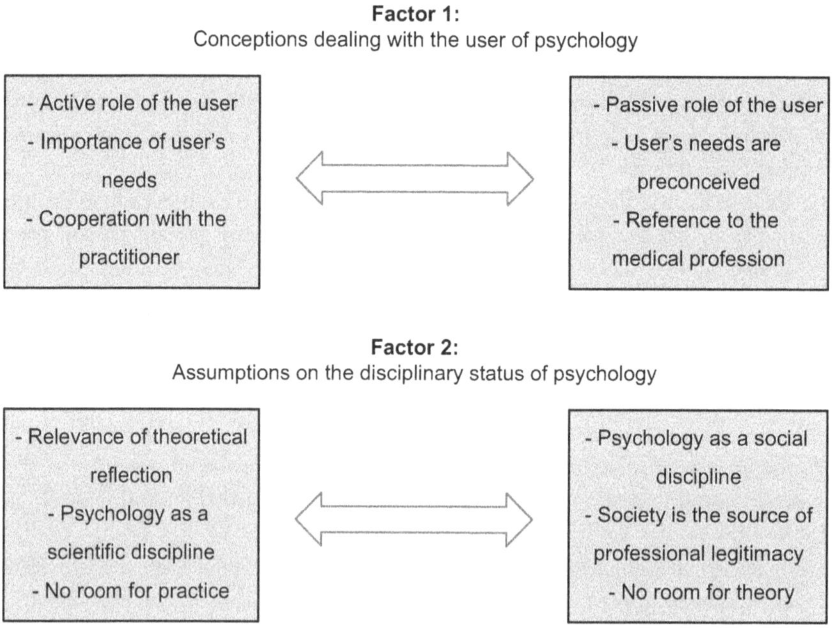

Factor 1:
Conceptions dealing with the user of psychology

Factor 2:
Assumptions on the disciplinary status of psychology

FIGURE 12.3 Polar dimensions of meaning emerging from the interpretation of clusters

considered in its peculiar features, but it seems to uncritically coincide with a sort of medical patient. In other words, instead of a proper reflection on the role of the psychological user, its conception and role are borrowed from a different professional field (namely, medicine).

In contrast, the other dimension emerging from factor 2 fundamentally deals with two different organizing aspects of psychology; it deals with different assumptions on the disciplinary status of psychology. On one hand, there are theoretical reflections on psychology and its foundations, a sort of meta-outlook on the discipline, which turns out to have poor connections with professional practice. This dimension conveys awareness of the problems of psychology as a scientific discipline, but lacks a reflection on the practical issues of the discipline. On the other hand, the social dimension may be considered as the organizing factor of psychology in its applied aspects, which means that psychology obtains legitimacy and direction from its belonging to a social context. However, such a social bent seems to somehow exclude a proper theoretical activity dealing with the relations that connect psychological work to the contexts where it is carried out.

Many limitations of the present research may be detected. Being an exploratory endeavor, the outcomes suffer from very limited, if any, generalizability or external validity. Indeed, the inquiry considered a small and non-representative sample of Italian psychologists recruited in a non-randomized mode. However, the goal of this research was to provide a preliminarily exploration of the issue at stake in order to provide grounds from which to formulate hypotheses which can be tested in the future. Therefore, the relevance of the present research lies in the distinction of recurring dimensions whose importance for the definition of psychology may be later tested with confirmatory methods and more reliable sample procedures. The dimensions outlined may suggest fruitful directions to explore in order to further understand the processes through which psychologists attribute meaning to their professional practice.

Notes

1 The basic conception of the world, as briefly noted in Chapter 4, presents a similar tension between those who support various forms of essentialism and those who refuse such positions. Adopting one position or another is important for the issue at stake.
2 As the reader may readily notice, the general framework is the usual S–R paradigm.
3 Hereafter, this term will be used in its technical meaning, as specified in the text.
4 Culture here is used a synonym of collusive processes.
5 In this perspective, the stimulus and the context may be considered as independent variables.
6 For more technical details about this issue, see below pp. 151–2.
7 www.opl.it
8 The original target question in Italian is: "Le chiediamo di pensare alla Sua esperienza professionale in rapporto alla psicologia come scienza e come professione, scrivendo per esteso le Sue riflessioni a riguardo."
9 In Italy, the first degree course in psychology was established in 1971, therefore some colleagues do not have a degree in psychology, but a postgraduate course in psychology.

10 The levels of this variable reflect key times when academic reforms regarding psychology graduate study occurred in Italy. Such reforms could supposedly influence psychologists' view of their discipline.
11 A lexeme is a minimal, abstract unit of language, that roughly corresponds to a set of forms taken by a single word.
12 The same procedure has been used for all of the clusters.
13 In Italian *pesare* (to weigh) is very similar to *pensare* (to think).

References

Battisti, N. (2006). Analisi del resoconto in psicologia clinica e cultura locale della professione. *8es Journées Internationales d'Analyse Statistique del Données Textuelles*: 121–133.
Bosio, A. C. (2011). *Fare lo psicologo. Percorsi e prospettive di una professione*. Milan: Cortina.
Carli, R. (1993). L'analisi della domanda collusiva. In R. Carli (ed.), *L'analisi della Domanda in Psicologia Clinica*. Milan: Giuffrè.
Carli, R. (2007). Notazioni sul resoconto. *Rivista di Psicologia Clinica*, 2: 186–206.
Carli, R. and Paniccia, R. M. (1981). *Psicosociologia delle organizzazioni e delle istituzioni*. Bologna: Il Mulino.
Carli, R. and Paniccia, R. M. (2002). *L'Analisi Emozionale del Testo. Uno strumento psicologico per leggere testi e discorsi*. Milan: Franco Angeli.
Carli, R. and Paniccia, R. M. (2006). L'analisi emozionale del testo (AET) e il caso K. Come impostare una verifica. *Rivista di Psicologia Clinica*: 45–59.
Dolcetti, F. R., Giovagnoli, F., Paniccia, R. M., and Carli, R. (2006). La cultura degli psicoterapisti e dei loro clienti a confronto. *8es Journées Internationales d'Analyse Statistique del Données Textuelles*.
Hoyningen-Huene: (1987). Context of discovery and context of justification. *Studies in History and Philosophy of Science*, 18(4): 501–515.
Norcross, J. C., Karpiak, C. P., and Santoro, S. O. (2005). Clinical psychologists across the years: The division of clinical psychology from 1960 to 2003. *Journal of Clinical Psychology*, 61(12): 1467–1483.
Normann, R. (1984). *Service Management. Strategy and Leadership in Service Business*. New York: Wiley.
Osgood, C. E., Suci, G. J., and Tannenbaum, H. (1957). *The Measurement of Meaning*. Urbana, IL: University of Illinois Press.
Reinert, M. (1993). Les "mondes lexicaux" et leur "logique" à travers l'analyse statistique d'un corpus de récits de cauchemars. *Langage et société*, 66: 5–39.
Tukey, J. W. (1980). We need both exploratory and confirmatory. *American Statistician*, 34(1): 23–25.
VandenBos, G. R. (2007). *APA Dictionary of Psychology*. Washington, DC: American Psychological Association.

13

CONCLUSIONS

The two dimensions so far highlighted – one dealing with the different conceptions of the users of psychological services, the other dealing with the social and theoretical organizing aspects of psychology – turn out to be rather central in the way that practitioners define psychology, at least in our sample. These dimensions should now be considered with regard to the theoretical interpretations of the previous chapters which described psychology as a unified or fragmented discipline.

The empirical study dealing with the reports of psychology practitioners, presented in the previous chapter, was designed with the goal of integrating and comparing the various theoretical aspects illustrated in Part 3. The aim of the present work is to give a complete view of psychology as a discipline, including theoretical and applied dimensions. In line with this aim and as a conclusion to the present work, the analysis of the practitioners' reports will be examined in light of the reflections regarding the different understandings of psychology provided by the authors in Part 3.

The proposal of Gregory Kimble (1996; see Chapter 6) seems to fit with one pole of factor 2, namely the dimension emerging from cluster 3, dealing with the understanding of psychology as a scientific discipline prioritizing theoretical reflection over practice. Indeed, Kimble considers psychology as a scientific discipline, for which he chooses the objective pole of the objective/subjective dichotomy. For Kimble, psychology is a scientific, naturalistic discipline devoted to the objective study of behavior. The analysis of behavior is abstract, in that it does not consider the content of behavior, but rather the syntactic aspects of it. This view is concordant with the considerations proposed by one pole of cluster 3. Moreover, Kimble's proposal explicitly tries to bridge the rift between the nomothetic and idiographic traditions, recalling again the dichotomy expressed by cluster 3. As with cluster 3, in Kimble's proposal there is no room for the discussion of the relationship between theory and practice, i.e., the ways psychological knowledge can be applied to practical, real problems. The author excludes the practical, applied side of psychology. Indeed, for Kimble psychology is a science, not a practice. For him the practical aspects of psychology seem to be confined to the common sense of practitioners, as practice does not put relevant problems regarding the application of theories into ecological contexts. This point is interesting, since the application of theory to practical problems is not necessarily linear, rather, it is my opinion that it requires the adaptation of theory to practical constraints.

What is missing in Kimble's analysis is a reflection on the way psychological knowledge can be properly applied to real problems. One of the aims of such a position is to obtain (scientific) credentials for psychology, connecting its status as a science to a naturalistic perspective. In this sense, Kimble's proposal also presents aspects emerging from cluster 5, namely psychologists' need to borrow scientific credentials from outside psychology, namely from medicine (in cluster 5), in order to strengthen the status of the discipline. For Kimble, psychology as a science seems to gain credentials through the imitation of hard sciences, and from the adoption of a naturalistic outlook (see Kimble's functional behaviorism). In cluster 5, psychology as a profession seems to obtain legitimacy through association with the medical profession. From this point of view, the two show a similar position.

Arthur Staats' psychological behaviorism (1996; see Chapter 7) seems to share some aspects emerging from cluster 3. Indeed, unified positivism reconnects two traditionally opposed ways of considering the object and the method of psychology, namely the objective and the subjective. Staats maintains that observation in psychology contains both objective and subjective aspects, reflecting the dichotomy emerging in cluster 3. Moreover, the author strongly links theory to practice and so the application of theory to practical problems is an issue under analysis. Indeed, practice is directly guided by theory, in terms of problem formulation and intervention procedures: problems are defined in behavioral terms and interventions are based on learning techniques. In this sense, this proposal has some of the aspects highlighted by cluster 2, which presents practice as the outcome of theoretical considerations about the relationship between the practitioner and the client. Here, the issue at stake is a theory about practice, contrary to Staats' Psychological Behaviorism. This is a kind of theory whose object deals with the way users and practitioners interact, it does not refer to basic psychological principles concerning human learning, as Staats does. In this sense, this author and the position emerging from cluster 2 differ.

Gregg Henriques' unified theory of psychology (2011; see Chapter 8) perfectly embodies the unsolved dialectics between objectivity and subjectivity or, in methodological terms, between monism and dualism. Again, this can be compared to some aspects which emerged from cluster 3. Such dialectics are rather clear in the reference to emergentism, which is a philosophical attempt to overcome the opposition between monism and dualism at an ontological level. Moreover, Henriques proposes a split between two aspects of psychology. Indeed, psychological formalism is different from human psychology. The two branches refer to distinct ways of scientifically understanding their objects: the "naturalistic" approach of psychology (psychological formalism), where the objective dimension is primary, as opposed to the "social" approach (human psychology), where the subjective dimension is primary. However, Henriques admits that practice is somehow different from theory, since the connection with the needs of those who benefit from psychological interventions makes professional psychology something different from the two above-mentioned branches. Indeed, the author highlights that the goals of the scientists (descriptive in nature) are completely different from those of the practitioners (transformative in nature), although theory and practice are connected. From this perspective, professional practice is an applied social science, grounded on scientific psychological knowledge. Such a position can be easily shared by most. However, what is missing here is the exact nature of this kind of connection: how does basic science provide grounds for the correct application of psychological knowledge? How does their connection work? How do they interact? Again, those and connected questions remain unanswered and the link between theory and practice seems to be uncritically assumed and left to psychologists' common sense or intuition. Again, the absence of a proper reflection on practice seems to associate Henriques' proposal with some aspects which emerged in cluster 3, namely the connection between theory and practice.

Norman Anderson's information integration theory (IIT) (2008; see Chapter 9) is openly an attempt to reconcile two traditionally opposed approaches: the nomothetic and the idiographic. Therefore, it refers to one of the main methodological dialectics in the social sciences, which can be found as the key theme of cluster 3, namely objectivity *versus* subjectivity. Again, such a dichotomy seems to be strongly embedded in psychological methodology, as is shown by cluster 3, and Anderson explicitly aims at resolving it with IIT. Moreover, via IIT Anderson does not formulate any reflection on the application of psychological knowledge, except those concerning experimental or research settings. This can also be deemed compatible with cluster 3. In more detail, the problems connected to the applicability of psychological knowledge to real world settings is left uncovered by Anderson who also leaves professional practice out of the discussion. Regarding this issue, an interesting point is that, among the limits of IIT, Anderson admits that his theoretical framework has no predictive power. Tolerating such a limit – which can have an enormous impact on professional practice – expresses how little consideration practical issues have for Anderson and colleagues.

Sternberg and colleagues' proposal (Sternberg, Grigorenko, and Kalmar, 2001; Sternberg and Grigorenko, 2003; see Chapter 10) identifies a distinction in aims between theory and practice, as Henriques (2011; Henriques and Sternberg, 2004) does. Theory and practice must be independent because they have different aims, respectively knowledge and change and, consequently, different procedures to achieve their goals. However, science and practice must be connected because scientific knowledge is understood as the starting point of practice. Sternberg maintains that practice has a sort of "monitoring function" over the application of scientific knowledge, its aim being to assess this knowledge, evaluating its practical relevance and the conditions of application in the real world. This is a position that can be shared by most. What is missing in this proposal are the details regarding the criteria which the practitioner can use in order to effectively play such a "monitoring" role. In other words, what features must scientific knowledge possess in order to be properly applied in ecological contexts? What are the constraints which practice must respect in order to properly, and effectively, use psychological knowledge in the real world? What is the difference between useful and useless psychological knowledge, with regards to its application in real contexts? How is this usefulness assessed? How do the contexts' features influence the applicability of psychological knowledge? Unfortunately, these and similar questions remain unanswered and require more research.

From this brief summary we can observe that the dialectics expressed in cluster 3 seem to be primary in the theoretical reflections proposed by the authors considered. In other words, the distinction between objective and subjective reflects a *leitmotiv* that spans the different theoretical proposals and characterizes one pole of the two main factors emerging from the factorial space, representing the cultural space of our sample of psychologists. Therefore, it may be assumed that such a dualism would play a key role in the connection between the theoretical, academic dimension of psychology (here represented by the theoretical models outlined) and the practical, professional dimension (whose emotional representations of psychology emerge in the empirical study). The fact that cluster 3 is characterized by the absence of a reflection on practical issues makes evident the difficulties for psychologists to reflect on practice. To simplify, we might say that practitioners practice without thinking, while scientists theorize without practicing.

It seems that in psychology there is a real need for the development of a theory about the practice, with the combined contributions of both scientists and practitioners. What are the reasons at the basis of such a situation? It is my opinion that most of them refer to the aspects that originate and feed the fragmentation of psychology (see Chapters 5 and 11), especially those dealing with the scientific status of the discipline. It may be assumed that the particular conception of scientific method, as it is understood in psychological academic settings, probably plays a central role in psychologists' reluctance to develop an appropriate theory of practice, i.e., a theoretical reflection on the application of psychological knowledge. In this regard, Machado, Lourenço and Silva (2000) maintain that in psychology scientists tend to overemphasize the importance of data gathering through the scientific method, while they tend to underestimate – or even refuse – the relevance of conceptual analysis, that is the reflection on the procedures used to develop scientific knowledge. In these authors' opinion, the overconfidence of most academic psychologists in the scientific technical procedures as means to mechanically collect data, together with a generally suspicious attitude toward philosophical speculation, led to a negative attitude toward those aspects of the scientific method that are unrelated to data gathering. Thus within the field of psychology an asymmetry developed between the sophistication of the technology of data gathering and analysis compared with the primitiveness of the conceptual, philosophical tools (Machado, Lourenço, and Silva, 2000: 2–6) used to clarify, sharpen, delimit, and coordinate the process of theory construction.

However, the two aspects must be intertwined: theory has its object in the empirical data – since it summarizes and gives meaning to the data collected – and conceptual analysis has its object in theory construction – since it proves its conceptual adequacy, i.e., it identifies errors, exposes incoherence, and finds nonsense. Such a situation evidently entails a narrow, dull view of the scientific method. A similar view is also shared by the psychologist Joseph Rychlack, who argues that the belief that the scientific method can only be applied within a mechanistic theoretical framework is a false assumption, connected to a superficial and non-sophisticated account of the scientific method (2005: 154–5).

To summarize, this sort of overemphasis and oversimplified version of the scientific method – inclined to exclude conceptual aspects supposedly unrelated to data gathering – may hinder the development of those conceptual aspects that would permit theory to be linked to practice. The task of creating a theory of practice requires a "sophisticated understanding of just what is involved in science" (Rychlack, 2005: 154), which would most likely be achieved from an in-depth philosophical reflection on psychological knowledge, which could become the foundation for the coherent development of theories about potential applications in the real world.

On the practitioners' side, misconceptions and misuses of the scientific method are likewise habitual. In general, psychological research has little impact on professionals everyday practice (Dawes, Faust, and Meehl, 1989; Wilson, Armoutliev, Yakunina, and Werth, 2009; Stewart, Wiltsey Stirman, and Chambless, 2012). Indeed, there is a general inflated confidence in subjective appraisal over scientific (i.e., objective or intersubjective) indexes in the clinical field. This is paradoxical, since the factors that may create problems in self-appraisal and judgmental accuracy are exactly those that scientific procedures are designed to counter (Dawes et al., 1989: 1673). Indeed, the goal of scientific method overtly is to manage data properly in order to reduce the impact of human biases, and obviously this is also valid for clinical practice. Thus, the trust placed in self-appraisal is misleading and declares a generally anti-scientific approach in psychological practice. In addition to this, professionals' training, theoretical orientation, and personal values may hinder the recognition of the validity of scientific evidence and procedures. In Robin Dawes and colleagues' opinion, this diffidence toward science may take the form of anti-statistical and/or dehumanizing statements. The anti-statistical statement typically assumes that the uniqueness of individuals is supposed to annul the explanatory power of statistical procedures which are based on the fact that individuals share common features with other people. However, it is this very characteristic which allows for the valuable predictive power of statistics (Dawes et al., 1989: 1672), which shows superiority compared with human judgment. These findings are well documented in psychological science (for example, Meehl, 1954; Dawes et al., 1989; Dawes, 2005). Thus, the anti-statistical statements usually rest on wrong assumptions about statistics' rationale and one of the aims of the scientific method, which is to reduce the impact of human biases. The dehumanizing statement is typically expressed in sentences such as "a person is not a number," or "people's behavior cannot be reduce to a formula." Such statements may be considered as variations of the anti-statistical statement that stress the fact that human events are somehow not understandable in their entirety. Although this might be true, as will be made clear later, this issue should not be overrated within psychological (as well as every other) practice. If something is left outside of our understanding, this does not mean that the portion of understanding we do obtain is not relevant for practical purposes! As Dawes et al. (1989) sharply affirm, this position "overlooks the human costs of increased error that may result" (p. 1672).

As an example, a recent empirical study by Stewart, Wiltsey Stirman, and Chambless (2012) confirmed that their sample of practicing psychologists raised many criticisms about a scientific approach in their own field, namely psychotherapy, and the relevance of its outcomes. The anti-statistical and the dehumanizing statements turn out to be confirmed by the views displayed by the authors. Here, it is worth noting that the participants, who are practitioners not involved in research, strongly criticize the procedures used by scientists as "artificial," "not generalizable," "not reflecting the realities of clinical practice." It is evident that such statements focus on methodological issues, with respect to which practitioners are completely unfamiliar. Such a criticism seems to be based on a general prejudice and/or misinformation concerning the scientific method, rather than on an in-depth knowledge and critical assessment of it. To the practitioners' eyes, the scientific method seems to look like a complicated bunch of rules and procedures whose goal is to gather data for academic purposes. The relevance of the scientific method in order to facilitate and to inform professionals' practices is evidently ignored or overlooked. The aversion to research-informed practice is also alarmingly evident in that many participants assert that "they know when their patients are improving … empirical verification is unnecessary" (Stewart et al., 2012: 109). The various aims of scientific research, including increasing unbiased knowledge and applying it to solve problems, seem to be neglected or misinterpreted by most practitioners, who see their practice as sharply distinct from science.

In Stewart and colleagues' opinion, the seriousness of this situation is often underrated in the psychological field, ignoring the consequences that such a gap would have between practice and science. In this regard, the psychologist Robyn Dawes proposes that, although the research obviously doesn't provide a complete manual telling the practitioner "how to proceed exactly with this client," it sets boundaries in ethical practice. In other words, research outcomes – provisionally identifying what works empirically and theoretically – provide minatory principles about what we ought not to do (2005: 1251): research findings somehow requires that one's practice is informed according to them, on the grounds of the evidence provided. In Dawes' opinion, this is justified by the existence of empirical and theoretical evidence supporting the explanatory and/or predictive superiority of a method or theory over others, which are not supported by similar evidence. In this sense, the respect of research findings represents an *ethical* aspect for the practice of psychology, whose goal is to improve the human condition. The isolation of practice from science would progressively make the practice of psychology ethically problematic, that is, not effective in reaching its self-imposed goals, namely to increase the knowledge of human and animal behavior in order to improve human conditions. In other words, psychological practice is able to achieve its goal effectively only by following the path of scientific research, whose outcomes are gathered and interpreted with procedures specifically designed to monitor and limit human biases. Labeling scientific research as "non relevant" for psychological practice would reduce psychology's effectiveness and would progressively lead to equating our discipline, at best, with mere common sense, having little or no practical relevance. Indeed, if psychological knowledge were equated with common sense knowledge, this would signify the scientific and practical illegitimacy of psychology.

In psychology the narrow conception of the scientific method so far described often coincides with the biased propensity for the nomothetic approach, as opposed to the idiographic approach.[1] Contrary to what is commonly assumed, these approaches are not really incompatible, as an accurate analysis of their ambit of application reveals. In fact, they serve different aims. For the nomothetic approach, what is interesting is the universality of (human) facts, while for the idiographic approach what is interesting is the uniqueness of that specific (human) fact. Thus, according to these approaches, mental or behavioral events are understood in different ways: as members of a class or category (i.e., as an expression of universal or probabilistic-statistical laws/processes) for the former, as display of irreducible uniqueness (i.e., as an expression of the uniqueness of that specific circumstance) for the latter. According to Meehl, the uniqueness of any event, be it psychological or physical, does not imply the impossibility of giving a reliable account based on its belonging to a class of events (1954). In other words, while all macroscopic events are absolutely unique, they may be characterized by a set of propositions which may grasp their relevant aspects. All events are unique; nonetheless, all events can be described in terms of their shared features, i.e., the features ascribable to their common belonging to a class of event. Thus, the syntactic (focused on the logical structure of knowledge) and semantic (focused on the nature and features of the events) perspectives turn out to be different though compatible points of view concerning the object.

Therefore, on one hand, the nomothetic approach permits a valid intersubjective knowledge to be obtained, but it lacks an object's detail. On the other hand, the idiographic approach permits an object's detail to be ascertained, but it lacks in generalizability. In other words, the more we get close to one desirable aspect of scientific inquiry, the more we go far from the other, and vice versa. Thus, these approaches are surely irreducibly different, but not necessarily incompatible. Rather, they can both be used in order to obtain information of a different nature on the object at stake.[2] Indeed, the nomothetic approach provides information about the processes concerning human behavior in general (considering very large groups of subjects). When psychologists want to investigate the variability between subjects (why the behavior of that subject differs from what is expected by his/her belonging to a specific group), the idiographic approach provides useful information. Such a collaborative relationship between the two approaches is illustrated in Figure 13.1.

Nomothetic approach

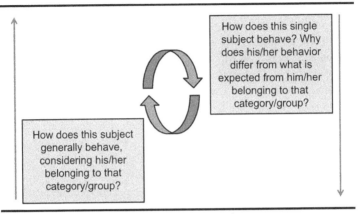

Idiographic approach

FIGURE 13.1 Compatibility between nomothetic and idiographic approaches

Such a wider understanding of these aspects of scientific method would allow for the integration of general aspects of psychological knowledge, detected and analyzed by basic science, with particular aspects relevant for a competent professional practice.

We may say, in accordance to Henriques and Sternberg, that in order to better articulate the relationship between theory and practice three aspects must be considered: psychology needs to define itself in order to clarify its mission, psychology needs to solidify its place as a primary health care discipline, psychology needs to clearly specify its boundaries with other disciplines (2004: 1054). The first point deals with the specification of the propelling forces of the discipline, while the second and the third deal with its identity. It is worth noting that these considerations are fairly theoretical, even if they primarily concern practice. In fact, these points can be worked out mostly through in-depth theoretical work about the status of psychology as an applied, scientific discipline. Here, it is worth remembering that the term "theoretical" is not equivalent to "it doesn't deal with practice." On the contrary, as already asserted, what psychology needs is a theoretical reflection about the foundation of psychological practice. Such a reflection can only originate from a sophisticated and critical use of the scientific method in order to connect the needs for rigor of basic science with the need for applicability of a science-based practice.

These are evidently methodological issues about the development and practice of psychology. Methodological issues are not in a vacuum: they are strongly connected to some kind of assumptions about the content and boundaries of "psychological reality," understood as the object of psychology. This means that methodology must entail some sort of ontological reflection, i.e., a reflection on what really exists. In other words, psychology has to risk providing ontological commitments about its objects of interest, even if such commitments are provisional, working hypotheses. This would mean drawing attention to those conceptual aspects which psychologists tend to ignore or underrate, as described above. Such an ontological commitment – although provisional – would suggest appropriate methods of inquiry. Indeed, according to the philosopher Daniel Robinson, without this interplay between ontology and epistemology there is no rational basis on which to choose a mode of inquiry (2007: 193). In this view, ontological assumptions influence theoretical construction, which in turn inform psychological technology, understood as the theoretical reflection about the problems produced by the application of practical procedures. It is reasonable to argue that appropriately managing the relationships between theory and practice requires in-depth philosophical reflections about what is supposed to exist and how we can affect it.

In conclusion, psychology seems to be rather fragmented in its different constituents and the two souls of psychology, namely theory and practice, do not seem to be sufficiently coherent. On the basis of what emerged in the present work, unity in psychology, as in many other sciences, does not seem to be a goal for its own sake. In other words, unity is not something to actively and directly seek out and cannot be considered an *a priori* goal of psychological research and theory development. This resonates with the psychologist Christopher D. Green, when he maintains that "Genuine unification, if it is to come, must come of open competition among theories, some of which will offer increased unification, some of which will not ... Surely, at the end of the day, we value truth over unity!" (Green, 1992: 1058). Whereas good theory–construction practices and the reliable use of the scientific method are certainly the primary tools for doing good science, if psychology is to be unified, and we do not know whether it will be, this will be the consequence of reliable empirical, theoretical, and philosophical research.

Notes

1 The nomothetic approach involves the study of groups of people or cases for the purposes of discovering those general and universally valid laws or principles that characterize the average person or case. On the other hand, the idiographic approach involves the thorough, intensive study of a single person or case in order to obtain an in-depth understanding of that person or case (VandenBos, 2007; see also Chapter 1).
2 See the proposal of Sternberg and colleagues about converging operations (Chapter 10).

References

Anderson, H. N. (2008). *Unified Social Cognition*. New York: Psychology Press.
Dawes, R. M. (2005). The ethical implications of Paul Meehl's work on comparing clinical versus actuarial prediction methods. *Journal of Clinical Psychology*, 61(10): 1245–1255.
Dawes, R. M., Faust, D., and Meehl, M. (1989). Clinical versus actuarial judgment. *Science*, 243: 1668–1674.
Green, C. D. (1992). Is unified positivism the answer to psychology's disunity? *American Psychologist*, 47: 1057–1058.
Henriques, G. R. (2011). *A New Unified Theory of Psychology*. New York: Springer.

Henriques, G. R. and Sternberg, R. J. (2004). Unified professional psychology: Implications for the combined-integrated model of doctoral training. *Journal of Clinical Psychology*, 60, 12: 1051–1063.

Kimble, G. A. (1996). *Psychology: The Hope of a Science*. Cambridge, MA: MIT Press.

Machado, A., Lourenço and Silva, F. J. (2000). Fact, concepts, and theories: The shape of psychology's epistemic triangle. *Behavior and Philosophy*, 28: 1–40.

Meehl: (1954). *Clinical versus Statistical Prediction. A Theoretical Analysis and a Review of the Evidence*. London: Oxford University Press.

Robinson, D. N. (2007). Theoretical psychology: What is it and who needs it? *Theory and Psychology*, 17: 187–198.

Rychlack, J. F. (2005). Unification in theory and method: Possibilities and impossibilities. In R. J. Sternberg (ed.), *Unity in Psychology. Possibility or Pipedream?* (pp. 145–157). Washington, DC: American Psychological Association.

Staats, A. W. (1996). *Behavior and Personality. Psychological Behaviorism*. New York: Springer.

Sternberg, R. J. and Grigorenko, E. L. (2003). Unified psychology. In A. E. Kazdin (ed.), *Methodological Issues and Strategies in Clinical Research* (3rd edn) (pp. 23–47). Washington, DC: American Psychological Association.

Sternberg, R. J., Grigorenko, E. L., and Kalmar, D. A. (2001). The role of theory in unified psychology. *Journal of Theoretical and Philosophical Psychology*, 21(2): 99–117.

Stewart, R. E., Wiltsey Stirman, S., and Chambless, D. L. (2012). A qualitative investigation of practicing psychologists' attitude toward research-informed practice: Implications for disseminating strategies. *Profession Psychology: Research and Practice*, 43(2): 100–109.

VandenBos, G. R. (2007). *APA Dictionary of Psychology*. Washington, DC: American Psychological Association.

Wilson, J. L., Armoutliev, E., Yakunina, E., and Werth, Jr., J. L. (2009). Practicing psychologists' reflections on evidence-based practice in psychology. *Professional Psychology: Research and Practice*, 40(4): 403–409.

APPENDIX

Chi2 values of main lexemes in clusters formation (Italian version; see Table 12.6)

Cluster 1		Cluster 2		Cluster 3		Cluster 4		Cluster 5	
Chi2	lexemes	Chi2	lexemes	Chi2	lexemes	Chi2	lexemes	Chi2	lexemes
67.89	progett<	85.55	client<	72.94	oggettiv<	35.86	uman<	44.46	lavora<
52.92	istituzion<	42.23	teori<	47.49	soggettiv<	33.34	mestier<	34.02	medic<
43.35	organizzazion<	21.94	interven<	44.09	assu<	33.34	stimol<	24.35	pazient<
38.37	cittadin<	20.15	pensier<	44.09	capacita	26.01	terap<	15.99	educa<
38.37	territor<	19.50	relazional<	36.60	limite<	24.09	cresc<	15.57	ospedal<
29.64	cultur<	19.49	util<	32.06	epistemolog<	22.79	metodo<	14.05	paga<
29.17	grupp<	16.55	complessita	32.06	filosofi<	18.17	risultat<	13.60	accett<
26.19	social<	14.84	ortopedic<	21.83	intuit<	16.54	lettur<	12.12	tirocin<
23.66	committen<	13.64	esplorare	19.35	natura	16.54	protocoll<	11.63	contratt<
21.38	famil<	13.53	tecnic<	16.95	variabil<	15.93	vita	11.63	soldi
19.62	adult<	13.27	perd<	15.84	scientific<	15.10	obbliga<	10.66	psicoterapeut<
18.86	convive<	12.01	condivi<	14.96	rigor<	11.50	verific<	10.22	universit<

INDEX

Taylor & Francis eBooks

Helping you to choose the right eBooks for your Library

Add Routledge titles to your library's digital collection today. Taylor and Francis ebooks contains over 50,000 titles in the Humanities, Social Sciences, Behavioural Sciences, Built Environment and Law.

Choose from a range of subject packages or create your own!

Benefits for you
- » Free MARC records
- » COUNTER-compliant usage statistics
- » Flexible purchase and pricing options
- » All titles DRM-free.

REQUEST YOUR FREE INSTITUTIONAL TRIAL TODAY **Free Trials Available**
We offer free trials to qualifying academic, corporate and government customers.

Benefits for your user
- » Off-site, anytime access via Athens or referring URL
- » Print or copy pages or chapters
- » Full content search
- » Bookmark, highlight and annotate text
- » Access to thousands of pages of quality research at the click of a button.

eCollections – Choose from over 30 subject eCollections, including:

Archaeology	Language Learning
Architecture	Law
Asian Studies	Literature
Business & Management	Media & Communication
Classical Studies	Middle East Studies
Construction	Music
Creative & Media Arts	Philosophy
Criminology & Criminal Justice	Planning
Economics	Politics
Education	Psychology & Mental Health
Energy	Religion
Engineering	Security
English Language & Linguistics	Social Work
Environment & Sustainability	Sociology
Geography	Sport
Health Studies	Theatre & Performance
History	Tourism, Hospitality & Events

For more information, pricing enquiries or to order a free trial, please contact your local sales team:
www.tandfebooks.com/page/sales

Routledge
Taylor & Francis Group

The home of
Routledge books

www.tandfebooks.com